THE NEW

Through Britain on Country Roads

Peter Brereton

Weidenfeld and Nicolson · London

Preface

THE PUBLICATION of *Through Britain on Country Roads* was encouraging. I received a host of letters from readers, many of them suggesting that there was a need for yet a further guide. *The New Through Britain on Country Roads* will, I hope, satisfy this demand. It has been written bearing in mind the many and varied suggestions of readers from all over the country as well as abroad.

I was aware when compiling the first guide that, for reasons of continuity, many of Britain's remote country roads and isolated villages had not been visited. The seventeen routes in *The New Through Britain on Country Roads* will, I hope, make good this omission. This latest guide, like the first, has been compiled on a double-page system, allowing the motorist, cyclist or rambler to explore out-of-the-way parts of England, Scotland and Wales with the information he needs at his finger-tips.

The work of a travel writer is dependent on the encouragement and advice he receives from others. In this respect gratitude is due both to Steve Dobell, editor of *Through Britain on Country Roads*, and to Jane Blackett, editor of *The New Through Britain on Country Roads*. Both editors worked tirelessly throughout the preparation of these guides.

I wish, also, to thank my sister for much helpful advice, as well as for her assistance in the more mundane task of checking the maps and route instructions.

Finally, I owe thanks to the countless people encountered along the way. The information given in a guide of this kind depends, to a large degree, on the help of those who live, literally, on the spot.

Price Grading of Hotel Accommodation

The letters A, B or C which follow the listed hotels refer to the lowest charge for bed and breakfast in a double room in 1988. This grading system should only be treated as a guide and it is advisable to check with the hotel before making a firm booking. Throughout all the routes the traveller will come across a variety of guest house and farm house accommodation. These establishments have not been listed but, normally, the price of these rooms will be at the lower end of the scale.

A £25–£35, B £15–£25, C up to £15

Illustration Acknowledgements

The photographs in this book are reproduced by kind permission of:

The J. Allan Cash Photolibrary: 54–5, 58–9, 60, 63, 64–5, 66–7, 68–9, 72, 75, 76, 78, 82–3, 99 below, 115, 117, 121 below, 125, 135, 158–9 below, 170–171 colour, 173, 183 above, 184, 192–3, 205, 219, 222–3 below, 226–7, 229, 230–231, 235, 237, 241, 245, 246–7, 250–251, 281, 286–7, 290–291, 295, 301, 305, 306, 309, 311, 313, 315, 316; *Derry Brabbs:* 85; *Martin Dohrn:* 175, 182–3 below, 274–5; *Colin Grant:* 37, 46–7, 110, 142; *Nick Meers:* 15, 20, 96, 139, 146, 153, 155; *Kenneth Scowen:* 28–9, 39, 42 above, 42–3 below, 91, 93, 98–9 above, 133, 167 below, 168, 170 inset, 180–181, 189, 194, 195, 207, 215, 243, 279, 282–3; *Sheila Thomlinson:* 257, 259, 263, 297; *Viewfinder:* 24 (Fil Price), 43 above, 88–9, 157, 159 above, 174, 270–271; *Weidenfeld & Nicolson Archives:* 12–13, 22, 34–5, 102–103, 128–9, 161, 163, 177, 199, 200, 212–13, 238, 225, 267; *Jason Wood:* 121 above, 126–7, 131, 220–221, 222–3 above, 253; *Tim Woodcock:* 32–3, 107, 167 above, 190–191.

The maps have been drawn by Technical Art Services.

Contents

Introduction

THIS BOOK describes seventeen routes throughout the length and breadth of Britain. These are shown in diagrammatic form on the outline map facing this page. Each of these routes starts and ends at a town of reasonable size and particular interest, where a variety of hotel accommodation is available. Each route is divided into sections of approximately thirty miles. Each section occupies two pages. These pages present a map of the route, complemented by instructions for finding the way, together with information about places of interest, accommodation and the general nature of the countryside.

Road numbers in Britain are preceded by the letters M (motorways), A (major roads), or B (secondary roads). The greater part of this country's road network, however, consists of unclassified roads. The chosen routes are confined as far as possible to the B or unclassified roads, although in the vicinity of towns or in the interest of continuity the occasional use of A roads has proved necessary.

The Route Maps

The maps on these pages are self-explanatory. Beside each map are written instructions, partly to amplify tricky points which cannot be shown in detail on the maps, and partly for the benefit of those who prefer written to visual presentation. These instructions indicate the distance in miles (to one tenth of a mile) from one point of change to another, as well as at least one of the names of the towns or villages shown on the signpost. At road junctions where no signpost exists or, as is sometimes the case on minor roads, the sign has been damaged or is indecipherable, this has been indicated with the words 'no sign'. Occasionally signposts are damaged or have been positioned incorrectly. It is impossible, therefore, to assure the reader that the named signs given in the guide are completely accurate – but it is hoped that their inclusion proves useful to complement the route instructions.

Finally it needs to be emphasized that roadworks or temporary diversions may entail the motorist diverting from the detailed route. But it is hoped that sufficient information has been given for the route to be rejoined without undue difficulty.

The Text

Towns and villages shown on the maps are mentioned in the accompanying text when there are points of special interest. Hotel or restaurant facilities are included where it is suggested that a comfortable night could be spent or a meal taken at reasonable cost. However, since this is not a comprehensive hotel guide, the reader may on occasions find a hotel of his choice that is not mentioned here. The purpose of listing hotels is only to reassure the traveller that although he may be far from a major town, he is always in a position to

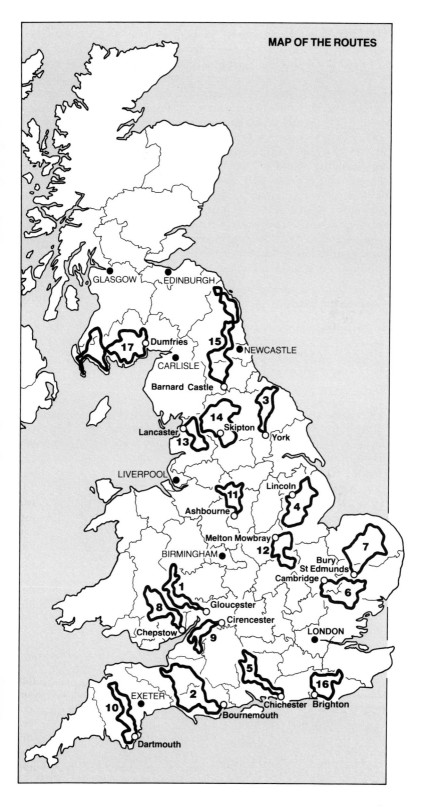

MAP OF THE ROUTES

GLASGOW
EDINBURGH

Dumfries
17
CARLISLE
15
NEWCASTLE

Barnard Castle
3
14 Skipton
Lancaster
13 York

LIVERPOOL

Lincoln
11
Ashbourne
4

Melton Mowbray
12
BIRMINGHAM
Bury St Edmunds
7

1
Cambridge
6
8 Gloucester
Cirencester
Chepstow
9
LONDON

5
EXETER
2
16
10
Chichester Brighton
Bournemouth

Dartmouth

7

anticipate a halt within a reasonable space of time along the route.

Hotel details include address (except in smaller places where this is not necessary) and telephone number. Trunk dialling codes are given in brackets. In addition each hotel has been given a price category with regard to the cost of a room on a bed and breakfast basis. These room costs have been categorized by a capital A, B, or C, and it is stressed that they refer to the cost of a double room. Naturally a single room will be relatively less expensive. The key to this grading system will be found on page 3. Costs in Britain as elsewhere may rise from year to year, but relative costs are unlikely to vary greatly, and for this reason it should be possible with this grading system to select hotels from the guide with approximate prices in mind. Brief details of places of interest along the route are given. However, it would be misleading to include opening times of properties, gardens, etc., for as the National Trust point out these vary from one property to another and at times they are closed for repairs. The National Trust publish annually a booklet entitled *Properties Open*, obtainable from 42 Queen Anne's Gate, London SW1H 9AS, T (01) 222 9251.

Starting Towns

In each case the town plan has been shown. Reference to the plan should help the reader to get clear of the town onto the minor road without difficulty.

Reference Points

The seventeen routes in *The New Through Britain on Country Roads* differ entirely from those in *Through Britain on Country Roads*. There are, however, occasions when a section of a route in the latter crosses one in the former. It is possible that the reader in possession of both guides might wish to transfer from one route to another. In order to facilitate this, reference points are given below referring to the page in the earlier guide where the routes cross.

Reference Points

Route No.	Ref. Point	Page No. in First Guide
1	Mortimer's Cross	267
2	Wedmore	121
5	Overton	205
7	Norwich	209
8	Brecon	245
9	Cirencester	229
10	Moretonhampstead	109
11	Ashbourne	309
14	Hawes	37
15	Hexham	179
16	Ditchling	281

Index

The index lists towns, villages and properties encountered along the route or referred to in the text. It also includes the names of people mentioned in the text. These names are distinguished from the names of towns and villages by their insertion in a lighter type.

1 Heart of England (West): Gloucestershire, Hereford and Worcester, Shropshire

THE ROUTE starts and ends in Gloucestershire. At its northern extremity it stretches into Shropshire. The majority of this 180-mile route, however, is confined to the county of Hereford and Worcester. This county was created in 1974 from the combined earlier counties of Herefordshire and Worcestershire. The west half, formerly Herefordshire, lies in hilly country close to the Welsh border, drained by the River Wye and its tributaries. Hereford cattle are famous throughout the world.

Initially, after passing by the Newent woods in Gloucestershire, the road loops through the heart of the Wye Valley. From here it stretches westward until reaching Garway, a remote hill village almost on the borders of Wales. The road to the north is at first by way of the Monnow Valley and later the Golden Valley, drained by the River Dore, with the abbey and gardens of the same name. Still further north, steep hills are crossed to Bredwardine and another delightful glimpse of the Wye.

Near the ancient town of Kington are traces of Offa's Dyke and later, after meandering through miles of unspoilt countryside, the road runs into Shropshire to the south of the Shropshire Hills. The northern extremity of the route is Craven Arms and from here the trend is almost due south, winding past many picturesque villages before veering to the east and re-entering the Wye Valley on the return journey to Gloucester.

Throughout the route, enriching the country roads, are ancient villages and churches, castles and fortified manor houses, National Trust properties and gardens, and a variety of delightful inns. Outstanding among the villages are, perhaps, Eardisland, Pembridge and Weobley. The churches at Abbey Dore and Peterchurch in particular ought not to be missed. Among the inns few enjoy a more charming setting than the New Harp on its garden bank above the Wye, while the New Inn at Pembridge and the Green Man at Fownhope are of much historic interest.

Gloucester

In the heart of the city of Gloucester is the magnificent cathedral, mainly Norman but built on the site of an 11c Benedictine monastery. The pinnacled central tower, 225 ft in height, houses the Great Peter bell, weighing more than three tons and believed to be the oldest of the large medieval bells in England. The Norman chapter house is said to be the site where William the Conqueror ordered the Domesday survey in 1085. The 14c cloisters are among the loveliest in England.

Footnote
In 1974 the county of Shropshire was redesignated Salop. After much public protest the name Shropshire has now been restored.

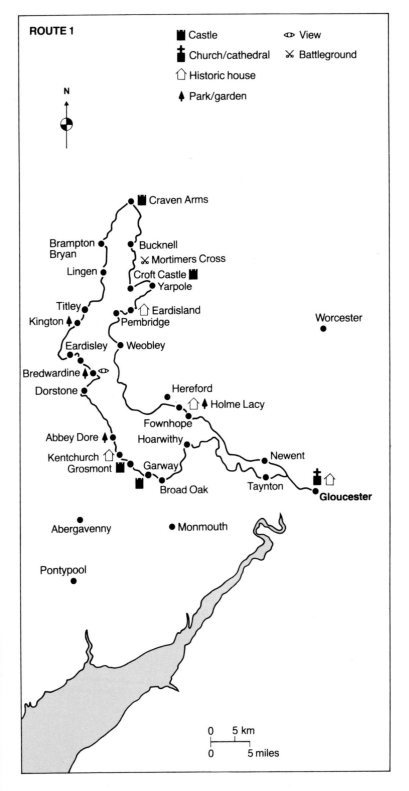

ROUTE 1

Castle

Church/cathedral

Historic house

Park/garden

View

Battleground

N

Craven Arms

Brampton Bryan

Bucknell

Mortimers Cross

Lingen

Croft Castle

Yarpole

Titley

Eardisland

Kington

Pembridge

Eardisley

Weobley

Bredwardine

Dorstone

Hereford

Holme Lacy

Fownhope

Abbey Dore

Hoarwithy

Kentchurch

Garway

Newent

Grosmont

Broad Oak

Taynton

Gloucester

Worcester

Abergavenny

Monmouth

Pontypool

0   5 km

0   5 miles

GLOUCESTER TOWN PLAN

KEY:

MAIN THROUGH ROUTES

ONE WAY STREETS ►►

TOURIST INFORMATION CENTRE 🅸

CAR PARK 🅿

Cathedral

WESTGATE STREET

NORTHGATE STREET

N

Castle Meads

SEVERN

The New Inn

🅸 • Guildhall

Robert Raikes House

The Docks

Museum

SOUTHGATE STREET

EASTGATE STREET

PARK

Garway's Norman church, near the River Monnow.

Apart from the cathedral this once Roman city contains a wealth of historic buildings and interesting museums, as well as many associations with famous people. Focal point of Gloucester is the Cross and St Michael's Tower, the intersection of the city's four main arteries – Northgate, Eastgate, Westgate, and Southgate Streets.

In Northgate Street is the timbered New Inn, built to accommodate pilgrims in 1450. The magnificent galleried courtyard now houses a variety of bars. Pride of Eastgate Street is the Guildhall, facing which is the Market Portico. This was the entrance to the earlier Eastgate market and was moved here in 1973 to front the modern shopping centre. In Southgate Street stands Robert Raikes House, the enchanting black and white gabled home of Robert Raikes, a pioneer of the Sunday School movement. The Fleece Hotel in Westgate Street, though mainly 16c, is notable for the Monk's Bar, a long Norman vault beneath the hotel. The Folk Museum at 99 Westgate Street is said to have been the house where Bishop Hooper spent his last night before his execution. The monument to the martyred Protestant bishop stands where he was burned at the stake off St Mary's Street.

Another notable museum is the City Museum and Art Gallery in Brunswick Road. At 9 College Court is the Beatrix Potter Centre, fictional home of the *Tailor of Gloucester*, a book which the authoress once described as the 'favourite among my little books'.

Finally, an interesting pedestrian trail known as the Via Sacra is recommended. The walk passes thirty places of interest, approximately along the line of the old city walls. A brochure referring to the numbered buildings along the route is available from the tourist office.

Fleece Hotel, Westgate St. T (0452) 22762.(B)

Wellington Hotel, Bruton Way. T (0452) 20022. (C)

Tourist Office, St Michael's Tower, The Cross. T (0452) 421188.

The Route

Though narrow and often hilly the roads are well surfaced. Fine views across the River Wye as the road meanders through the Wye Valley on either side of the river.

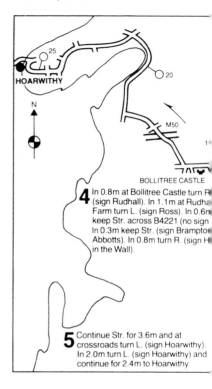

BOLLITREE CASTLE

4 In 0.8m at Bollitree Castle turn R (sign Rudhall). In 1.1m at Rudha Farm turn L. (sign Ross). In 0.6m keep Str. across B4221 (no sign In 0.3m keep Str. (sign Brampton Abbotts). In 0.8m turn R. (sign H in the Wall).

5 Continue Str. for 3.6m and at crossroads turn L. (sign Hoarwithy). In 2.0m turn L. (sign Hoarwithy) and continue for 2.4m to Hoarwithy.

Taynton (Glos)

Perched on a hill to the left of the road in this remote countryside is a unique little church, the only one in England to have been built during the Commonwealth. The original was burned to the ground by Royalist troops, fearing it might make a fortified position for the enemy. In 1647, by order of Parliament, the Church of St Mary was rebuilt on a site once known as Parson's Hill.

Aston Ingham (Hereford and Worcs)

The little village is surrounded by wooded hills, the fir-clad May Hill (971 ft) to the south being the dominating feature.

Linton (Hereford and Worcs)

The church has an imposing 14c tower and an even earlier stone seated porch. Half a mile to the south the map indicates Talbot's Well, a reminder that nearby are the remaining earthworks of Eccleswall Castle, seat of one of the 'band of brothers', the Talbot immortalized in *Henry V*:

Familiar in his mouth as household words,
Harry the King, Bedford and Exeter,
Warwick and Talbot, Salisbury and Gloucester,
Be in their flowing cups freshly remembered.

Bollitree (Hereford and Worcs)

The sturdy castle walls tower over the moat that now serves as a duck pond, a delightful and tranquil scene.

Hoarwithy (Hereford and Worcs)

This enchanting village on the River Wye nestles beneath the church built a century ago by William Poole, vicar here for forty six years. An extraordinary feature of the church is the high Italianate tower. The village inn has a picturesque setting in a meadow near the river.
New Harp Inn, T (043 270) 213. (C)

Bollitree Castle.

3 Turn L. on to B4222 (sign Aston Crews). In 1.1m at Aston Crews (Penny Farthing Inn) turn R. on to minor road (sign Linton). In 0.2m keep Str. (sign Linton) for 1.2m to Linton. Here turn L. (sign Bromsash) and in 1.5m keep Str. on to minor road (sign Ross).

1 From Gloucester (The Cross) take Westgate St and follow signs Ross (see Town Plan). In 1.0m bear L. on to A40 (sign Ross). In 1.3m bear R. on to B4215 (sign Newent). In 2.5m (after passing Rufford church) turn L. (no sign). Continue Str. for 0.9m to Tibberton. Keep Str. (sign Taynton) for 1.6m to Taynton.

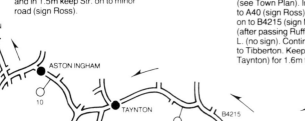

2 In 0.5m bear R. (sign Newent) and immediately bear L. on to B4216 (sign Huntley). In 0.2m keep Str. on to minor road (sign Glasshouse). Keep Str. for 1.0m over Castle Hill to inn at Glasshouse. Turn R. (sign Clifford's Mesne) for 1.1m to Clifford's Mesne (Yew Tree Inn). Bear R. (no sign) and in 0.2m turn L. (sign Aston Ingham). Keep Str. for 1.0m to Aston Ingham.

The Route

Initially the road runs westward through quiet traffic-free countryside until reaching Garway. From here the course is north west, first through the Monnow Valley and on reaching Abbey Dore by way of the Golden Valley all the way to Dorstone.

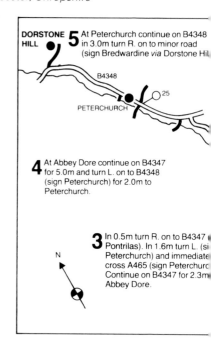

5 At Peterchurch continue on B4348 in 3.0m turn R. on to minor road (sign Bredwardine *via* Dorstone Hil

4 At Abbey Dore continue on B4347 for 5.0m and turn L. on to B4348 (sign Peterchurch) for 2.0m to Peterchurch.

3 In 0.5m turn R. on to B4347 Pontrilas). In 1.6m turn L. (si Peterchurch) and immediate cross A465 (sign Peterchurc Continue on B4347 for 2.3m Abbey Dore.

Garway (Hereford and Worcs)

Farmhouses are scattered across the hillside. The River Monnow flows beneath, little more than a mile away, and with it is Skenfrith Castle in the border land of Wales. The Norman church is found at the far extremity of the village, signed to the left of the road and lying in meadows.

Kentchurch (Hereford and Worcs)

Here is yet another delightful scene in the heart of the Monnow Valley. Nearby, across the river in Wales, are the ruins of Grosmont Castle, scene of much border conflict. Kentchurch Court, home of the Scudamores over centuries, stands in one of the few remaining deer parks of the area. The church, with a medieval cross by the porch, occupies a charming position by a stream. Although largely Victorian, many older features remain. In the chancel are the figures of John Scudamore and his large family with an inscription that reads:

His mournful widow to his worth still debtor
Built him this tomb, but in her heart a better.

Abbey Dore (Hereford and Worcs)

The Cistercian Abbey of Dore was founded in 1147. No traces of the original building remain but the present church retains features of the later abbey, begun in 1180. The abbey lies amid orchards on the River Dore at roughly the southern extremity of the Golden Valley through which the route passes. In the 17c the construction of the roof was entrusted to the renowned King's Carpenter, John Abel, a task completed with Herefordshire oak.

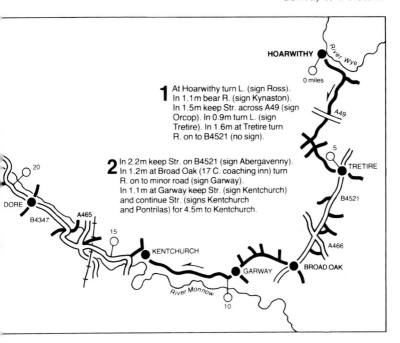

1 At Hoarwithy turn L. (sign Ross). In 1.1m bear R. (sign Kynaston). In 1.5m keep Str. across A49 (sign Orcop). In 0.9m turn L. (sign Tretire). In 1.6m at Tretire turn R. on to B4521 (no sign).

2 In 2.2m keep Str. on B4521 (sign Abergavenny). In 1.2m at Broad Oak (17 C. coaching inn) turn R. on to minor road (sign Garway). In 1.1m at Garway keep Str. (sign Kentchurch) and continue Str. (signs Kentchurch and Pontrilas) for 4.5m to Kentchurch.

To the north of the abbey are the Abbey Dore Court Gardens. The gardens of three acres contain fine shrubs and herbaceous borders, a herb garden, a walled kitchen garden and a river walk.

Peterchurch (Hereford and Worcs)

Known as the capital of the Golden Valley, Peterchurch is the proud possessor of a very ancient church. The Saxon altar stone is a reminder that the Church of St Peter was begun in 786 AD, an event celebrated annually on St Peter's Day. An interesting feature of the village is the John Smith Charity Almshouses (early 18c) which at one time undertook to 'provide accommodation of six ancient women who had been good livers, and to pay each of the poor women 2s. 6d per week'.

Dorstone (Hereford and Worcs)

Here the route leaves the Golden Valley at its northern extremity, the road rising steeply across Dorstone Hill before descending to Bredwardine. In the valley by the village are yet further earthworks, remains of another of the many castles strung along the valley. Up on the hill, signed to the left, is Arthur's Stone, a prehistoric burial chamber covered by a stone some twenty feet long.

The Route

The route is narrow and steep as it crosses the Brilley Hills. Later, beyond Kington, it runs by way of Wapley Hill and Coombe Wood, pleasant wooded scenery.

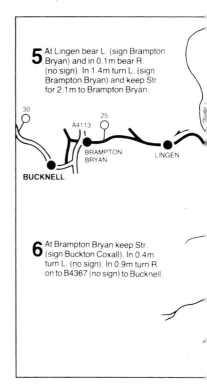

5 At Lingen bear L. (sign Brampton Bryan) and in 0.1m bear R. (no sign). In 1.4m turn L. (sign Brampton Bryan) and keep Str. for 2.1m to Brampton Bryan.

6 At Brampton Bryan keep Str. (sign Buckton Coxall). In 0.4m turn L. (no sign). In 0.9m turn R. on to B4367 (no sign) to Bucknell.

Bredwardine (Hereford and Worcs)

There is a marvellous view of the river from the bridge of this Wye beauty spot. Along the banks of the river are earthworks of a castle once, perhaps, the home of Sir Robert Vaughan who died at Agincourt. In the beautiful Norman church there is a representation of the helmeted knight. Close to Bredwardine Bridge are the Brobury House Gardens and Gallery, open to the public during the summer months. Eight acres of gardens contain fine conifers, terraces, pools and herbaceous borders. In the gallery are displays of watercolours from about 1820, and more than 100,000 antique prints.

Eardisley (Hereford and Worcs)

The long main street is lined with picturesque half-timbered black and white cottages. At the end of the street two inns face each other. One of these, the Tram Inn, is so called because at one time ponies were used for hauling coals along nearby rails. Little black and white cottages behind the inn were once their stables.

Kington (Hereford and Worcs)

An old town reputed to have been named after Edward the Confessor. The narrow main street leads down to an old stone bridge across the River Arrow. Just before reaching Kington, up on Brilley Mountain, to the right of the road are 358 acres of wooded farmland preserved by the National Trust. Also preserved are a number of interesting timber-framed farmhouses. Above Kington are the Hergestcroft Gardens, which have an impressive collection of trees and shrubs as well as a rockery and greenhouses.

Swan Hotel, Church St, T (0544) 230510. (C)

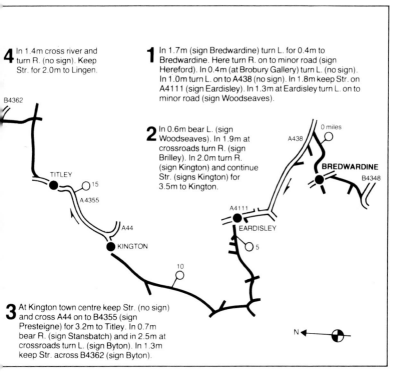

4 In 1.4m cross river and turn R. (no sign). Keep Str. for 2.0m to Lingen.

1 In 1.7m (sign Bredwardine) turn L. for 0.4m to Bredwardine. Here turn R. on to minor road (sign Hereford). In 0.4m (at Brobury Gallery) turn L. (no sign). In 1.0m turn L. on to A438 (no sign). In 1.8m keep Str. on A4111 (sign Eardisley). In 1.3m at Eardisley turn L. on to minor road (sign Woodseaves).

2 In 0.6m bear L. (sign Woodseaves). In 1.9m at crossroads turn R. (sign Brilley). In 2.0m turn R. (sign Kington) and continue Str. (signs Kington) for 3.5m to Kington.

3 At Kington town centre keep Str. (no sign) and cross A44 on to B4355 (sign Presteigne) for 3.2m to Titley. In 0.7m bear R. (sign Stansbatch) and in 2.5m at crossroads turn L. (sign Byton). In 1.3m keep Str. across B4362 (sign Byton).

Titley (Hereford and Worcs)

Offa's Dyke constructed by the King of Mercia as a protection from marauding Welshmen ran from here southward towards Kington. There are many prominent stone battlemented houses – even the 19c church stands beneath a battlemented tower.

Lingen (Hereford and Worcs)

There is a delightful church with a tower more than 300 years old. Chestnut trees grace the churchyard. To the south east of Lingen are the ruins of Limebrook Priory, founded in the time of Richard the Lionheart.

Brampton Bryan (Hereford and Worcs)

Another pretty village with many delightful black and white cottages. This was the home of the Harley family who first settled here in the person of Sir Robert Harley in 1309. The gatehouse of the castle he built still lies in the park of the hall by the church. A later Robert Harley (1661–1724) was the prominent Tory statesman. It was this family that gave its name to London's famous street of medical specialists.

The Route

The minor roads from Onibury to Leinthall Starkes run almost due south through unspoilt countryside. The route instructions need to be followed carefully here as signposts at the various junctions are all too often missing.

Bucknell (Salop)

The first village encountered in Shropshire. It lies on the River Redlake on the fringe of the lovely Shropshire Hills. Dominating features to the north are Black Hill (1,448 ft) and Hopton Titterhill by the ruins of Hopton Castle.

Craven Arms (Salop)

This former coaching stage now straddles the busy A44. The village is handy for visiting Stokesay Castle that stands above the River Onny a mile to the south. Stokesay Castle, built by a wealthy Ludlow wool merchant around 1300, is notable for the tower and for the timber Elizabethan gatehouse, one of very few of its kind to have survived.
Craven Arms Hotel.
T (058 82) 3331. (B)

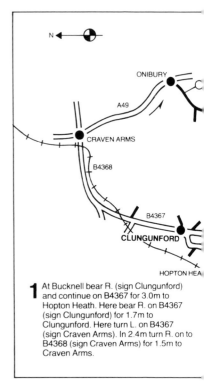

1 At Bucknell bear R. (sign Clungunford) and continue on B4367 for 3.0m to Hopton Heath. Here bear R. on B4367 (sign Clungunford) for 1.7m to Clungunford. Here turn L. on B4367 (sign Craven Arms). In 2.4m turn R. on to B4368 (sign Craven Arms) for 1.5m to Craven Arms.

Mortimer's Cross
(Hereford and Worcs)

Little to note here except that this was the scene of Hereford's bloodiest conflict – the decisive

Stokesay Castle.

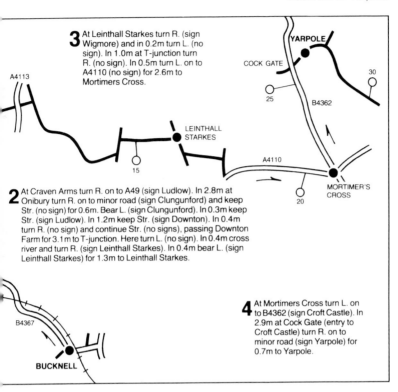

3 At Leinthall Starkes turn R. (sign Wigmore) and in 0.2m turn L. (no sign). In 1.0m at T-junction turn R. (no sign). In 0.5m turn L. on to A4110 (no sign) for 2.6m to Mortimers Cross.

2 At Craven Arms turn R. on to A49 (sign Ludlow). In 2.8m at Onibury turn R. on to minor road (sign Clungunford) and keep Str. (no sign) for 0.6m. Bear L. (sign Clungunford). In 0.3m keep Str. (sign Ludlow). In 1.2m keep Str. (sign Downton). In 0.4m turn R. (no sign) and continue Str. (no signs), passing Downton Farm for 3.1m to T-junction. Here turn L. (no sign). In 0.4m cross river and turn R. (sign Leinthall Starkes). In 0.4m bear L. (sign Leinthall Starkes) for 1.3m to Leinthall Starkes.

4 At Mortimers Cross turn L. on to B4362 (sign Croft Castle). In 2.9m at Cock Gate (entry to Croft Castle) turn R. on to minor road (sign Yarpole) for 0.7m to Yarpole.

battle of the Wars of the Roses that resulted in the crowning of Edward Mortimer as King Edward IV. A monument nearby tells how 4,000 men were killed here.

Croft Castle (Hereford and Worcs)

To the left of the B4362 an impressive avenue lined by chestnut trees leads to the castle. This is not, however, the entry for the public who must use Cock Gate a mile further along the road. The castle, preserved by the National Trust, is named after the family who built it, sold it in 1750, and bought it back in 1923. This one-time Marcher castle is square in shape with towers at the corners of the enclosed courtyard. On view in the castle are fine collections of furniture and family portraits. The church, roughly the

same age as the castle, stands on the lawn beside it. The most splendid monument is the 16c altar tomb to Sir Richard Croft, wearing the armour he used at Tewkesbury. The surrounding park is renowned for some of the finest oaks in England.

Yarpole (Hereford and Worcs)

There is mention of this ancient village in the Domesday Book. It lies, quiet and aloof from the main road, along a stream fringed with black and white houses and others washed in a variety of colours. A medieval building with archways stands right on the stream. It is called the Old Bakehouse, but over the centuries it has fulfilled a number of other functions, among them use as the village jail and an illicit Quaker meeting house.

The Route

The road runs north to south through the heart of the county. At Bridge Sollers, if time permits, it is worth diverting east along the A438 for two miles. Here is The Weir (National Trust), an 18c house with steep river-bank garden.

Eardisland (Hereford and Worcs)

There is a lovely view of this picturesque village from the bridge that straddles the River Arrow. Here delightful Georgian houses, fronted by lawns, face each other across the stream. Oldest building in the village is Staick House, at its northern extremity. This large timber-framed house, partly built in the 14c, was once a mote house. The manor house, Burton Court, lies two miles to the south of Eardisland. Though privately owned, it is open on occasions to the public, containing an impressive medieval hall and an interesting collection of period costumes.
Cross Inn. T (054 47) 249. (C)

Pembridge (Hereford and Worcs)

In common with the neighbouring villages, Eardisland and Weobley, Pembridge has a wealth of black and white half-timbered houses. Focal point of the village is the 16c market house, its tiled roof supported by eight pillars. Next to it is the New Inn, a name that belies the age of the charming black and white building which was established as a coaching inn in 1311. At one time the building bore the odd title 'The Inn Without A Name'. One of the bedrooms was once used as a courtroom, and the cellars beneath contained a prison. Steps from the Market House lead up to the Church of Saint Mary the Virgin. A notable feature of the church is the Bell House, the finest of the seven Hereford detached belfries. Among many notable buildings scattered around the village is the Greyhound Inn, early 16c with an

1 In Yarpole turn R. (sign Kingsland) and keep Str. for 3.0m to Kingsland. Here continue Str. (sign Eardisland). In 0.3m turn L. on to A4110 (sign Hereford). In 1.1m bear R. (sign Eardisland).

2 In 0.3m turn R. on to A44 (sign Eardisland) for 1.0m to Eardisland. Here keep Str. on A44 for 2.4m to Pembridge.

3 At Pembridge New Inn turn L. on to minor road. In 0.8m turn R. (sign Broxwood). Keep Str. for 2.6m to Broxwood and here keep Str. (sign Hereford). In 0.4m turn L. (sign Weobley) for 3.0m to Weobley.

The New Inn at Pembridge.

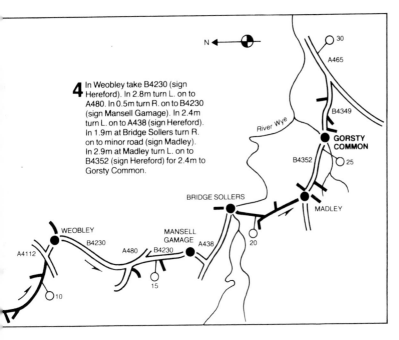

N

30
A465

4 In Weobley take B4230 (sign Hereford). In 2.8m turn L. on to A480. In 0.5m turn R. on to B4230 (sign Mansell Gamage). In 2.4m turn L. on to A438 (sign Hereford). In 1.9m at Bridge Sollers turn R. on to minor road (sign Madley). In 2.9m at Madley turn L. on to B4352 (sign Hereford) for 2.4m to Gorsty Common.

B4349

River Wye

GORSTY COMMON

B4352   25

BRIDGE SOLLERS

MADLEY

WEOBLEY   MANSELL
    B4230   GAMAGE   A438   20
A4112   A480   B4230

15

10

overhanging storey, and the Trafford and Duppa Almshouses, both 17c and modernized internally. The Old Steppes, once the rectory but now a village store, has wood carvings on the gable illustrating fruit, flowers and dragons.
New Inn. T (054 47) 427. (C)

Weobley (Hereford and Worcs)

Tucked well away from the main roads, there is a feeling on entering this compact village that one has stepped back into medieval times. Weobley is sometimes known as the capital of the black and white. Certainly the majority of the shops, houses and inns are of black and white half-timbered construction, the occasional modern red-brick houses being hidden from this central scene. The main street, appropriately named Broad Street, has a sunken rose garden and contains only a handful of small shops and restaurants. The

Church of St Peter and St Paul stands proudly at the edge of the village. There is a marble statue of Colonel John Birch (died 1691), a Parliamentary Commander who later turned Royalist and settled at Weobley after the Civil War. There are some pleasant inns, among them the Unicorn, which has been owned by the same family for over 100 years, and the Red Lion. Close to the Unicorn is a private house 'The Throne' where King Charles I rested after the Battle of Naseby.
Red Lion Hotel. T (0544) 318220. (A)
Unicorn Inn. T (0544) 318230. (B)

Mansell Gamage (Hereford and Worcs)

The Norman church needs to be approached by a steep grassy path to the left of the road. To the east of the village is a great house, Garnons, the lovely setting of the grounds making it a popular local point-to-point venue.

23

The Route

The return route avoids the centre of Hereford. Regrettably this beautiful city has some ugly sprawling suburbs through which the route inevitably has to pass. Fortunately there are only two or three miles of these – just enough to enhance one's appreciation of the beauty of the country roads through which the majority of the route passes.

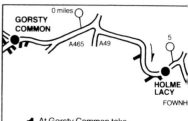

1 At Gorsty Common take B4349 and in 2.0m turn L. on to A465 (sign Hereford). In 2.0m at roundabout turn R. on to A49 (sign Ross). In 0.3m turn L. on to B4399 (sign Holme Lacy) for 4.2m to Holme Lacy.

3 At Fownhope continue on B422 and in 5.7m keep Str. across A449 (sign Newent). In 1.1m at Upton Bishop turn L. on to B422 (sign Newent). In 5.5m at Newent keep Str. on to B4215 (sign Gloucester).

Holme Lacy (Hereford and Worcs)

There are a handful of black and white houses and a green with chestnut trees. The village is named after Walter de Lacy who settled here after the Norman Conquest. Later, in the 14c, another Norman family, the Scudamores, arrived and in 1675 built one of Hereford's greatest mansions that stands in an oak-studded park overlooking the River Wye. Here the Scudamores lived until 1830 when this branch of the family died out. Holme Lacy house now serves as a hospital. The church occupies a delightful position on the banks of the River Wye, signposted from the village and a good mile away from it. Here there are many fine tombs of the Scudamores, among them the altar tomb of John Scudamore (1571) with alabaster effigies of the knight in armour and of his wife. The church has also a fine east window with St Michael and a host of angels. To the north west of Holme Lacy is Dinedor Hill, an iron age hill fort at the top.

The parish church at Holme Lacy.

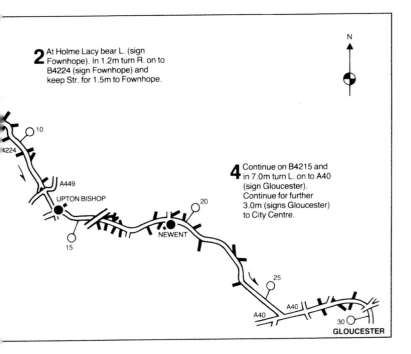

2 At Holme Lacy bear L. (sign Fownhope). In 1.2m turn R. on to B4224 (sign Fownhope) and keep Str. for 1.5m to Fownhope.

4 Continue on B4215 and in 7.0m turn L. on to A40 (sign Gloucester). Continue for further 3.0m (signs Gloucester) to City Centre.

Fownhope (Hereford and Worcs)

Black and white timbered houses mingle with others of plain stone and red-brick in this charming village in the Wye Valley. The church, larger than most in villages of this size, is known as the 'Little Cathedral'. It has a Norman tower that carries a 14c broach spire roofed with wooden tiles. The Green Man Inn is of particular interest. It dates from 1485 when it appeared in the deeds as 'The Naked Boy' – an association, some believe, with chimney-sweeps. The inn served as a coaching-house in the days when the main road from Hereford to Gloucester ran through Fownhope. In the eighteenth and nineteenth centuries the Petty Sessional Court was held here. Still to be seen are the cell and the Judge's bedroom. A famous landlord was Tom Spring, bare-fist prize fighter and heavyweight champion of England, who was born at Fownhope. There is a quaint inscription over the entrance: 'You travel far, you travel near, it's here you find the best of beer; you pass the east, you pass the west, if you pass this you pass the best'. The Green Man is certainly worth a visit.

Green Man Inn. T (043 277) 243. (B)

Newent (Glos)

The road back to Gloucester by-passes the centre of the little town. Worth a diversion if time permits. There is a fine medieval church. The Tudor market house is gabled and rests on oak pillars.

2 Dorset, Somerset

We leave the sprawling suburbs of Bournemouth at Sandbanks Ferry and within minutes touch down on the Isle of Purbeck. We have been transported, it seems, to another world.

The Isle of Purbeck, a peninsula rather than an island, the grey village of Corfe Castle at its centre, is an area of heath dotted with farms, hamlets and spinal hill ranges that run parallel to the sea. Purbeck marble and stone are quarried, materials that give charm to many village buildings.

The county of Dorset – principal rivers the Stour and Frome – embraces countryside as unspoilt and unchanged as any in England. A feature of the coast is the long and narrow Chesil Bank, a gravel and shingle ridge between Bridport and Weymouth. The novels of Thomas Hardy (1840–1928) have made familiar the beauty of Dorset's countryside to millions who have never had the opportunity to see it. The route passes the house where the author was born and where he wrote his first novels, *Under the Greenwood Tree* (1872) and *Far from the Madding Crowd* (1874). Countless Dorset villages, churches and inns form the background to his novels. Many of these lie along the route in an area that he termed Wessex after the former kingdom of the West Saxons founded around 500 AD.

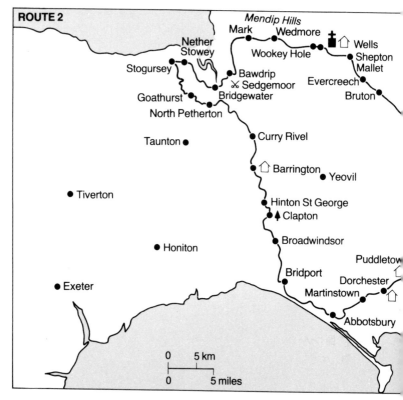

From Bridport the road runs north, and at Broadwindsor there is the reminder that Charles II fled to Dorset in an unsuccessful attempt to cross the Channel after his defeat at Worcester. Shortly the road runs into Somerset, famed for dairy products and cider. Its chief rivers are the Exe and Parrett, with the Mendip Hills to the north and the Quantocks to the west. The coastline is one of low cliffs, fringing marshy land protected from the sea by dykes and sluices.

Somerset is steeped in history, and travelling through mile after mile of country roads is like turning the pages of the history books. First thoughts focus on Alfred the Great (*circa* 848–901) and his battles with the marauding Danes. In about 878 the man described as 'the wisest, best and greatest king that ever reigned in England' was forced to seek refuge in Somerset, building a fort at Athelney as a kind of guerrilla headquarters. It was here that the episode of the burning of the cakes took place. The old English song of the scolding he received is worth repeating:

> Can't you mind the cakes man?
> And don't you see them burn?
> I'm bound you'll eat them fast enough,
> As soon as 'tis thy turn.

All this took place near the road at Burrow Bridge and nearby was unearthed, centuries later, an ornament of gold with a crude portrait engraved 'Alfred had me wrought'. Alfred's Jewel is kept in the Ashmolean Museum, Oxford.

Only a few miles to the north of Burrow Bridge is Sedgemoor, scene

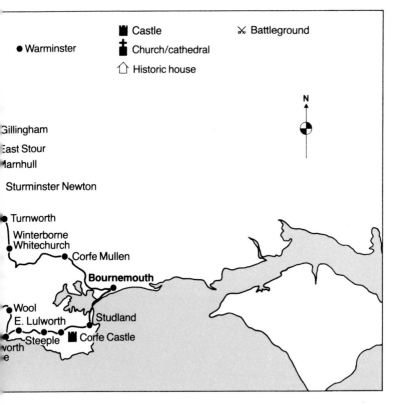

⬛ Castle	⚔ Battleground
✚ Church/cathedral	
⌂ Historic house	

● Warminster

N

Gillingham
East Stour
Marnhull

Sturminster Newton

● Turnworth
Winterborne
● Whitechurch
● Corfe Mullen
Bournemouth
● Wool
E. Lulworth
Studland
Steeple ⬛ Corfe Castle
worth
e

of the last battle to be fought on English soil in 1685. It was here that the Duke of Monmouth was defeated, a result that culminated in the Bloody Assize when 320 Monmouth supporters were executed and hundreds more transported. Sedgemoor, now farmland, lies a few miles to the east of Bridgwater.

The route continues past the lovely cathedral city of Wells and the charming Somerset towns of Shepton Mallet and Bruton before returning to Dorset at Gillingham. There is a further reminder of Hardy at the inn at Marnhull. From the market town of Sturminster Newton progress continues southward, meandering past many remote villages of the Winterbourne before returning to Bournemouth.

Bournemouth

The town provides an excellent starting point. There is a wealth of accommodation ranging from luxury hotels to boarding houses.

Bournemouth is among Britain's largest and most popular seaside resorts. The beautiful bay of golden sands is backed by cliffs and promenades. Picturesque wooded clefts or 'chines' interrupt the line of cliffs. There are pine woods. The Upper and Lower Central Gardens follow the course of the Bourne stream, giving weight to Bournemouth's claim to be the 'Garden City of the Sea'.

St Peter's Church, Hinton Road, is graced by a spire more than 200 ft high. Among a number of museums are the Rothesay, with a marine collection, furniture and paintings; the Big Four Museum which includes a working model railway; and the British Typewriter Museum where 350 typewriters are on display. The Russell Cotes Art Gallery is famous for its collection of unusual 19c pictures. There are four theatres in the town.

Hotel Cecil, Parsonage Road. T (0202) 293336. (A)

Avon Royal, Christchurch Road. T (0202) 292800. (B)

Tree Tops, Christchurch Road. T (0202) 23157. (C)

Tourist Office, Westover Road, T (0202) 291715.

A fine display of daffodils on the cliffs of Bournemouth.

28

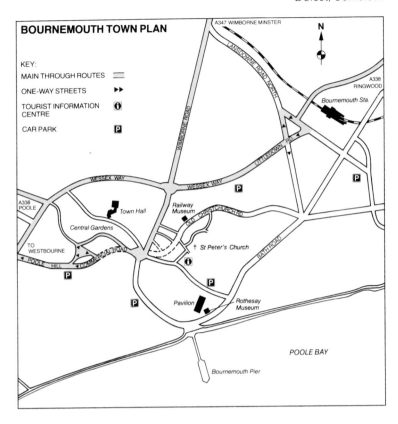

BOURNEMOUTH TOWN PLAN

KEY:

MAIN THROUGH ROUTES

ONE-WAY STREETS ►►

TOURIST INFORMATION
CENTRE

CAR PARK P

A347 WIMBORNE MINSTER

N

A338
RINGWOOD

Bournemouth Sta.

WESSEX WAY

WESSEX WAY

A338
POOLE

Town Hall

Central Gardens

TO
WESTBOURNE

POOLE HILL

COMMERCIAL ROAD

Railway
Museum

OLD CHRISTCHURCH RD

† St Peter's Church

BATH ROAD

Pavilion

Rothesay
Museum

POOLE BAY

Bournemouth Pier

The Route

On occasional summer weekends, sections of the road between Corfe Castle and Lulworth may be closed for military exercises. On these rare occasions noticeboards will indicate 'Road Closed'. In such an event it is recommended that Wool is approached from Corfe Castle by the A351 and A352 via Wareham. The route runs, initially, through the heart of the Isle of Purbeck. Later it veers northwards to Gallows Hill (fine views) before running west to Clouds Hill.

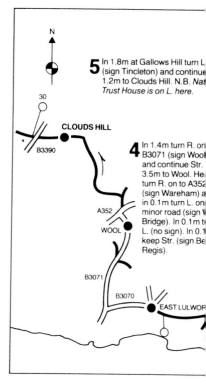

5 In 1.8m at Gallows Hill turn L. (sign Tincleton) and continue 1.2m to Clouds Hill. N.B. *Nat Trust House is on L. here.*

4 In 1.4m turn R. on B3071 (sign Wool and continue Str. 3.5m to Wool. He turn R. on to A352 (sign Wareham) a in 0.1m turn L. on minor road (sign W Bridge). In 0.1m t L. (no sign). In 0.1 keep Str. (sign Be Regis).

Sandbanks Ferry
(Dorset)

During the short ferry crossing to the Isle of Purbeck there is a good view of Poole Harbour (right). Dominating the harbour is Brownsea Island, 500 acres of heathland and woodland, together with marshland frequented by wildfowl and many quiet beaches. The island, privately owned until 1961, is now the property of the National Trust. The Dorset Naturalists Trust manage a 200–acre Nature Reserve. The castle, built on the site of Henry VIII's blockhouse, has been leased to the John Lewis Partnership as a holiday centre. Brownsea Island had been called the 'cradle of the boy scouts'. It was here in 1907 that a party of twenty boys, led by Lord Baden-Powell, pitched tents and the Boy Scout movement was born.

Studland (Dorset)

A coastal village with fine golden sands that fringe Studland Bay. To the south is the great chalk hill of Ballard Down. Westward,

dominating Black Down, the huge protruding rock known as The Agglestone has been claimed as a prehistoric relic in the pattern of Stonehenge.
Knoll House Hotel.
T (092 944) 251. (A)

Corfe Castle (Dorset)

In the heart of the Isle of Purbeck the village crouches beneath the towering castle walls, one of the most spectacular castle ruins in England. The castle has known much bloodshed. It was on this site in Saxon times that Queen Elfrida murdered her stepson to enable her son Ethelred to come to the throne. In the dungeons of the castle King John starved twenty-two French noblemen to death for supporting his nephew's claim to the throne. In 1646, now a Royalist stronghold, the castle was reduced to ruins by the

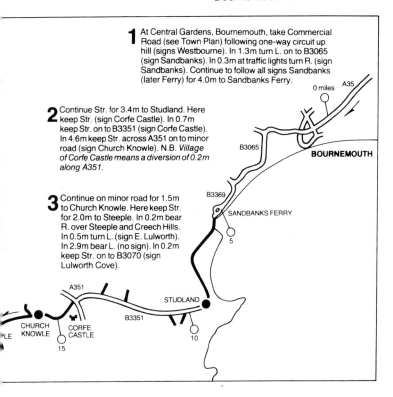

1 At Central Gardens, Bournemouth, take Commercial Road (see Town Plan) following one-way circuit up hill (signs Westbourne). In 1.3m turn L. on to B3065 (sign Sandbanks). In 0.3m at traffic lights turn R. (sign Sandbanks). Continue to follow all signs Sandbanks (later Ferry) for 4.0m to Sandbanks Ferry.

2 Continue Str. for 3.4m to Studland. Here keep Str. (sign Corfe Castle). In 0.7m keep Str. on to B3351 (sign Corfe Castle). In 4.6m keep Str. across A351 on to minor road (sign Church Knowle). N.B. *Village of Corfe Castle means a diversion of 0.2m along A351.*

3 Continue on minor road for 1.5m to Church Knowle. Here keep Str. for 2.0m to Steeple. In 0.2m bear R. over Steeple and Creech Hills. In 0.5m turn L. (sign E. Lulworth). In 2.9m bear L. (no sign). In 0.2m keep Str. on to B3070 (sign Lulworth Cove).

Roundheads. The church with its 15c tower bears an inscription to 'Edward the Martyr, King of Wessex, treachourously stabbed at Corves Gate in 798 AD by his stepmother Elfrida'.

The village contains many delightful buildings constructed from grey Purbeck stone. The Fox Inn, near the car park, was built in 1568 and claims to be the oldest of the village inns.
Banks Arms Hotel.
T (0929 480) 206. (C)

Steeple (Dorset)

In common with the neighbouring villages of Church Knowle and Tyneham, Steeple is a small remote village that shelters beneath the Purbeck Hills. All three villages possess small churches. At Steeple the church with its Norman doorway lies to the left of the road. The church has

an early connection with the United States. Edmund Laurence, who lived at Steeple Manor, married in the early 17c Agnes, heiress of the Washington family. The coat of arms over the east doorway of the transept incorporates the stars and stripes. George Washington, first President of the United States, was descended from this family and it is thought that this Washington shield may have influenced the design for the Stars and Stripes of America.

Lulworth Cove (Dorset)

At a point where the B3070 joins the B3071 the route turns northward to Wool. A mile to the south, however, is that famous beauty spot, Lulworth Cove. The tiny harbour is almost circular with a narrow entrance. It is overlooked by towering cliffs.

Wool (Dorset)

Little remains of Bindon Abbey,
signed to the right of the route.
Across the river, by Wool bridge,
is the old manor house – manor
and abbey linked, fictionally, by
the honeymoon of Thomas
Hardy's *Tess of the d'Urbervilles.*

Clouds Hill (Dorset)

The cottage, owned by the
National Trust, is signed to the left
of the route. This is the cottage
that Lawrence of Arabia first
rented when he posed as Private
Shaw and was stationed with the
Tank Corps nearby. The cottage is
open to the public during the
summer months. Here can be seen
his sitting room and library.
Among interesting relics are his
gramophone and records as well
as photographs taken during his
Arabian campaign.

The spectacular ruins of Corfe Castle.

The Route

*After climbing the heights
between Dorchester and
Abbotsbury the road runs
high above and parallel to
Chesil Beach.*

Puddletown (Dorset)

The town lies on the River Piddle
and was originally named,
appropriately, Piddletown. Thirty
years ago, for reasons of propriety,
the council decreed that the
village would in future be known
as Puddletown. In the square are
a number of picturesque thatched
cottages. The church, mainly 15c,
has a chapel with fine monuments
to the Martin family who over
generations lived at one of
Dorset's finest houses,
Athelhampton. The house lies a
mile to the east on the A35.
Features are the great hall with its
open timber roof; the state
bedchamber; the long gallery
library; and some lovely gardens
with an original dovecote. It is
open to the public on occasions.

Puddletown forms the
background for Thomas Hardy's
Far from the Madding Crowd.
Hardy Cottage, owned by the
National Trust, lies a little further
along the route at Higher
Bockhampton (signed left). The
thatched cottage, built by Hardy's
grandfather in 1800, was
described by Dorset's best known
writer:

> It faces west and round the back and
> sides
> High beeches, bending, hang a veil
> of boughs,
> And sweep against the roof.

The room where Hardy was
born in 1840 and the one in
which he wrote *Far from the
Madding Crowd* in 1874 can
been seen.

3 In Abbotsbury continue on B3157
(sign Bridport) for 3.8m to Swyre.
Continue on B3157 for further 3.0m
to Burton Bradstock. Continue on
B3157 for 2.3m and at roundabout
keep Str. (sign Bridport town centre)
for 0.6m to town centre.

BRIDPORT

B3157

BURTON BRADSTOCK

SWYRE

B3157

ABBOTSBURY

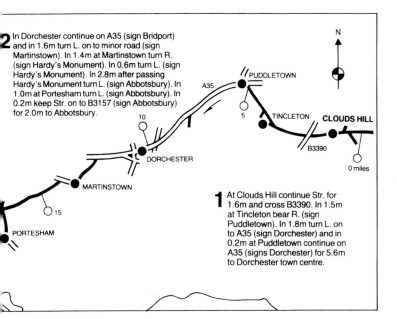

2 In Dorchester continue on A35 (sign Bridport) and in 1.6m turn L. on to minor road (sign Martinstown). In 1.4m at Martinstown turn R. (sign Hardy's Monument). In 0.6m turn L. (sign Hardy's Monument). In 2.8m after passing Hardy's Monument turn L. (sign Abbotsbury). In 1.0m at Portesham turn L. (sign Abbotsbury). In 0.2m keep Str. on to B3157 (sign Abbotsbury) for 2.0m to Abbotsbury.

1 At Clouds Hill continue Str. for 1.6m and cross B3390. In 1.5m at Tincleton bear R. (sign Puddletown). In 1.8m turn L. on to A35 (sign Dorchester) and in 0.2m at Puddletown continue on A35 (signs Dorchester) for 5.6m to Dorchester town centre.

Thatched cottages in Puddletown.

35

Dorchester (Dorset)

This former Roman town lies at the heart of the picturesque Frome Valley. An ancient earthworks, Maumbury Ring, lies within the town. It was once a sacred circle and then a Roman amphitheatre. Traces of a Roman wall are incorporated in the Borough garden walls. Dorchester was the scene of Judge Jeffreys' Bloody Assize in 1685 after the Monmouth rebellion. The house where the judge lived in High West Street faces the Crown Court where the Tolpuddle Martyrs faced trial in 1834. St Peter's Church, also in High West Street, stands on the site of an old Roman temple. The Dorset County Museum includes a history of the county and the Hardy Collection. The Dorset Military Museum lies on the Bridport Road, with exhibits of Dorset regiments and yeomanry.
George Hotel, High Street.
T (0305) 83147. (B)

Martinstown (Dorset)

Sometimes known as Winterborne St Martin, there is a broad main street with bridges over the river leading to pretty thatched cottages. A little further along the route is the Hardy Monument, a tower eighty ft. high standing upon one of Dorset's highest hills. This is the memorial to Vice-Admiral Hardy, flag-captain of the *Victory* at Trafalgar. It was erected in 1864, commanding on clear days views across the English Channel that range from Start Point in Devon to the Isle of Wight.

Abbotsbury (Dorset)

From the church of St Nicholas there is a glimpse of the remains of the abbey buildings, in particular the gatehouse. A more impressive survivor, also seen from here, is the great abbey barn with its massive buttresses. A sign points to the swannery, established by the monks in the 14c. Here more than 500 swans as well as wild geese and ducks can be seen. A lane off the main street of the village bears a sign to the little 15c seamen's Chapel of St Katherine which crowns the hill above the village. To the west of Abbotsbury, also signposted, are the sub-tropical gardens that lie above Chesil Beach, renowned for exotic trees, camelias, magnolias and azaleas. *Ilchester Arms Hotel*, Market St. T (0305) 871243. (A)

Burton Bradstock (Dorset)

The picturesque thatched Three Horseshoes Inn stands on the right of the main road. The lane past this inn leads to the church by way of some delightful thatched terraced cottages, washed in a variety of colours.

Bridport (Dorset)

The town stands two miles from the sea, encircled by hills, with the River Brit winding to the little harbour at West Bay. There are some pleasant old houses along the street that runs from the Georgian town hall to the sea. The main street, running east to west, is spacious and also is lined with some fine Georgian buildings. Over the centuries the town prospered through rope-making. It was said that all the Queen's ships were equipped with Bridport rope when Elizabeth reigned.
Bridport Arms, West Bay.
T (0308) 22994. (C)

The coastline near Lulworth Cove.

The Route

The road from Hinton St George is narrow and poorly signed, crossing the Roman Fosse Way just before reaching Seavington St Michael.

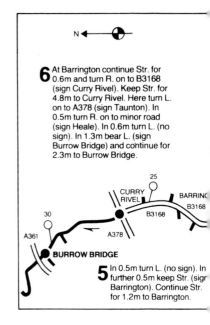

6 At Barrington continue Str. for 0.6m and turn R. on to B3168 (sign Curry Rivel). Keep Str. for 4.8m to Curry Rivel. Here turn L. on to A378 (sign Taunton). In 0.5m turn R. on to minor road (sign Heale). In 0.6m turn L. (no sign). In 1.3m bear L. (sign Burrow Bridge) and continue for 2.3m to Burrow Bridge.

5 In 0.5m turn L. (no sign). In further 0.5m keep Str. (sign Barrington). Continue Str. for 1.2m to Barrington.

Broadwindsor (Dorset)

A small terraced stone cottage in the centre of the village has a tablet stating that: 'King Charles II slept here September 23/24 1651'. This was the occasion of the King's flight from Worcester and his unsuccessful attempt to obtain a promised boat at Charmouth. The cottage is on the site of an inn, subsequently burned down.

Clapton (Somerset)

After leaving Drimpton the road crosses the border into Somerset. Here are the Clapton Court Gardens and Clapton Mill, both open to the public on occasions. Clapton Mill was the flour mill featured in the BBC's *A Small Country Living* radio series in 1985. It can be seen just as it was when built on an earlier mill site in 1864. It is run by a family whose ownership dates back to 1870.

Hinton St George (Somerset)

Many of the buildings in this delightful village, in common with the neighbouring village of Montacute, are constructed of golden stone from Ham Hill, giving Hinton St George a golden glow when the sun shines. In the High Street there is a 15c preacher's cross bearing the figure of St John the Baptist. In the Church of St George there are monuments to the Poulett family who once lived at Hinton House to the west of the village.

Barrington (Somerset)

Here is Barrington Court, one of the National Trust's finest possessions. The house, built of honey-coloured stone, has a south front that stands proud and almost defiant with its several gabled pinnacled roofs above dormer windows. The present building is thought to date from the mid-16c. During the 19c it fell into disrepair and it was not until the 1920s that restoration took place. The surrounding gardens were designed by Gertrude Jekyll.

Curry Rivel (Somerset)

Pride of the village is the Church of St Andrew. The church guide points out that the figures around the church – they include a hound, a bagpiper and a fiddler – are grotesques, not gargoyles, because they do not contain water spouts. Within the church is a splendid monument to Marmaduke Jennings and his son Robert, dressed as troopers with their families beneath them.

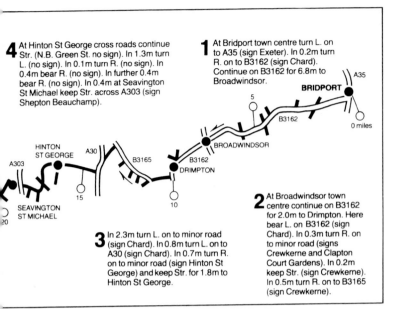

4 At Hinton St George cross roads continue Str. (N.B. Green St. no sign). In 1.3m turn L. (no sign). In 0.1m turn R. (no sign). In 0.4m bear R. (no sign). In further 0.4m bear R. (no sign). In 0.4m at Seavington St Michael keep Str. across A303 (sign Shepton Beauchamp).

1 At Bridport town centre turn L. on to A35 (sign Exeter). In 0.2m turn R. on to B3162 (sign Chard). Continue on B3162 for 6.8m to Broadwindsor.

3 In 2.3m turn L. on to minor road (sign Chard). In 0.8m turn L. on to A30 (sign Chard). In 0.7m turn R. on to minor road (sign Hinton St George) and keep Str. for 1.8m to Hinton St George.

2 At Broadwindsor town centre continue on B3162 for 2.0m to Drimpton. Here bear L. on B3162 (sign Chard). In 0.3m turn R. on to minor road (signs Crewkerne and Clapton Court Gardens). In 0.2m keep Str. (sign Crewkerne). In 0.5m turn R. on to B3165 (sign Crewkerne).

Burrow Bridge
(Somerset)

Beside the bridge is the inn, appropriately named the King Alfred. For here, also beside the bridge across the River Parrett, is a hill known as Burrow Mump, once fortified by King Alfred against his Danish enemies.

Craft shop in Curry Rivel.

The Route

From North Petherton the route skirts the northern edge of the Quantock Hills to Nether Stowey, then by traffic-free roads until the final stretch from Cannington to Bridgwater.

North Petherton
(Somerset)

The minor road veers westward here, passing the church but avoiding the village centre. The church has a grand 15c pinnacled tower, 120 feet in height. The village is expanding and is now a dormitory for the nearby town of Bridgwater.

Goathurst (Somerset)

Halswell House stands in its park to the south of the village, a sanctuary for red deer and possessor of one of Somerset's largest heronries. Memorials to the former lords of the manor, the Tyntes, can be seen in the church. One of these memorials depicts a 17c knight with his wife and all of his nine children kneeling beside him.

Spaxton (Somerset)

After passing through Barford Park, the route reaches a crossroads known as 'Four Forks' on the outskirts of Spaxton. In the pleasant Lamb Inn details are plentiful regarding the chapel of the Agapemone religious cult that stands nearby – an Abode of Love established in 1859 by a Brother Prince and developed on his death forty years later by one of his disciples, the Reverend J.H. Smyth-Pigott.

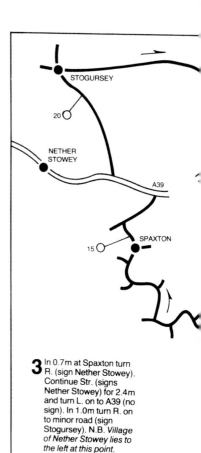

3 In 0.7m at Spaxton turn R. (sign Nether Stowey). Continue Str. (signs Nether Stowey) for 2.4m and turn L. on to A39 (no sign). In 1.0m turn R. on to minor road (sign Stogursey). N.B. *Village of Nether Stowey lies to the left at this point.*

Nether Stowey
(Somerset)

The minor road route by-passes the centre of this charming village, but it is certainly worth visiting if time permits. Nether Stowey stands on the slopes of the Quantock Hills, from where a small stream bubbles past picturesque cottages alongside the village's broadest street. Opposite the First and Last Inn is the cottage where Samuel Taylor Coleridge stayed from 1796 to 1799. The parlour where he wrote *The Ancient Mariner* is preserved

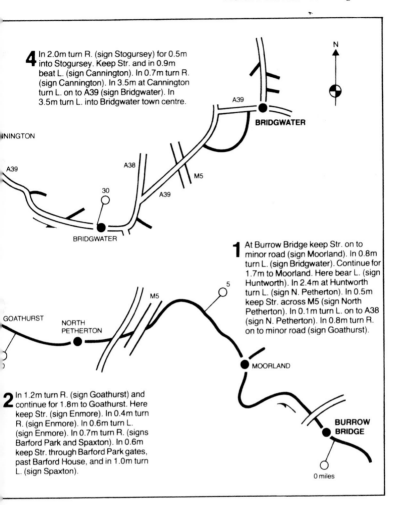

4 In 2.0m turn R. (sign Stogursey) for 0.5m into Stogursey. Keep Str. and in 0.9m beat L. (sign Cannington). In 0.7m turn R. (sign Cannington). In 3.5m at Cannington turn L. on to A39 (sign Bridgwater). In 3.5m turn L. into Bridgwater town centre.

1 At Burrow Bridge keep Str. on to minor road (sign Moorland). In 0.8m turn L. (sign Bridgwater). Continue for 1.7m to Moorland. Here bear L. (sign Huntworth). In 2.4m at Huntworth turn L. (sign N. Petherton). In 0.5m keep Str. across M5 (sign North Petherton). In 0.1m turn L. on to A38 (sign N. Petherton). In 0.8m turn R. on to minor road (sign Goathurst).

2 In 1.2m turn R. (sign Goathurst) and continue for 1.8m to Goathurst. Here keep Str. (sign Enmore). In 0.4m turn R. (sign Enmore). In 0.6m turn L. (sign Enmore). In 0.7m turn R. (signs Barford Park and Spaxton). In 0.6m keep Str. through Barford Park gates, past Barford House, and in 1.0m turn L. (sign Spaxton).

by the National Trust and open to the public on most afternoons.

Stogursey (Somerset)

Little remains of the castle built by the de Courcy family. The Landmark Trust, however, have now acquired the property and the 17c cottage built on the gatehouse has been restored. The finest building of the village is St Andrew's Priory Church, in an excellent state of preservation and containing much Norman work. Also dedicated to St Andrew is the

Well, signed off the main street (right). St Andrew's Well was regarded as a sacred spring from ancient times. Its archway was built by the Earl of Egremont more than 200 years ago. In 1847 the well was described as providing 'the only good public drinking water, having never been known to fail'.

Bridgwater (Somerset)

It was at Bridgwater in 1685 that the citizens proclaimed the Duke of Monmouth to be King – a short-

Coleridge Cottage in Nether Stowey.

Above right: Robert Blake's statue, Bridgwater.

Below: Sedgemoor, where the Duke of Monmouth was defeated in 1685.

lived decision as the rebellious leader's forces were crushed at Sedgemoor, some four miles east of the town. Here James Scott Monmouth was captured and later beheaded at Tower Hill. Bridgwater's most famous son is Robert Blake, born in 1598 in a house that is now preserved as a Blake Museum. In the centre of the town is Blake's impressive statue, a fine memorial to a man who distinguished himself as a General in the Civil War and later as an Admiral of the Fleet against the Dutch.

The Route

Initially the road runs mainly eastwards, crossing the Somerset flats to the north of the Polden ridge, through what is now drained marshland until reaching Wells at the foot of the Mendips.

Bawdrip (Somerset)

A feature of the church of St Michael and All Angels is an inscription behind the altar that refers to the Lovell family. It was their daughter, Eleanor, who died mysteriously on her wedding day and became the subject of a ballad *The Mistletoe Bough*. The story tells how on her wedding eve she hid in a chest. When the heavy lid was closed she was trapped there and never found. On the wall of the church is a panel of oak, engraved with Tudor roses, a grim reminder of the tale:

> An old oak chest that had long lain hid
> Was found in the castle; they raised the lid,
> And a skeleton form lay mouldering there,
> In the bridal wreath of the lady fair.

Woolavington (Somerset)

This was once a quiet village, graced by a courthouse, windmill and duck pond. These features have now, regrettably, been swallowed up by a multitude of red-brick housing estates. The road from Woolavington leads northwards, crossing the River Brue by way of the ancient Bason Bridge.

Mark (Somerset)

The village straggles along Mark Causeway for at least a mile. At its

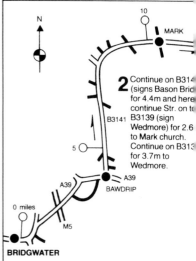

2 Continue on B314 (signs Bason Brid for 4.4m and here continue Str. on to B3139 (sign Wedmore) for 2.6 to Mark church. Continue on B313 for 3.7m to Wedmore.

BRIDGWATER

1 At Bridgwater town centre leave on A38 (sign Bristol). Very shortly bear R. on to A39 (sign Glastonbury). In 1.8m turn R. on to minor road (sign Bradney). In 1.3m bear R. past Bawdrip church (no sign). In 0.3m turn R. on to A39 (no sign). In 0.4m turn L. on to B3141 (sign Woolavington).

eastern extremity is a large and splendid church. By the church gates is an ancient inn, The Packhouse, adjoining which is the house where the Conservative politician and best-selling author Jeffrey Archer spent his boyhood years. When the roof of the inn was replaced an interesting discovery was made – a pair of studded labourer's shoes believed to date back to before 1800. They are of a type known as 'straights' and it was not until after this date that shoes of this type were curved to fit left and right feet.

Wedmore (Somerset)

Perhaps the village name derives from 'Wet Moor'. It has a charming aspect by the church in the heart of the village. A medieval cross graces both the churchyard and a part of Wedmore known as the Borough. To the south of the village, at Mudgley, King Alfred

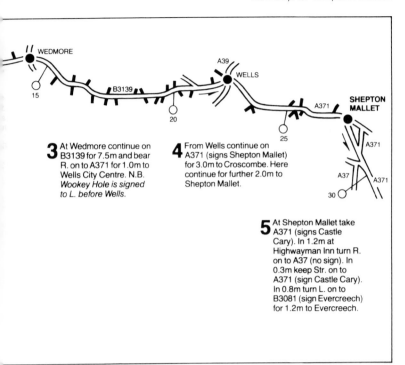

3 At Wedmore continue on B3139 for 7.5m and bear R. on to A371 for 1.0m to Wells City Centre. N.B. *Wookey Hole is signed to L. before Wells.*

4 From Wells continue on A371 (signs Shepton Mallet) for 3.0m to Croscombe. Here continue for further 2.0m to Shepton Mallet.

5 At Shepton Mallet take A371 (signs Castle Cary). In 1.2m at Highwayman Inn turn R. on to A37 (no sign). In 0.3m keep Str. on to A371 (sign Castle Cary). In 0.8m turn L. on to B3081 (sign Evercreech) for 1.2m to Evercreech.

had a palace where he signed the Peace of Wedmore with the Danes. One thousand years later the treaty was commemorated in the church:

Alfred the King at Wedmore made peace
Death of Alfred 901 Edward VII 1901

Wookey Hole (Somerset)

Although the route runs by the village of Wookey Hole, the famous Wookey Hole subterranean cavern and fascinating Ebbor Rocks lie a mile or two to the north (signed later by way of the A371)

Wells (Somerset)

Sheltered beneath the Mendip Hills is this charming cathedral city. The cathedral has an imposing west front, faced with tier upon tier of sculpture and surmounted by 14c and 15c

towers. Many splendid buildings surround the cathedral. Among these are St Cuthbert's Church, of Saxon foundation with a magnificent tower; the Bishop's Palace, where the swans on the moat pull a bell rope when hungry; the Vicar's Close, one of the oldest streets in Europe; and the 15c Bishop Bubwith's Almshouses. Among many old inns are the Crown Inn, where Penn is reputed to have preached from a window; and the Gate House, oldest of all the inns and part of the cathedral gateway.
Crown Hotel, Market Place. T (0749) 73457. (A)
Ancient Gate House, Saddler St. T (0749) 72029. (B)

Shepton Mallet (Somerset)

This lovely old town of the Mendips is named appropriately – a Sheep Town allied with the name of the 12c lord of the manor, a Mallet. There is a fine market cross with stone paved floor and six arches set up, we are told, by Walter Buckland and his wife in 1500 who 'beg our prayers forever'. Next to the cross, and even older, are the Shambles. This row of covered market stalls is believed to have stood here for more than five centuries.

The Shrubbery, Commercial Road. T (0749) 2555. (B)

Right: the imposing west front of Wells Cathedral.

Below left: Gateway to the Bishop's Palace.

Below right: Vicar's Close, one of the oldest streets in Europe.

The Route

There are panoramic views from Creech Hill between Evercreech and Bruton. Delightful unspoilt countryside thereafter.

Evercreech (Somerset)

The first reference to this ancient village is in a charter of Edward the Confessor. St Peter's Church is notable for its 110 ft Perpendicular tower. On the exterior south walls are gargoyles executed by a stonemason in 1842. During the work he had altercations with the vicar, the publican, and two village women and portrayed them as a hideous monster (the vicar), a monkey (the publican), and two gossiping cats.

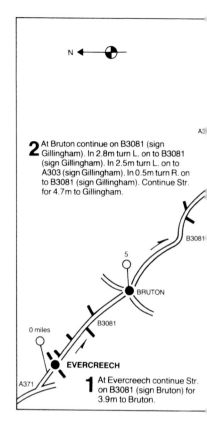

2 At Bruton continue on B3081 (sign Gillingham). In 2.8m turn L. on to B3081 (sign Gillingham). In 2.5m turn L. on to A303 (sign Gillingham). In 0.5m turn R. on to B3081 (sign Gillingham). Continue Str. for 4.7m to Gillingham.

1 At Evercreech continue Str. on B3081 (sign Bruton) for 3.9m to Bruton.

Bruton (Somerset)

The route crosses the bridge over the River Brue in Bruton. It is worth pausing here. A mere hundred yards downstream is a little pack bridge, now a footbridge, scarcely three feet wide. From here also, high on the green hills above, is a view of the dovecote. This is preserved by the National Trust and is almost all that remains of a one-time Augustinian abbey. The dovecote is a tower-like structure of stone with four gables and mullion windows, built early in the 16c. The pride of Bruton is its church and spectacular 15c tower. The buildings of King's School Bruton, originally a monastic establishment, occupy a central position in the town.

Gillingham (Dorset)

The road crossed into Dorset some five miles before descending to this small industrial town. Although surrounded by delightful country on every side, much of Gillingham is now red-brick. At one time it was central to a huge forest, and to the east of the town was the King's Palace, hunting lodge of kings around the time of Henry I.
Stock Hill House, Wyke.
T (074 76) 3626. (A)

East Stour (Dorset)

An old farmhouse by the church on the A303, built in grey stone, was the home of the novelist

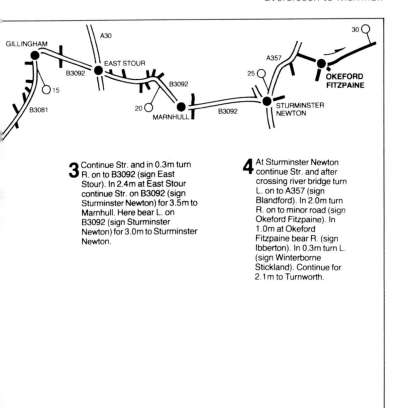

3 Continue Str. and in 0.3m turn R. on to B3092 (sign East Stour). In 2.4m at East Stour continue Str. on B3092 (sign Sturminster Newton) for 3.5m to Marnhull. Here bear L. on B3092 (sign Sturminster Newton) for 3.0m to Sturminster Newton.

4 At Sturminster Newton continue Str. and after crossing river bridge turn L. on to A357 (sign Blandford). In 2.0m turn R. on to minor road (sign Okeford Fitzpaine). In 1.0m at Okeford Fitzpaine bear R. (sign Ibberton). In 0.3m turn L. (sign Winterborne Stickland). Continue for 2.1m to Turnworth.

Henry Fielding (1707–1754) author of *Tom Jones*. It was not, however, until after he moved to London in 1735 that Fielding wrote his first novel, *Joseph Andrews*.

Marnhull (Dorset)

The route passes the charming Crown Inn and 14c church, the bulk of the village lying to the right. Parts of the semi-thatched Crown Inn date back to the 17c. The inn appears in Hardy's *Tess of the d'Urbervilles* as the Pure Drop Inn. An interesting gravestone inscription at the church commemorates one John Warren and his wife who were great smokers, John dying aged 94 in 1752:

> Here under this stone
> Lie Ruth and old John,
> Who smoked all his life,
> And so did his wife.
> And now there's no doubt
> But their pipes are both out.
> Be it said without joke
> That life is but smoke,
> Though we live to fourscore
> 'Tis a whiff and no more.

Among the many picturesque cottages central to Marnhull is the Dial House, a listed building that dates from the 17c. Now the post office, in earlier days it served as a school and a bank.
Crown Inn. T (0258) 820224. (C)

49

The Route

From Sturminster the road runs almost due south through the Winterborne Valley, sheltered by wooded hills on both sides. The final few miles into Bournemouth run through suburbs that cannot be described as attractive.

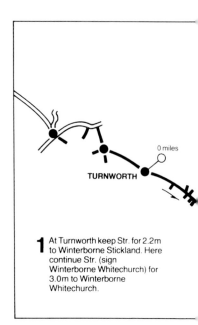

1 At Turnworth keep Str. for 2.2m to Winterborne Stickland. Here continue Str. (sign Winterborne Whitechurch) for 3.0m to Winterborne Whitechurch.

Sturminster Newton (Dorset)

The little town is busy on Mondays when the cattle market takes place near a wooden building known as the Corn Exchange. There is a fine single track bridge across the Stour controlled by traffic lights. A plaque on the bridge reads:

> Any person wilfully injuring any part of this County Bridge will be guilty of Felony and upon conviction liable to be Transported for Life

The church and churchyard occupy a peaceful position above the river and adjacent meadows. Around the church is a network of footpaths and lanes, all with picturesque shops and cottages, many of them thatched. A house of particular interest is Vine House in Penny Street. This broad fronted building with stone mullioned windows dates from the 17c. It was here, as a boy, that the renowned Dorset dialect poet William Barnes was employed as a solicitor's clerk.

Okeford Fitzpaine (Dorset)

A small village of deep narrow lanes and dainty cottages. It

features in the Hardy novel *The Woodlanders* as Oakbury Fitzpiers.

Turnworth (Dorset)

Separated from Okeford Fitzpaine by Okeford Hill, this tiny village nestles in a fold of the downs, sheltered by woods in the heart of Dorset's lovely countryside. Hardy described the manor house as a 'hole of great beauty'. In fact this house was demolished in 1959.

Winterborne Stickland (Dorset)

The church, part Norman, stands beneath a fine pinnacled tower among a cluster of thatched cottages in this quiet village. A mile further along the road is Winterborne Clenston. Here there is little more than the new church

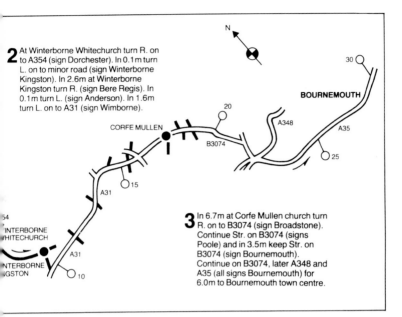

2 At Winterborne Whitechurch turn R. on to A354 (sign Dorchester). In 0.1m turn L. on to minor road (sign Winterborne Kingston). In 2.6m at Winterborne Kingston turn R. (sign Bere Regis). In 0.1m turn L. (sign Anderson). In 1.6m turn L. on to A31 (sign Wimborne).

3 In 6.7m at Corfe Mullen church turn R. on to B3074 (sign Broadstone). Continue Str. on B3074 (signs Poole) and in 3.5m keep Str. on B3074 (sign Bournemouth). Continue on B3074, later A348 and A35 (all signs Bournemouth) for 6.0m to Bournemouth town centre.

with the old manor and tithe barn shaped like a cross.

Winterborne Whitechurch (Dorset)

Yet another of the Winterborne villages – there are at least sixteen in Dorset. This Winterborne was the birthplace of John Wesley's father, Samuel, son of the local vicar. Later Samuel was also ordained, moving to Epworth, Lincs, where John Wesley was born. St Mary's Church has been much restored but stands beneath a 15c tower.

Winterborne Tomson (Dorset)

Immediately before turning on to the A31 a signpost to the left directs to an old gabled farmhouse. By the side of the farm and adjacent to its outbuildings is the tiny church of St Andrew on a site which has been used for worship for more than 800 years. Eventually the church was abandoned, a derelict and forlorn wreck, overrun by donkeys and dogs and gnawed by rats. In 1932, however, the Society for the Protection of Ancient Buildings restored it in memory of one of its members, Albert Powys, who is buried in the churchyard. No services take place here but it is a delight to step into this building with its remarkable barrel roof and high box pews.

Corfe Mullen (Dorset)

The church stands above meadows, often flooded, on the main road, close to the River Stour. The rest of this large village, however, straggles away from the river to the south.

3   North Yorkshire, Cleveland

PRIOR TO 1974 the county of Yorkshire was divided into Ridings. Then reorganization gave birth to the separate counties of North, South and West Yorkshire. The county of Cleveland, also created in 1974, embraces areas on both banks of the River Tees formerly included in Durham and the North Riding of Yorkshire.

The greater part of this route is confined to North Yorkshire, in particular the lovely North Yorkshire Moors National Park. The northernmost stretches of the route run from east to west through the fringe of Cleveland. It is interesting to note that despite all this reorganization North Yorkshire remains England's largest county.

The early part of the route, from Oswaldkirk to Staithes, runs roughly north east through the heart of the North Yorkshire Moors National Park. The latter part, from Guisborough to Coxwold, runs almost due south on the western fringes of the park, the Cleveland and Hambleton Hills always at hand.

Nowhere else in England, perhaps, can match this part of the country for wildness of scenery. Within the National Park there are more than 1,000 miles of public footpaths and bridleways quite apart from the extensive network of country roads.

Almost half of the National Park is open moorland, providing the richest supply of heather to be found in the country, at its best when in full bloom in August and September. Throughout the moors sheep graze on unfenced roads and can also be found wandering through the moorland villages. Only cautious drivers are welcome here. Red grouse thrive on the moorland heather. The stone-built shooting butts by the side of the roads are only put to use during the season (12 August to 10 December).

Apart from scenery and wildlife, a feature of the moors are the stone crosses. There are said to be at least thirty named crosses within the park, many of ancient origin but most of them set up in medieval times to assist walkers to navigate this remote wilderness. Among those passed along the route is Ralph Cross, chosen by the National Park Committee as the emblem of the park and lying at its centre.

The coastline scenery that marks the eastern boundary of the park is superlative, with Boulby Cliff, just north of Staithes and 666 ft above the sea, the highest point along the English coast. Staithes village has much of the charm of Clovelly in Devon and Polperro in Cornwall. It is less of a tourist trap, however, and consequently more natural than the villages of the south west.

Perhaps the most beautiful section of the route lies where the road returns southwards from Swainby through Osmotherley to Hawnby. All three villages lie close to the Cleveland Way, ideal centres for ramblers wishing to explore further.

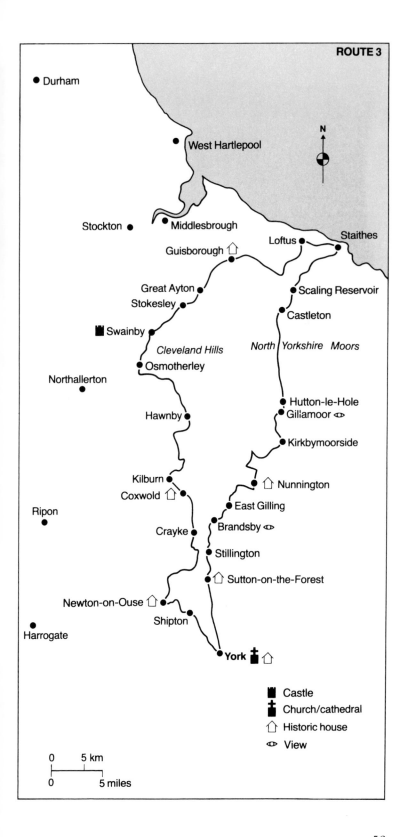

ROUTE 3

Durham

West Hartlepool

N

Stockton   Middlesbrough

Loftus   Staithes

Guisborough ⌂

Scaling Reservoir

Great Ayton

Stokesley

Castleton

Swainby

Cleveland Hills

North Yorkshire Moors

Northallerton

Osmotherley

Hawnby

Hutton-le-Hole

Giliamoor ⚌

Kirkbymoorside

Kilburn

Coxwold ⌂

⌂ Nunnington

East Gilling

Ripon

Brandsby ⚌

Crayke

Stillington

Sutton-on-the-Forest ⌂

Newton-on-Ouse ⌂

Shipton

Harrogate

York ✝ ⌂

▉ Castle

✝ Church/cathedral

⌂ Historic house

⚌ View

0   5 km

0   5 miles

York

Paulinus, the first Bishop of York, baptized King Edwin at a wooden church here in 627 AD. Six hundred years later, on the site of this church, York Minster was begun, developing over more than two centuries. The Minster is famous for its grand west front and stained glass, among the finest in Europe.

Large sections of the 14c city walls survive, along them four gateways, or bars as they are called here – Bootham, Micklegate, Monk and Walmgate – necessary bastions of defence in more turbulent days.

Over the centuries York has, of course, had many visitors. In 71 AD it began as a Roman fortress. When the Vikings came their brief tenure gave York its name, a derivation of Jorvik. Apart from its historical associations, lovely cathedral and well-preserved city walls, York has much else to offer. Among many attractions are Stonegate, a traffic-free shopping area rich in medieval and Georgian architecture; Clifford's Tower, the 13c keep of York Castle; the Treasurer's House (National Trust), built on the site of the Roman legionary fortress; and the Mansion House, the only house in England used solely as the official private residence of the Lord Mayor during his term of office.

Among many museums are the National Railway Museum and the famous Castle Folk Museum with its fascinating area of reconstructed streets, shops, schools, prison cells and inns.

Viking Hotel, North St. T (0904) 59822. (A)
Post House, Tadcaster Rd. T (0904) 707921. (A)
Abbots Mews, Marygate Lane. T (0904) 34866. (B)

Staithes, in a picturesque setting.

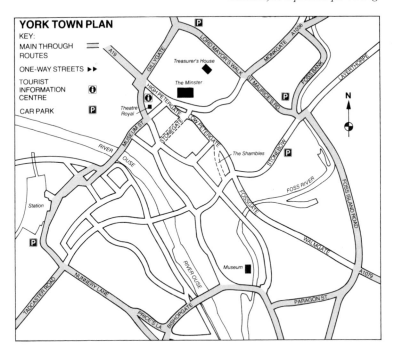

Town House, Holgate Rd. T (0904) 36171. (B)
Tourist Office, Exhibition Square. T (0904) 21756

The Route

The first eight miles are through the plain of York. Thereafter, from Sutton-on-the-Forest, delightful rural scenery with wooded hills on all sides.

6 In 2.9m turn R. (sign Kirkbymoorside). 0.4m turn R. (sign Kirkbymoorside). In 0.4m at Welburn turn L. (sign Kirkbymoorside). In 0.3m turn R. on to A170 (sign Kirkbymoorside). In 1.2m t L. (sign Town Centre) for 0.2m to Kirkbymoorside centre.

KIRKBYMOORSIDE

A170

25

30

NUNNINGTON

OSWALDKIRK

20 EAST GILLING

4 At East Gilling continue Str. on B1363. In 1.8m at Oswaldkirk bear R. (sign Helmsley). In 0.1m turn R. on to B1257 (sign Malton). In 0.9m turn L. on to minor road (sign Nunnington).

Sutton-on-the-Forest
(N. Yorks)

A spacious village, the cottages fronted by green verges with added colour when the daffodils are in bloom. The church and Sutton Park face each other. The Irish writer Laurence Sterne (1713–1768) was vicar here for twenty years, beginning his novel *Tristram Shandy* which he was to complete at Coxwold (page 67). Sutton Park is an early Georgian house built in 1730. It is open to the public on occasions during the summer months. The contents of the house include Chippendale, Sheraton and French furniture. The surrounding park was designed by Capability Brown with gardens created by the owners that contain a fine rose garden, shrubs, herbaceous borders and a lily pond.
Rose and Crown Inn.
T (0347) 810351. No accommodation but excellent bar meals and dining room.

Stillington (N. Yorks)

Another picturesque village with a broad main street lined by greens.

Brandsby (N. Yorks)

The church is signed to the right, almost a mile from the village. It is worth visiting for the superb view of the wooded Howardian Hills to the east. All Saints Church was built around 1770 and is surmounted by a magnificent open cupola. Within the church is some fine oak panelling, the mouse signifying that here is yet more of the work of Robert Thompson, The 'Mouseman of Kilburn' (pages 66–7).

East Gilling (N. Yorks)

Hidden in thick woods above the village is Gilling Castle, now a preparatory school for nearby Amplethorpe but open to the public on specified occasions. The village is a delight, lying beneath the Hambleton Hills to the north and the Howardian Hills to the

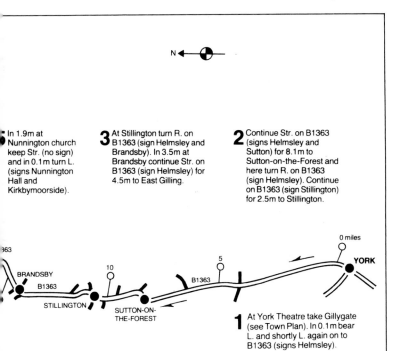

5 In 1.9m at Nunnington church keep Str. (no sign) and in 0.1m turn L. (signs Nunnington Hall and Kirkbymoorside).

3 At Stillington turn R. on B1363 (sign Helmsley and Brandsby). In 3.5m at Brandsby continue Str. on B1363 (sign Helmsley) for 4.5m to East Gilling.

2 Continue Str. on B1363 (signs Helmsley and Sutton) for 8.1m to Sutton-on-the-Forest and here turn R. on B1363 (sign Helmsley). Continue on B1363 (sign Stillington) for 2.5m to Stillington.

1 At York Theatre take Gillygate (see Town Plan). In 0.1m bear L. and shortly L. again on to B1363 (signs Helmsley).

south, with sparkling streams that cascade past the cottages and pleasant inn. The oldest parts of the Church of the Holy Cross are contained in the nave and date from the 11c.

Nunnington (N. Yorks)

Stands above the River Rye, the pride of the village being Nunnington Hall which since 1952 has been owned by the National Trust. The most distinguished name associated with Nunnington is Lord Preston, a Stuart supporter who retired here discreetly, remodelling the south front of the house and being responsible for much of the interior design on view today. Lord Preston died here in 1695.

Kirkbymoorside (N. Yorks)

An old market town with a broad main street and a variety of old inns. Among these is the George and Dragon Hotel that adjoins the timbered Black Swan Inn which dates from 1632 and has a porch beneath an overhanging room. The town stands to the immediate south of the North Yorkshire moors, a placid place that stands aloof from the busy A170 which runs from east to west to the south of the town.
George and Dragon Hotel.
T (0751) 31637. (C)

The Route

Runs from north to south through the heart of the heather-clad moors. The final stretch from Scaling to Staithes is a beautiful road between the Roxby and Easington Becks – a narrow stretch fortunately not much in use.

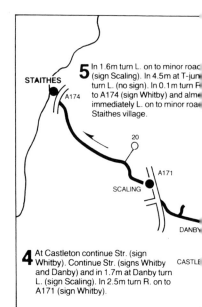

5 In 1.6m turn L. on to minor road (sign Scaling). In 4.5m at T-jun turn L. (no sign). In 0.1m turn F to A174 (sign Whitby) and almo immediately L. on to minor road Staithes village.

4 At Castleton continue Str. (sign Whitby). Continue Str. (signs Whitby and Danby) and in 1.7m at Danby turn L. (sign Scaling). In 2.5m turn R. on to A171 (sign Whitby).

Gillamoor (N. Yorks)

An enchanting out-of-the-way village on the fringe of the moors. From the east of the churchyard there is a magnificent view of the River Dove and the Farndale valley, bedecked with wild daffodils in spring. On the exterior

The beautiful Farndale Valley, from Gillamoor.

N ←

1 At Kirkbymoorside town centre keep Str. (sign Gillamoor) and in 0.1m turn L. (sign Gillamoor). Keep Str. (signs Gillamoor) for 2.5m to Gillamoor.

3 Continue Str. through moors (signs Castleton) for 11.6m to Castleton.

2 At Gillamoor turn R. (sign Hutton-le-Hole). In 0.7m bear R. (sign Hutton-le-Hole). In 1.1m turn L. (sign Castleton).

59

church wall to the east of the porch is a tablet inscribed: 'Here lie deposited the ashes of James Smith of Farndale, stonemason. He was a sound workman – and in consequence selected to rebuild this chapel which he completed with his own hands in the summer of 1802.' Shortly after leaving Gillamoor the road runs north through the heart of the moors, within half a mile of Hutton-le-Hole.

Hutton-le-Hole (N. Yorks)

Worth the half-mile diversion. The village cottages fan out in a V-shape, the prongs divided by Hutton Beck which flows swiftly down from Spaunton Moor. Several little footbridges span the stream. There are large expanses of green where sheep graze among the village buildings. The Crown Inn dates from 1695 and

close to it is the Ryedale Folk Museum, filled with local agricultural and domestic implements used in these parts over centuries. At Rosedale Head, between Hutton-le-Hole and Castleton, note Ralph Cross (left), a remarkable nine-foot tall stone cross that stands in the geographical centre of the moors.

Castleton (N. Yorks)

Lies in the midst of the Esk Valley. There was once a Norman castle here. The earthworks can be seen to the west of the church, overlooking the Esk.
Moorlands Hotel.
T (0287) 60206. (C)

Danby (N. Yorks)

The road continues northward from the village. However, it is worth visiting the Moors Centre (half a mile off the route). This former shooting lodge is open daily with a large exhibition area and a programme of illustrated talks, slides and films – everything, in fact, one needs to learn about the National Park.

Scaling (Cleveland)

At this point the road crosses into the edge of the county of Cleveland. The Scaling Reservoir lies to the south of the A171, hemmed in by moors on every side. Sailing is allowed here and nearby is a pleasant inn, the Bunch of Grapes.

Staithes (N. Yorks)

Essential to park above the village as there is no room for cars at the foot of the steep hill that descends to the water's edge. From the car park a sign 'To the Beach' indicates the start of a footpath that zigzags down past a jumble of quaint cottages perched precariously on the side of the hill. A network of narrow cobbled streets twists between houses of every shape, size and hue. The picturesque Cod and Lobster Inn is said to have been washed away by high seas on at least three occasions. Near to the inn is a small house, once a grocer's shop, where the explorer James Cook (1728–79) was apprenticed before running away to Whitby and signing on as a cabin boy. Those seeking accommodation in this fine coastal area might be advised to divert some nine miles to Whitby (see *Through Britain on Country Roads*, page 164). The two hotels below are highly recommended.
Royal Hotel, West Cliff.
T (0947) 602234. (B)
Saxonville, Ladysmith Avenue.
T (0947) 602631. (B)

Dairy equipment in the Ryedale Folk Museum, Hutton-le-Hole.

The Route

The first part is inevitably by an A road and initially, around Loftus and Liverton, rather dull. After Great Ayton the Cleveland Hills dominate the scene to the east.

Loftus (Cleveland)

A busy little mining town built on a steep hillside. There is little to note either here or at the nearby villages of Liverton and Moorsholm.

Guisborough (Cleveland)

This lies to the north of the wooded Cleveland Hills with a broad main street, tree-lined with cobbled verges and an old market cross. The glory of the town is the Priory, founded in about 1119 by Robert de Bruce, a monastery that dominated the town throughout the Middle Ages. Although most of the monastic buildings can only be picked out by stone relics, the Norman gateway survives as does the magnificent east end of the church that towers over the scene. The other distinctive feature is the dovecote, added in the 16c. At present (1987) English Heritage are excavating. Among the early remains, at a depth of six feet, fragments of pottery were found which showed that Saxon occupation preceded the Norman priory.

Newton under Roseberry (Cleveland)

The village lies on the western fringe of the moors. To the east is Roseberry Common with Roseberry Topping (1,051 ft) an impressive landmark.

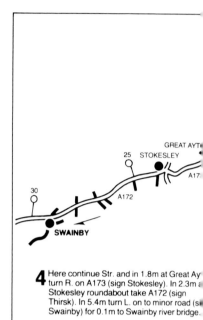

4 Here continue Str. and in 1.8m at Great Ayton turn R. on A173 (sign Stokesley). In 2.3m at Stokesley roundabout take A172 (sign Thirsk). In 5.4m turn L. on to minor road (sign Swainby) for 0.1m to Swainby river bridge.

Great Ayton (N. Yorks)

The first sight of the village is not impressive. However, it is well worth following the signs to the village centre, for here is a peaceful scene, full of historic interest. There is a large, semi-circular village green and the River Leven flows beside the main street. The Royal Oak, an old coaching inn, faces the green with a 1771 sundial over the porch. On the green a noticeboard depicts a Heritage Trail, linking places associated with Captain Cook in the surrounding countryside. The explorer's early education was in the little brown school-house near the green, now a Cook Museum with an inscription telling that the boy's fees were paid by his father's employer. In Bridge Street is a monument hewn out of stone from Hicks Point, the explorer's first sighting of Australia and named after one of his officers. The monument stands on the site where the Cook family's cottage stood before it was dismantled

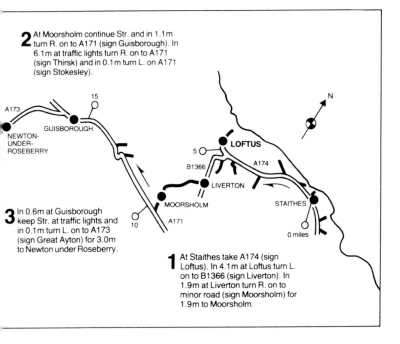

2 At Moorsholm continue Str. and in 1.1m turn R. on to A171 (sign Guisborough). In 6.1m at traffic lights turn R. on to A171 (sign Thirsk) and in 0.1m turn L. on A171 (sign Stokesley).

A173

15

GUISBOROUGH

NEWTON-UNDER-ROSEBERRY

N

5 LOFTUS

B1366

A174

LIVERTON

MOORSHOLM

STAITHES

10

A171

0 miles

3 In 0.6m at Guisborough keep Str. at traffic lights and in 0.1m turn L. on to A173 (sign Great Ayton) for 3.0m to Newton under Roseberry.

1 At Staithes take A174 (sign Loftus). In 4.1m at Loftus turn L. on to B1366 (sign Liverton). In 1.9m at Liverton turn R. on to minor road (sign Moorsholm) for 1.9m to Moorsholm.

and shipped to Australia. In the graveyard of the church is the tomb of Cook's mother and sisters. Above the village on Easby Moor is the Cook Memorial, erected in 1827, forty-eight years after the explorer was killed at Owkyee.

Stokesley (N. Yorks)

A pleasant market town that lies to the immediate left of the route. The River Leven flows beside one of the streets, crossed by several bridges.

Bridge across the River Leven at Stokesley.

The Route

Spectacular moorland scenery throughout. Between Swainby and Osmotherley is the pine-fringed Codbeck Reservoir.

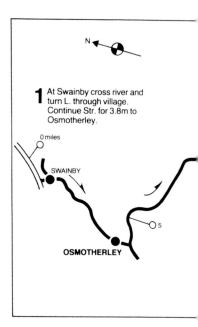

1 At Swainby cross river and turn L. through village. Continue Str. for 3.8m to Osmotherley.

Swainby (N. Yorks)

A charming and spacious village where the Scugdale Beck flows, dividing Swainby into two distinct lines of cottages. To the left a cul-de-sac ascends sharply to Whorl Hill. Here on the left is the gatehouse of Whorlton Castle (1400). Over the archway are the carved shields of Meynell, Darnley and Grey. A former occupant of the castle was the Earl of Lennox, father of Henry Stuart Darnley (1545–67), the ill-fated second husband of Mary Queen of Scots. A little further along the road (right) is the little church with a roofless nave and Norman chancel.

Osmotherley (N. Yorks)

A large yet enchanting village where stone-built houses stand near the village green. Here is the cross where John Wesley (1703–91) once preached. The Cleveland Hills lie to the east with the Hambleton Hills to the south, making the village an ideal centre for ramblers. The Cleveland Way, opened in 1969 and one of England's best-loved footpath walks, encircles Osmotherley.

Hawnby (N. Yorks)

A little hamlet set on the wooded slopes of the Hambleton Hills overlooking the Rye Valley. It was a surprise to find this pleasant hotel in such a secluded area. *Hawnby Hotel.* T (043 96) 202. (B)

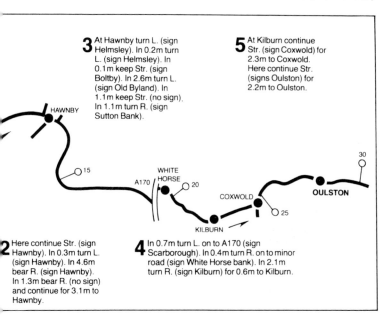

3 At Hawnby turn L. (sign Helmsley). In 0.2m turn L. (sign Helmsley). In 0.1m keep Str. (sign Boltby). In 2.6m turn L. (sign Old Byland). In 1.1m keep Str. (no sign). In 1.1m turn R. (sign Sutton Bank).

5 At Kilburn continue Str. (sign Coxwold) for 2.3m to Coxwold. Here continue Str. (signs Oulston) for 2.2m to Oulston.

HAWNBY

15

A170

WHITE HORSE 20

COXWOLD

KILBURN

25

OULSTON

30

2 Here continue Str. (sign Hawnby). In 0.3m turn L. (sign Hawnby). In 4.6m bear R. (sign Hawnby). In 1.3m bear R. (no sign) and continue for 3.1m to Hawnby.

4 In 0.7m turn L. on to A170 (sign Scarborough). In 0.4m turn R. on to minor road (sign White Horse bank). In 2.1m turn R. (sign Kilburn) for 0.6m to Kilburn.

Black Hambleton and Cleveland Way, near Osmotherley.

Kilburn (N. Yorks)

Before descending the steep hill to Kilburn the road passes the famous White Horse (right). This figure was carved in chalk in 1857 by the village schoolmaster and his pupils. The horse, 314 ft long and 228 ft high, serves as a landmark visible for miles. From the car park a one-and-a-half mile trail round the horse begins, the paths marked by red arrows. Kilburn's fame relies chiefly, however, on Robert Thompson, the 'Mouseman of Kilburn' who was born here in 1876. His carving from oak timber was of such rare quality that by his death in 1955 his work could be seen in 700 churches, among them Westminster Abbey and York Minster. His trademark, a carved mouse, is explained by a conversation once held with a fellow carver: 'I was carving a beam on a church roof when another carver, Charlie Barker, murmured something about us being as poor as church mice, and on the spur of the moment I decided to carve one. Afterwards

The Kilburn White Horse.

I decided to adopt the mouse as a trademark.' Examples of Thompson's craft can be seen in several of the churches along this route. His workshops still stand in Kilburn and are on view to the public.

Coxwold (N. Yorks)

In the opinion of many, Coxwold is one of Yorkshire's loveliest villages. The main street is steep, broad and tree-lined with stone houses and honey-coloured cottages, fronted by greens and cobbled verges. Oliver Cromwell's daughter Mary married the Earl of Fauconberg, and the 17c inn bearing the family crest is called after him. The almshouses, single-storeyed with mullioned windows, were endowed by Lady Fauconberg. Another famous name associated with the village is that of the novelist Laurence Sterne. It was here that he completed *Tristram Shandy*, naming his house at the end of the village Shandy Hall. It is open to the public as a museum.
Fauconberg Arms.
T (034 76) 214. (C)

The Route

These final few miles of the route traverse the fertile plain of York by way of quiet traffic-free roads.

1 At Oulston continue Str. (no sign). In 1.1m keep Str. (sign Crayke) for 1.7m to Crayke.

Crayke (N. Yorks)

Almost the last village before returning to the plain of York, the houses climbing the hill with its battlemented church and imposing tower. Also on the hill are fragments of the Norman castle that once dominated the plain. When the body of St Cuthbert was moved from Lindisfarne to Durham in 995 it was said to have rested here at the church, accounting for the name of the village inn, the Durham Ox.

Newton-on-Ouse (N. Yorks)

It is a surprise to come upon a massive house in the midst of the flat plain of York. Beningbrough Hall (National Trust) was built in 1716, a tall rectangular building of mellow brick linked to balancing pavilions. Outstanding features are the two-storey hall and staircase with stair treads more than seven feet wide. The National Portrait Gallery exhibits one hundred 17th and 18th century portraits at the hall.

The battlemented church at Crayke.

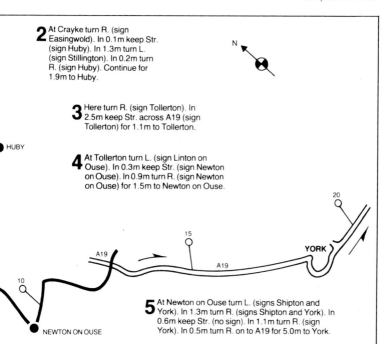

2 At Crayke turn R. (sign Easingwold). In 0.1m keep Str. (sign Huby). In 1.3m turn L. (sign Stillington). In 0.2m turn R. (sign Huby). Continue for 1.9m to Huby.

3 Here turn R. (sign Tollerton). In 2.5m keep Str. across A19 (sign Tollerton) for 1.1m to Tollerton.

● HUBY

4 At Tollerton turn L. (sign Linton on Ouse). In 0.3m keep Str. (sign Newton on Ouse). In 0.9m turn R. (sign Newton on Ouse) for 1.5m to Newton on Ouse.

A19

15

20

YORK

A19

10

NEWTON ON OUSE

5 At Newton on Ouse turn L. (signs Shipton and York). In 1.3m turn R. (signs Shipton and York). In 0.6m keep Str. (no sign). In 1.1m turn R. (sign York). In 0.5m turn R. on to A19 for 5.0m to York.

Beningbrough Hall, Newton-on-Ouse.

69

4 Lincolnshire

THE ROUTE is confined entirely to Lincolnshire, a county which with the reorganization of 1974 lost a sector on the Humber in the north to Humberside.

Shortly after leaving Lincoln the route runs from north to south through the heart of the peaceful countryside of the Wolds, a forty-mile stretch of chalk uplands that have been designated an area of outstanding natural beauty. The Bluestone Heath Road, between Scamblesby and Tetford, provides a lofty vantage point giving a panorama of the beautiful Wolds countryside. To the south is Tennyson country. It is an area featured in much of his poetry and it was at Somersby that the poet was born and spent his boyhood and early manhood. He expresses his love of his country home with lines written when anticipating a visit from his friend, Arthur Hallam, to the vicarage:

> Witch-elms that counterchange the floor
> Of this flat lawn with dusk and bright;
> And thou with all thy breadth and height
> Of foliage, towering sycamore;
> How often, hither wandering down,
> My Arthur found your shadows fair,
> And shook to all the liberal air
> The dust and din and steam of town.

The road now runs south westward past Horncastle, once famous for its horse fair, and the spacious village of Tattershall with its splendid church and National Trust-owned castle. From here the road runs through the Fens, fertile agricultural land criss-crossed by flood banks and water channels, some of which date from Saxon times. Houses gabled in the Dutch style are a feature here, as are windmills, in particular the well-preserved mill at Heckington.

After crossing the Fens the road returns once more to a rolling landscape with many beautiful villages that compare favourably with those of the Wolds. The extreme western part of the route almost enters Leicestershire. Only a mile diversion is needed to view Belvoir Castle in all its wooded grandeur. In this latter part of the route there are prominent wooded hills around Denton and Woolsthorpe, while later the villages of Hough-on-the-Hill, Fulbeck and Stragglethorpe are of particular beauty. Before returning to Lincoln the final village to note is Doddington, the Hall there being among the finest on view in the county.

Lincoln

At one time the city was among the most important Roman centres in Britain. Lindum Colonia was a fortress on the hilltop where the cathedral and castle were later to be built. Newport Arch (start of the route) is a monumental gate of Roman origin, as is the lower Westgate.

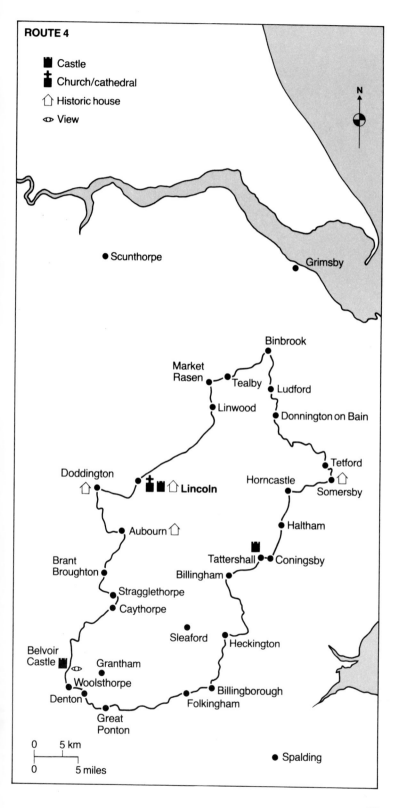

Later came the Saxons, then the Danes, as street names like Danes-gate and Saltergate testify. It is the Norman influence, however, that predominates. It was they who began the cathedral and built the castle where the keep, Lucy's Tower, still stands. The glory of Lincoln is the cathedral, begun in 1072, the triple pinnacled towers crowning the hill-top. The early structure was damaged, first by fire and later by earthquake. It was not until 1192 that the building as seen today began to take shape.

Alongside the keep of the Norman castle is the Observatory Tower, a 19c addition. Among other Norman buildings are Jew's Court and Jew's House, adjoining each other in Steep Hill, and Aaron's House, further up Steep Hill. The Guildhall in High Street, also of Norman origin, has a fine open timber roof where the civic insignia include the Richard II and Henry VII swords.

Other buildings of interest include the remains of the Old Bishop's Palace (13c), to the south side of the cathedral, and the timbered medieval Green Dragon Inn. The High Bridge shops are built on a 12c bridge, the oldest bridge in Britain still to carry buildings. Among the museums are the City and County Museum, housed in the oldest surviving Franciscan chapel in Britain, with local and natural history collections; the Usher Gallery, with paintings of the area and a Tennyson exhibition room; and the National Cycle Museum.

White Hart Hotel, Bailgate. T (0522) 26222. (A)
Duke William, Bailgate. T (0522) 33351. (B)
Hillcrest, Lindum Terrace. T (0522) 26341. (B)
Tourist Office, Castle Hill. T (0522) 29828.

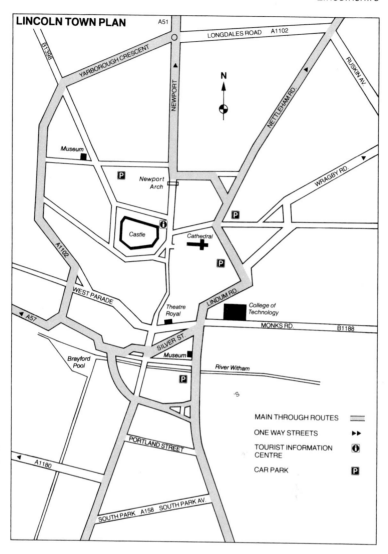

LINCOLN TOWN PLAN

MAIN THROUGH ROUTES

ONE WAY STREETS ▶▶

TOURIST INFORMATION CENTRE ⓘ

CAR PARK Ⓟ

The Bluestone Heath Road near Tetford Hill, on the Lincolnshire wolds.

The Route

Flat and a little dull for the first few miles. Fine wooded country as the road runs from Market Rasen to Tealby and the Wolds.

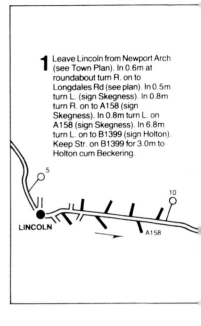

1 Leave Lincoln from Newport Arch (see Town Plan). In 0.6m at roundabout turn R. on to Longdales Rd (see plan). In 0.5m turn L. (sign Skegness). In 0.8m turn R. on to A158 (sign Skegness). In 0.8m turn L. on A158 (sign Skegness). In 6.8m turn L. on to B1399 (sign Holton). Keep Str. on B1399 for 3.0m to Holton cum Beckering.

Holton-cum-Beckering (Lincs)

A quiet little village, the church approached by a path of yew trees. To the south meanders a stream, separating Holton from the smaller hamlet of Beckering. Much of the church was restored a century ago, a feature being the variety of dark paintings on the walls.

Linwood (Lincs)

The church dedicated to St Cornelius, the third century Roman bishop, lies in a secluded lane by Eleanor Wood and Lyndewode Wood to the south of the village. Linwood gets its name from John Lyndewode, woolstapler, of whom there is a brass (1419) in the church. One of John's seven sons, William, was a favourite of Henry VI and helped to found Eton College. Linwood Warren, to the north east, has been preserved as a nature reserve, an area of birch and pine that harbours a variety of wild birds.

Market Rasen (Lincs)

A busy market town surrounded by woods and sheltered to the east by the high Lincolnshire Wolds. The church, much restored with a 15c tower, stands by the square. The racecourse to the east of the town is a popular National Hunt venue.
Limes Hotel, Gainsborough Road.
T (0673) 842357. (A)

Tealby (Lincs)

Stands near the north of the high Lincolnshire Wolds. There is a marvellous view of the village from the church with its impressive square pinnacled tower. Spread out below are the houses with pantile rooftops and the school beneath a quaint spire. Bayons Manor, home of Alfred Lord Tennyson's grandfather, stood here until its demolition in 1964. The poet's brother Charles was a curate at the church.

Binbrook (Lincs)

One of the larger villages of the Wolds and set in their heart – a spacious place with a large square which no longer, however, holds a market. The Royal Australian Air Force were stationed here during the Second World War.

Castle Buildings at Lincoln.

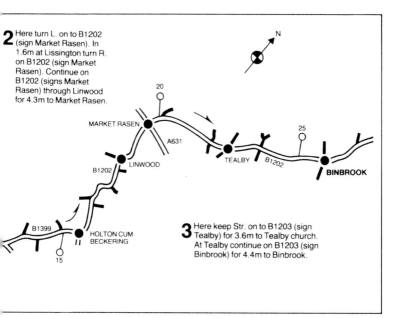

2 Here turn L. on to B1202 (sign Market Rasen). In 1.6m at Lissington turn R. on B1202 (sign Market Rasen). Continue on B1202 (signs Market Rasen) through Linwood for 4.3m to Market Rasen.

3 Here keep Str. on to B1203 (sign Tealby) for 3.6m to Tealby church. At Tealby continue on B1203 (sign Binbrook) for 4.4m to Binbrook.

The Route

The peaceful country roads run from north to south through the heart of the Wolds. Fine views from Bluestone Heath that runs along the spine of Tetford Hill between Scamblesby and Tetford. On the right, here, a notice points to surrounding features and villages.

Ludford (Lincs)

The road skirts the fringe of the village which lies on the busy road from Louth to Market Rasen. On the left of the road to Burgh on Bain are the wrought iron gates of Girsby Park which once surrounded Girsby Manor, now demolished.

Burgh on Bain (Lincs)

To the south of the village is Baxter Square Farm where relics of the Bronze Age have been discovered. In the chancel of the church is a tablet recording that its restoration is in memory of Flora Fox, one-time occupant of Girsby Manor.

Donnington on Bain (Lincs)

It is worth pausing at the water-mill (left) before entering the village. The small church, 13c or 14c, has a fine tower built in 1779. On the north wall of the chancel is a brass plate commemorating Thomas Kent (died 1638) which concludes:

The learned modest pious Thomas Kent
Late Rector of this Church, as whilome were
His good old father and his brother deare,
Fame hath his praise, ye world his life welle spent,
His spirit heaven, his bones this monument.

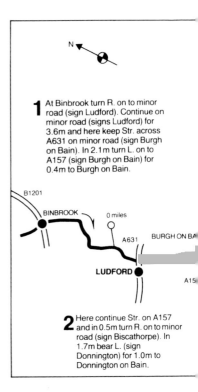

1 At Binbrook turn R. on to minor road (sign Ludford). Continue on minor road (signs Ludford) for 3.6m and here keep Str. across A631 on minor road (sign Burgh on Bain). In 2.1m turn L. on to A157 (sign Burgh on Bain) for 0.4m to Burgh on Bain.

2 Here continue Str. on A157 and in 0.5m turn R. on to minor road (sign Biscathorpe). In 1.7m bear L. (sign Donnington) for 1.0m to Donnington on Bain.

Watermill, Donnington on Bain.

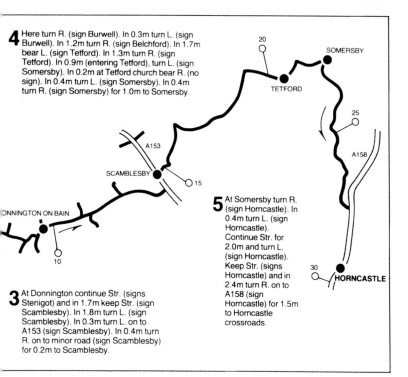

4 Here turn R. (sign Burwell). In 0.3m turn L. (sign Burwell). In 1.2m turn R. (sign Belchford). In 1.7m bear L. (sign Tetford). In 1.3m turn R. (sign Tetford). In 0.9m (entering Tetford), turn L. (sign Somersby). In 0.2m at Tetford church bear R. (no sign). In 0.4m turn L. (sign Somersby). In 0.4m turn R. (sign Somersby) for 1.0m to Somersby.

3 At Donnington continue Str. (signs Stenigot) and in 1.7m keep Str. (sign Scamblesby). In 1.8m turn L. (sign Scamblesby). In 0.3m turn L. on to A153 (sign Scamblesby). In 0.4m turn R. on to minor road (sign Scamblesby) for 0.2m to Scamblesby.

5 At Somersby turn R. (sign Horncastle). In 0.4m turn L. (sign Horncastle). Continue Str. for 2.0m and turn L. (sign Horncastle). Keep Str. (signs Horncastle) and in 2.4m turn R. on to A158 (sign Horncastle) for 1.5m to Horncastle crossroads.

Tetford (Lincs)

Wooded hills surround Tetford, a village that lies amid a circle of lanes.
White Hart Hotel.
T (065 883) 255. (C)

Somersby (Lincs)

Set in a wooded hollow, the most prominent buildings are the church, a battlemented house that faces the church and was built in 1722, and the former rectory where Alfred Lord Tennyson was born in 1809. Recalling his love of the place he wrote of:

> The seven elms, the poplars four
> That stand beneath my father's door.
> (*Ode to Memory*)

Even before the ravages of Dutch elm disease the trees to which the poet referred had vanished. But the long rambling yellow building, almost opposite the church, still stands. There is a bust of the poet in the church. He spent his first twenty-six years here, looking back on his departure with nostalgia:

> I turn to go; my feet are set
> To leave the pleasant fields and farms;
> They mix in one another's arms
> To one pure image of regret. (*In Memoriam*)

Horncastle (Lincs)

The route turns southwards at the edge of Horncastle, a pleasant town that stands between the Wolds and the Fens. Here was the site of a Roman fort, Bonovallum. It was once the scene of a famous horse fair described by George Borrow in *The Romany Rye* (1857).
Bull Hotel, Bull Ring.
T (065 82) 3331. (C)

The Route

Pleasant country roads to Tattershall. Thereafter the road runs through the heart of the flat Lincolnshire Fens, with some charming villages along the way.

Haltham (Lincs)

Lies between the River Bain to the west and Haltham Beck and Wood to the east. On the right is a picturesque thatched Elizabethan inn, the Marmion Arms. The nave of the church has a 13c arcade with arches and stone seats at the base of the pillars.

Coningsby (Lincs)

Before reaching the centre of this small town on the River Bain the prominent church tower comes into view. Its particular significance is the huge clock face, 16 ft in diameter and said to be the largest clock in the world with a single hour hand. The dial of the clock is so big that one can tell the time from a great distance.

Tattershall (Lincs)

In the spacious square, once the market place, is the War Memorial and beside it the Cromwell Cross, rising above four stone steps with the shield of Ralph Cromwell. Towering above the village is the great keep, more than 100 ft high, the remains of the castle built by Cromwell between 1435 and 1445. Ralph Cromwell was one of Shakespeare's 'band of brothers' who fought at Agincourt, later becoming Lord Treasurer to Henry VI. This great tower of four storeys topped by four hexagonal corner towers stands above the moat. In the church is a brass of Ralph Cromwell, a headless armoured figure. The terraced brick-built Bede Almshouses under a pantile

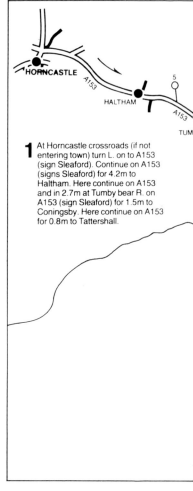

1 At Horncastle crossroads (if not entering town) turn L. on to A153 (sign Sleaford). Continue on A153 (signs Sleaford) for 4.2m to Haltham. Here continue on A153 and in 2.7m at Tumby bear R. on A153 (sign Sleaford) for 1.5m to Coningsby. Here continue on A153 for 0.8m to Tattershall.

The imposing keep of Tattershall Castle.

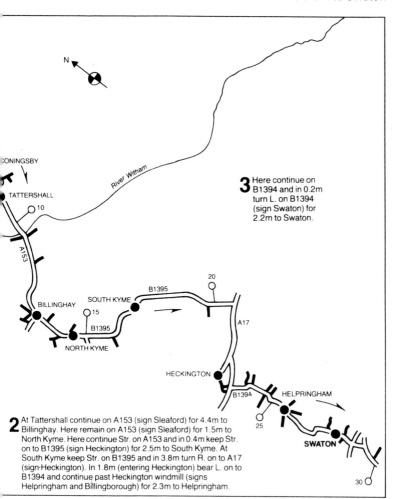

3 Here continue on B1394 and in 0.2m turn L. on B1394 (sign Swaton) for 2.2m to Swaton.

2 At Tattershall continue on A153 (sign Sleaford) for 4.4m to Billinghay. Here remain on A153 (sign Sleaford) for 1.5m to North Kyme. Here continue Str. on A153 and in 0.4m keep Str. on to B1395 (sign Heckington) for 2.5m to South Kyme. At South Kyme keep Str. on B1395 and in 3.8m turn R. on to A17 (sign·Heckington). In 1.8m (entering Heckington) bear L. on to B1394 and continue past Heckington windmill (signs Helpringham and Billingborough) for 2.3m to Helpringham.

roof stand to the north of the church amid pleasant gardens. First built in 1440, they have been restored recently.

Billinghay (Lincs)

From this large village the road runs southwards directly through the Fens to North and South Kyme. Nothing in particular to note in any of these villages.

Heckington (Lincs)

The route runs southwards before entering the centre of the village. Heckington is worth visiting as here is one of the finest 14c churches in England. It is a big church, 150 ft long and standing beneath a tower with four pinnacles and a spire. Returning to the route is seen (right) the well preserved eight-sailed tower windmill, built in 1830.

Helpringham (Lincs)

One of the larger Fen villages. Pleasant cottages, slate-roofed and red-tiled, stand near a green with chestnut trees.

Swaton (Lincs)

The small village is dwarfed by the huge grey eight-pinnacled tower of the church.

The Route

From Billingborough the road runs more or less due west. The flat open Fen country is left behind, the road giving way increasingly to wooded vales and hills.

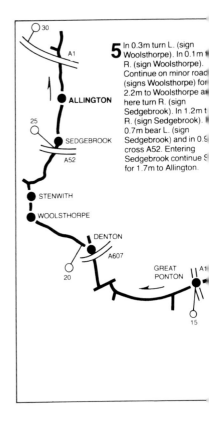

5 In 0.3m turn L. (sign Woolsthorpe). In 0.1m R. (sign Woolsthorpe). Continue on minor road (signs Woolsthorpe) for 2.2m to Woolsthorpe a here turn R. (sign Sedgebrook). In 1.2m t R. (sign Sedgebrook). 0.7m bear L. (sign Sedgebrook) and in 0.9 cross A52. Entering Sedgebrook continue S for 1.7m to Allington.

Horbling (Lincs)

A picturesque village where charming little cottages are approached from the road by little bridges across a stream shaded by chestnut trees.

Billingborough (Lincs)

Stands to the edge of the Fens, a long street of pleasant old houses and inns. The Tudor Hall, built of grey stone beneath a number of chimneys, hides behind the trees.

Folkingham (Lincs)

A spacious village where the broad main street, lined with stone-built houses and inns, leads to the square and the prominent Greyhound Inn. The village was at one time an important coaching centre, this inn from the time of Queen Anne with its facade of mellow red-brick being the focal point. Folkingham now, however, is a quiet and somewhat isolated place and although the inn still bears its sign it is an inn no more, now serving as an antique shop. The Church of St Andrew, close to the inn, has a noble 15c tower crowned by sixteen pinnacles. Before entering the village (right) are the ruins of the old Correction House, built in 1809 on the site of Folkingham Castle. Set on a mound, all that remains is the austere grey stone gateway.

Ingoldsby (Lincs)

No connection with the verse tales of Richard Barham. The village name is said to derive from a Danish chief, Ingold. A mile or two to the west is Ingoldsby Wood where, at Round Hills, there is a rounded earthwork more than 100 yards in diameter.

Boothby Pagnell (Lincs)

Lies in wooded countryside on the River Glen. In the grounds of the modern Hall are the remains of an unfortified Norman manor house.

Marston (Lincs)

Although barely two miles from the Great North Road, Marston is a quiet village on the meadows by the River Witham. The church has a fine broach spire. There are memorials to the family who have occupied the Hall by the church over many generations.

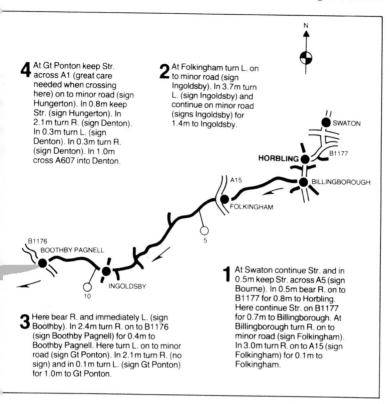

4 At Gt Ponton keep Str. across A1 (great care needed when crossing here) on to minor road (sign Hungerton). In 0.8m keep Str. (sign Hungerton). In 2.1m turn R. (sign Denton). In 0.3m turn L. (sign Denton). In 0.3m turn R. (sign Denton). In 1.0m cross A607 into Denton.

2 At Folkingham turn L. on to minor road (sign Ingoldsby). In 3.7m turn L. (sign Ingoldsby) and continue on minor road (signs Ingoldsby) for 1.4m to Ingoldsby.

SWATON

B1177

HORBLING

BILLINGBOROUGH

A15

FOLKINGHAM

B1176

BOOTHBY PAGNELL

INGOLDSBY

10

5

1 At Swaton continue Str. and in 0.5m keep Str. across A5 (sign Bourne). In 0.5m bear R. on to B1177 for 0.8m to Horbling. Here continue Str. on B1177 for 0.7m to Billingborough. At Billingborough turn R. on to minor road (sign Folkingham). In 3.0m turn R. on to A15 (sign Folkingham) for 0.1m to Folkingham.

3 Here bear R. and immediately L. (sign Boothby). In 2.4m turn R. on to B1176 (sign Boothby Pagnell) for 0.4m to Boothby Pagnell. Here turn L. on to minor road (sign Gt Ponton). In 2.1m turn R. (no sign) and in 0.1m turn L. (sign Gt Ponton) for 1.0m to Gt Ponton.

Hough on the Hill (Lincs)

The church with Saxon tower stands above the square, across which is the stone-built inn and adjoining red-brick village shop. Hough on the Hill is in every respect a charming and secluded hill-top village. On the green hillside to the south of the church there was once a priory founded by Henry I.

Caythorpe (Lincs)

A large village on the main road from Lincoln to Grantham.

Fulbeck (Lincs)

The bulk of Fulbeck lies to the west of the Lincoln to Grantham road. It is considered to be among Lincolnshire's prettiest villages. Here picturesque cottages nestle along the lanes of the hillside. Splendid wrought iron gates and an avenue of lime trees lead to the stone-built Hall, built as the home of the Fane family after their move from another manor house in 1733. There are many memorials to this family in the church. Among these is a tribute from Sir Francis Fane to a servant, Thomas Ball, who died in 1673 after travelling with his master:

... into Holland, Denmark, Germany, Lorraine, Switzerland, Italy, Naples, France, and Flanders, where he considered ye Courts, and camps of most of ye European princes, their splendour and mutabilitie, concluding with ye preachers there was nothing new under ye sun and yet all was vanity, and only one thing necesary, to fear God and keep his Commandments. Soe doth F.F. who fixed this stone.

The River Witham at Marston.

Great Ponton (Lincs)

The road crosses the River Witham into this large village that lies near the busy A1.

Denton (Lincs)

There is a good view of this charming close-knit village from the point where the road descends sharply to Denton. On the left is a fine 19c gatehouse, the entry to the park and the house which replaced the earlier manor house. In the park a spring, St Christopher's Well, feeds a number of lakes. The village cottages of brown stone with red roofs make a charming picture. Down a cul-de-sac on the edge of the park are the church and picturesque inn, the Welby Arms, named after the lords of the manor.

Woolsthorpe (Lincs)

A pretty estate village on the River Devon, across which are the wooded heights of Belvoir Castle in Leicestershire. The short diversion is recommended. This home of the Duke and Duchess of Rutland stands on an isolated spur, the battlemented walls and towers dominating the Vale of Belvoir. The name Belvoir (beautiful view) dates back to Norman times. The present building was inspired by the fifth Duchess of Rutland who rebuilt the castle after a fire in 1816. Her statue stands in the Elizabethan saloon with its marvellous painted ceiling. Treasures in the castle include paintings by Poussin, Holbein, Reynolds and Rubens. The Statue Gardens are built into the hillside below the castle, the terraces taking their name from the sculptures on view. Medieval jousting tournaments and falconry displays take place annually.

The Route

Runs south to north through many picturesque villages until reaching Doddington. From here the final few miles to Lincoln are less interesting.

Stragglethorpe (Lincs)

Farmhouses and picturesque pantiled cottages are the main feature of this remote village between the River Brant and Sand Beck. The church is tucked away, neighbour of a large farm complex. High timber box pews give this small church an olde worlde air. There are some moving lines to Sir Richard Earle who died in 1697 when only twenty-four:

> While the mother this sad structure rears
> A double dissolution there appears;
> He into dust dissolves, she into tears.

Brant Broughton (Lincs)

The village lies astride a long main street close to the River Brant. Church and manor house stand at each of the extremities of Brant Broughton.

Aubourn (Lincs)

The River Witham flows round the village, with the Hall nearby and a picturesque mill.

Thorpe on the Hill (Lincs)

This hillside village lies half a mile from the A46, once the Roman Fosse Way. Much of the church is modern but there are relics of Norman work to be seen in the tower.

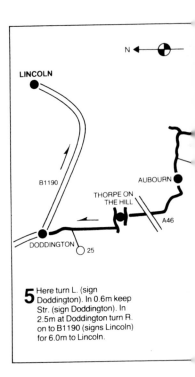

5 Here turn L. (sign Doddington). In 0.6m keep Str. (sign Doddington). In 2.5m at Doddington turn R. on to B1190 (signs Lincoln) for 6.0m to Lincoln.

Doddington (Lincs)

Doddington Hall and Gardens are open to the public. This splendid Elizabethan mansion, approached by a gabled gatehouse, is built of mellow red-brick and Ancaster stone. It is surrounded by the original walled gardens, in summer decked with old-fashioned roses, laced pinks and flag iris. In the church are monuments to the Jarvis family, owners of Doddington Hall.

Back at Lincoln, some of the buildings in Steep Hill date back to the 12c.

2 Here turn R. (sign Caythorpe). In 1.5m at Caythorpe turn L. on to A607 (sign Lincoln) for 1.9m to Fulbeck. Here at Fox Inn turn L. (no sign) and in 0.2m turn L. (no sign). In 0.1m turn R. (no sign). In 2.4m turn R. (sign Brant Broughton for 1.0m to Stragglethorpe.

Here continue Str. and in 0.7m keep Str. across A17 (sign Brant Broughton) for 0.6m to Brant Broughton.

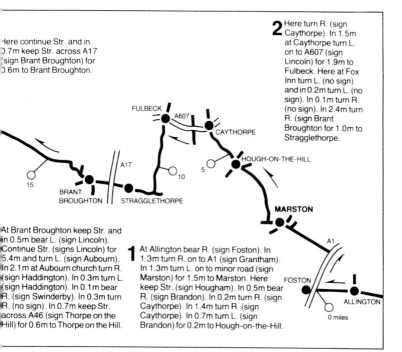

At Brant Broughton keep Str. and in 0.5m bear L. (sign Lincoln). Continue Str. (signs Lincoln) for 5.4m and turn L. (sign Aubourn). In 2.1m at Aubourn church turn R. (sign Haddington). In 0.3m turn L. (sign Haddington). In 0.1m bear R. (sign Swinderby). In 0.3m turn R. (no sign). In 0.7m keep Str. across A46 (sign Thorpe on the Hill) for 0.6m to Thorpe on the Hill.

1 At Allington bear R. (sign Foston). In 1.3m turn R. on to A1 (sign Grantham). In 1.3m turn L. on to minor road (sign Marston) for 1.5m to Marston. Here keep Str. (sign Hougham). In 0.5m bear R. (sign Brandon). In 0.2m turn R. (sign Caythorpe). In 1.4m turn R. (sign Caythorpe). In 0.7m turn L. (sign Brandon) for 0.2m to Hough-on-the-Hill.

5 Sussex, Hampshire, Berkshire

ALTHOUGH THE 150-mile route begins in West Sussex, the great part of it is confined to the county of Hampshire, crossing into Berkshire for only a few miles around Kintbury.

Hampshire lies west of Sussex on the English Channel. The administrative headquarters of the county are in the cathedral city of Winchester, the route running through Twyford a few miles to the south of the city. The south west of Hampshire incorporates the New Forest, a royal hunting ground in Saxon times later enlarged by the Norman kings. Chief rivers are the Test, Itchen and Avon. This route avoids the New Forest, an area mapped and described in the first volume of *Through Britain on Country Roads*. Instead it runs through the heart of the Hampshire Downs, a lovely sparsely populated area where sheep are reared and on lower ground wheat, hay and fruit are grown and cattle pastured. The landscape varies. Along the river valleys are lush pastures, often backed by fine trees, small copses and occasional low wooded hills. Often the road undulates. It climbs several hundred feet south of Kingsclere and later, above Combe in Berkshire, there are glorious views from Inkpen and Walbury Hills at altitudes of almost 1,000 ft above sea level. At this point, incidentally, a signpost indicates footpaths to the Test Way and Totton, forty-four miles away near Southampton, and the Wayfarers' Walk and Emsworth, seventy miles away near Havant.

Among great houses along the route are Goodwood House in Sussex and the National Trust-owned Mottisfont Abbey in Hampshire. At Burghclere in Hampshire the road passes the Sandham Memorial Chapel, also National Trust, with the superb murals of Sir Stanley Spencer. At Corhampton is a famous little Saxon church, the oldest in Hampshire.

There are many picturesque villages. Outstanding among them, perhaps, are East Marden for its peaceful tranquillity, Buriton, Abbotts Ann, and lovely Meonstoke by the river. Few hotels can enjoy a more charming aspect than the Dundas Arms at Kintbury. Among the many pleasant inns along the route are the White Horse at Chilgrove and the Boot Inn at Houghton.

Chichester

The four main streets of this delightful market town meet at the Market Cross, given by Bishop Storey in 1501 and one of the finest in England. A stroll around the centre of the city is rewarding, particularly as this area has now been pedestrianized. There is much to see.

At the cathedral with its pinnacled tower and lofty spire, splendid architecture and art treasures ancient and modern feast the eye. Here can be seen the Shrine of St Richard of Chichester, Romanesque stone carvings, Tudor paintings, and monuments by the British sculptor

ROUTE 5

⌂ Historic house
♠ Park/garden
◉ View

N

Reading

Kintbury
Newbury
Combe
Burghclere
◉ Kingsclere

Tangley
Hurstbourne
Tarrant
Weyhill
Overton

Aldershot

Micheldever

Kings Worthy
Itchen Abbas
Winchester
Tichborne
Cheriton
Hursley
Morestead
Bramdean
Otterbourne ⌂ Twyford
Corhampton
Buriton

Sussex Downs

Southampton
Hambledon
East Marden
Singleton
West Dean ♠
Funtington
Houghton
⌂ Goodwood
Chichester

0   5 km
0   5 miles

John Flaxman (1755–1826). Among modern treasures are works by Graham Sutherland and John Piper.

Chichester is an ancient Roman township, and the remains of the Roman palace built *circa* 80 AD at nearby Fishbourne are unique outside Italy. Features of the palace are the mosaic floors, underfloor heating and a bath suite.

Chichester's harbour numbers among the most picturesque in England. It comprises some fifty miles of shoreline and seventeen miles of navigable channel, catering for a host of power boats and colourful sailing vessels.

The Chichester Festival Theatre, built in 1962, is famous for the plays and concerts performed here. The District Museum, close to the Market Cross, is housed in a Georgian corn store. The museum recalls the history of the district from prehistoric to modern times. A notable feature is the figure of a Roman soldier in full armour.

Only five minutes walk from the cathedral a splendid Queen Anne house is the home of the Pallant House Gallery. It stands in a reconstructed Georgian garden with furnished historic rooms, art treasures and 18c porcelain and glass.

Dolphin and Anchor Hotel, West St. T (0243) 785121. (A)

Bedford Hotel, Southgate. T (0243) 785766. (B)

Goodwood's famous race course.

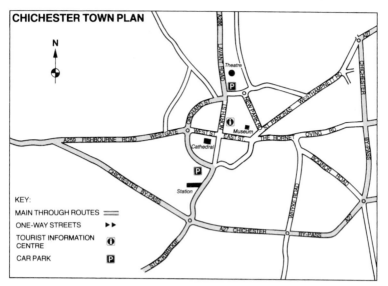

CHICHESTER TOWN PLAN

KEY:

MAIN THROUGH ROUTES

ONE-WAY STREETS

TOURIST INFORMATION
CENTRE

CAR PARK

Ship Hotel, North St. T (0243) 782028. (B)
Tourist Office, St Peter's Market, West St. T (0243) 775888.

The Route

*Glorious wooded
countryside throughout.
The road through the West
Dean Estate and Chilgrove
is narrow. Later, before
reaching Buriton, the road
runs through the Queen
Elizabeth Forest.*

Goodwood (Sussex)

The road passes the race course,
which is set in such splendid
scenery that it has been styled
'Glorious Goodwood'. Near the
race course (left of road) is one of
the ramparts of the ancient
Britons, an old camp named
Trundle. Goodwood House
(signed to the right of road) is the
home of the Earl of March, son of
the ninth Duke of Richmond. The
landscaped grounds of this
gracious house contain
Goodwood Country Park, a
protected area of outstanding
natural beauty. The house, open
to the public on specified
occasions, has many treasures.
Among these are paintings by
Canaletto, Van Dyck, Kneller and
Stubbs, Sèvres porcelain, French
furniture and many mementoes of
famous people.

Singleton (Sussex)

To the immediate south of this
pretty village is the Weald and
Downland Open Air Museum.
Here historic buildings have been
reconstructed in forty acres of
natural beauty with a millpond
and wooded walks. Among
exhibits are medieval houses, a
Tudor market hall and a village
school.

West Dean (Sussex)

West Dean College (left of road),
a centre for teaching arts and
crafts, is not open to the public.

3 At E. Marden turn R. (sign N. Marden). In
0.5m turn L. (sign Compton). In 0.5m
continue Str. (sign Compton). In 1.6m at
Compton turn R. on to B2146 (sign
Petersfield). In 0.6m turn L. on to minor
road (sign Finchdean). In 2.2m turn R.
(sign Chalton). In 0.9m turn L. (sign
Chalton). In 0.1m bear R. (no sign). In
3.4m at Buriton turn L. (sign Petersfield).

4 In 0.7m keep Str. across A3 (sign
Ramsdean). In 1.7m turn R. (sign
Ramsdean). In 0.3m at Ramsdean keep
Str. (sign Langrish). In 0.5m turn R. (sign
Petersfield) for 0.7m to Langrish.

Around the college, however, are
thirty-five acres of informal
gardens which are open. On view
are specimen trees, a walled
garden, a wild garden, and a 300-
ft pergola gazebo. There is an
exhibition of garden history and a
collection of lawn mowers.

Chilgrove (Sussex)

Although the route by-passes the
centre of the village the
picturesque White Horse Inn
stands to the right of the road.
White Horse Inn and Restaurant.
T (024 359) 219. No
accommodation.

East Marden (Sussex)

There are four Mardens in this
lovely country of wooded hills and
valleys. Here, at East Marden,
picturesque houses cluster below
the small flint church surmounted
by a weather-cock. By the church
is the village pump, sheltered by a
round thatched roof. In spring this
secluded hollow is ablaze with
daffodils.

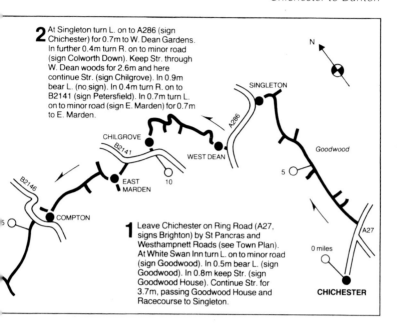

2 At Singleton turn L. on to A286 (sign Chichester) for 0.7m to W. Dean Gardens. In further 0.4m turn R. on to minor road (sign Colworth Down). Keep Str. through W. Dean woods for 2.6m and here continue Str. (sign Chilgrove). In 0.9m bear L. (no sign). In 0.4m turn R. on to B2141 (sign Petersfield). In 0.7m turn L. on to minor road (sign E. Marden) for 0.7m to E. Marden.

1 Leave Chichester on Ring Road (A27, signs Brighton) by St Pancras and Westhampnett Roads (see Town Plan). At White Swan Inn turn L. on to minor road (sign Goodwood). In 0.5m bear L. (sign Goodwood). In 0.8m keep Str. (sign Goodwood House). Continue Str. for 3.7m, passing Goodwood House and Racecourse to Singleton.

Buriton (Hants)

The heart of Buriton lies only 200 yards to the right of the route, a worthwhile diversion. Here is the duck pond, shaded by willow trees; the Church of St Mary, largely Norman; and the manor house. Towering above the whole scene is lofty Butser Hill, site of a stone-age camp and farm. At the manor the historian Edward Gibbon (1737–94) spent his boyhood years. It was not until 1788 that he completed his master work, *The Decline and Fall of the Roman Empire*.

Goodwood House.

The Route

Initially by way of woods and meadows, following the course of the River Itchen. After crossing the motorway more quiet country roads between Micheldever and Overton.

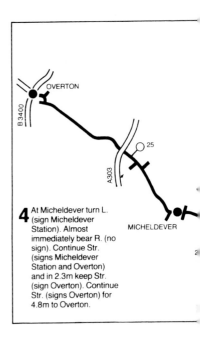

4 At Micheldever turn L. (sign Micheldever Station). Almost immediately bear R. (no sign). Continue Str. (signs Micheldever Station and Overton) and in 2.3m keep Str. (sign Overton). Continue Str. (signs Overton) for 4.8m to Overton.

Bramdean (Hants)

Some pleasant old houses are grouped here. Before entering the village is an Elizabethan manor house (right). To the south of Bramdean is Brookwood Park where a Roman pavement was excavated and given to Winchester. A little to the west of the village is the source of the River Itchen, a charming stream which flows westward to Winchester, flanked by several pretty villages along the route.

Cheriton (Hants)

Lies in a sheltered valley where the River Itchen is already growing. To the east is Cheriton Wood where the forces of the Parliamentarian General Waller lay in ambush in 1644. The Royalists, under Lord Hopton, were taken by surprise and routed. Some 2,000 men were killed and buried in communal graves. The burial mounds are still visible around the village.

Tichborne (Hants)

The village name is believed to derive from Saxon days – a settlement 'at the Itchen bourne', a village on the banks of a tributary of the Itchen. In 1871 this quiet out-of-the-way village received dramatic publicity due to the longest trial ever to be held on British soil. It was the trial for perjury of a man who claimed to be Roger Tichborne, heir to the baronetcy and the Tichborne estate. The Trial of the Tichborne Claimant lasted ten months. Local opinion as to the veracity of the claim was divided. The court, however, decided that it was false and that the claimant was the son of a Wapping butcher. He was sentenced to fourteen years penal servitude. On a quite different note is the 13c legend of the Tichborne Dole. At that time, it is said, Lady Marbella, wife of Sir Roger Tichborne, made a dying request that bread should be distributed to the local poor each Lady Day. Sir Roger agreed to the proposal, somewhat callously offering as much corn as his wife could crawl around. Incapable of walking, Lady Marbella crawled around a twenty-three-acre field, the source of the Tichborne Dole and an area still known as The Crawls.

Itchen Abbas (Hants)

Together with the smaller village of Itchen Stoke, it stands on the northern bank of the River Itchen amid lush meadows and majestic trees. It is small wonder that

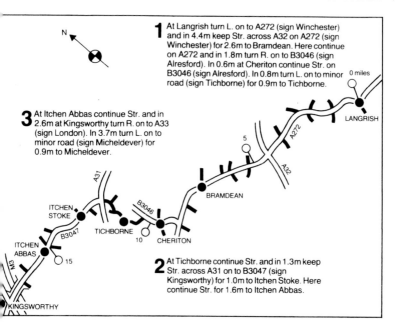

1 At Langrish turn L. on to A272 (sign Winchester) and in 4.4m keep Str. across A32 on A272 (sign Winchester) for 2.6m to Bramdean. Here continue on A272 and in 1.8m turn R. on to B3046 (sign Alresford). In 0.6m at Cheriton continue Str. on B3046 (sign Alresford). In 0.8m turn L. on to minor road (sign Tichborne) for 0.9m to Tichborne.

3 At Itchen Abbas continue Str. and in 2.6m at Kingsworthy turn R. on to A33 (sign London). In 3.7m turn L. on to minor road (sign Micheldever) for 0.9m to Micheldever.

2 At Tichborne continue Str. and in 1.3m keep Str. across A31 on to B3047 (sign Kingsworthy) for 1.0m to Itchen Stoke. Here continue Str. for 1.6m to Itchen Abbas.

Charles Kingsley loved this place and here wrote much of his *Water Babies* in 1863. A mile away, on the other side of the river, is Avington House.

Kingsworthy (Hants)

A pleasant village, though busy as it lies near the motorway.

Micheldever (Hants)

The medieval church has a grand tower of flint and stone, topped by a variety of gargoyles. To the west of the village are ancient earthworks at Norsebury Ring.

Overton (Hants)

There is a broad main street and some old inns in this little town, once an important coaching centre at the end of the first stage from London to the west. St Mary's Church, first built in 1180 and much restored, has a 15c south door of particular interest. It is unusual in that it is hinged in the centre. Above the doors of the porch are water-mark portraits of Queen Elizabeth II and Prince Charles when a boy (visible only when the inner porch lights are switched on).

The attractive village of Micheldever.

93

The Route

Between Burghclere and Kintbury the road runs past Woolton Hill and The Chase (right), where 131 acres of woodland are preserved by the National Trust. Splendid panoramic views from White Hill above Kingsclere and the hills above Combe. Further entrancing wooded countryside lies between Combe and Tangley.

Kingsclere (Hants)

The downs above this small town provide superb gallops for race horses. It was across them that Derby winners like Ormond and Flying Fox were trained. Kingsclere today is a sleepy little town with a Norman church.

Burghclere (Hants)

Although the route avoids the centre of Burghclere it does pass the National Trust-owned Sandham Memorial Chapel (right). The Oratory of All Souls was erected as a memorial to H.W. Sandham, killed in the First World War. This brick-built shrine rises between two wings designed as almshouses. Here are to be seen the magnificent murals of Stanley Spencer (1891–1959) inspired by his wartime experiences at Salonika. They portray the lives of front-line soldiers and the largest work behind the altar, the Resurrection on the Salonika Front, is considered to be among Spencer's finest achievements.

Kintbury (Berks)

This small Berkshire town stands on the Kennet and Avon Canal close to the boundaries of Hampshire and Wiltshire. The most charming aspect is found around the Kintbury Mill and the Dundas Arms, by the canal and stream. This hotel, incidentally, is

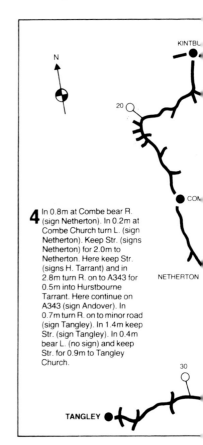

4 In 0.8m at Combe bear R. (sign Netherton). In 0.2m at Combe Church turn L. (sign Netherton). Keep Str. (signs Netherton) for 2.0m to Netherton. Here keep Str. (signs H. Tarrant) and in 2.8m turn R. on to A343 for 0.5m into Hurstbourne Tarrant. Here continue on A343 (sign Andover). In 0.7m turn R. on to minor road (sign Tangley). In 1.4m keep Str. (sign Tangley). In 0.4m bear L. (no sign) and keep Str. for 0.9m to Tangley Church.

renowned for its French cuisine. Few hotels can boast such a picturesque setting.
Dundas Arms. T (0488) 58263. (A)

Combe (Berks)

Until local goverment reorganization Combe and Inkpen lay within the boundaries of Hampshire. Here there are only a handful of houses and a small 12c church tucked down a leafy lane. Towering above the village are Walbury and Inkpen Hills, the former almost 1,000 ft and Berkshire's highest point. On Inkpen Hill is the Combe Gibbet, where George Broomham of Inkpen and Dorothy Newman of Combe were hanged in 1676 for the murder of two of their children.

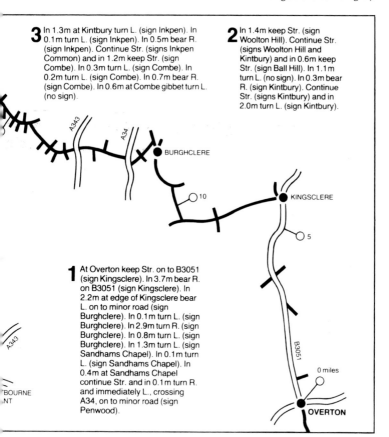

3 In 1.3m at Kintbury turn L. (sign Inkpen). In 0.1m turn L. (sign Inkpen). In 0.5m bear R. (sign Inkpen). Continue Str. (signs Inkpen Common) and in 1.2m keep Str. (sign Combe). In 0.3m turn L. (sign Combe). In 0.2m turn L. (sign Combe). In 0.7m bear R. (sign Combe). In 0.6m at Combe gibbet turn L. (no sign).

2 In 1.4m keep Str. (sign Woolton Hill). Continue Str. (signs Woolton Hill and Kintbury) and in 0.6m keep Str. (sign Ball Hill). In 1.1m turn L. (no sign). In 0.3m bear R. (sign Kintbury). Continue Str. (signs Kintbury) and in 2.0m turn L. (sign Kintbury).

1 At Overton keep Str. on to B3051 (sign Kingsclere). In 3.7m bear R. on B3051 (sign Kingsclere). In 2.2m at edge of Kingsclere bear L. on to minor road (sign Burghclere). In 0.1m turn L. (sign Burghclere). In 2.9m turn R. (sign Burghclere). In 0.8m turn L. (sign Burghclere). In 1.3m turn L. (sign Sandhams Chapel). In 0.1m turn L. (sign Sandhams Chapel). In 0.4m at Sandhams Chapel continue Str. and in 0.1m turn R. and immediately L., crossing A34, on to minor road (sign Penwood).

Hurstbourne Tarrant (Hants)

The prettiest part of the village is found along the B3048 to the south east where the school and thatched cottages are fronted by a little stream and faced on the other side of the road by the Church of St Peter. Two remarkable men are associated with the village and in particular with Rookery Farm which lies on the main road at the southern extremity. Joseph Blount lived here and often entertained his friend William Cobbett (1762–1835), who wrote much of his *Rural Rides* at the farmhouse. On the garden wall of Rookery Farm the initials WC and the date 1825 are inscribed. The wall is known as the Wayfarer's Table for it was here that the generous Blount would place plates of bread and bacon for the relief of passing agricultural labourers. Blount died in 1863, almost thirty years after Cobbett, and generous to the last, ordered that his tombstone should be big and flat enough for the village children to play marbles on. *Essebourne Manor Hotel.* T (026 476) 444. (A)

Tangley (Hants)

The little church stands to the end of the village and is famous for its 400-year-old font, the only one made of lead to be found in Hampshire. The oldest objects in Tangley can be seen in the churchyard, small sarsen stones similar to the larger prehistoric boulders prevalent in Wiltshire.

Combe Gibbet on Inkpen Hill.

1 In 0.3m at Tangley village continue Str. (sign Chute). In 0.1m bear R. (no sign) and at Cricketers' Arms bear L. (no sign). In 0.2m at T-junction turn L. (sign Weyhill). In 2.6m at Clanville keep Str. (sign Weyhill). In 1.2m keep Str. (sign Andover). In 0.2m at Weyhill church turn L. on to A303 and immediately R. on to minor road (sign Abbotts Ann). In 1.2m keep Str. (sign Abbotts Ann). In 0.8m turn R. (sign Abbotts Ann). In 0.1m turn L. (sign Abbotts Ann) into Abbotts Ann.

The Route

Quiet country roads throughout. South of Abbots Ann the road climbs past Danebury Hill (right), the finest Iron Age stronghold to be seen in Hampshire.

Weyhill (Hants)

Situated on the busy A303, across which the country road passes directly. The church lies to the left of the road with a prominent churchyard cross. The ancient base excavated by a rector is surmounted by a cross transported from Jerusalem. A centuries-old fair is held in the village in mid-October.

Abbotts Ann (Hants)

The name suggests charm and Abbotts Ann lives up to it. It is a village with many picturesque thatched cottages and a lovely church. There was once a Roman settlement here and the pavements are displayed in the British Museum. A feature of the church is the memorial garlands, hanging on the internal walls and attached to white paper gloves. The earliest garland dates from 1740, the first of many memorial tokens to young men and women who have led blameless lives. The garlands are carried at the burial service and later left for permanent remembrance on the walls.

Houghton (Hants)

Picturesque thatched cottages cluster along the meadows by the River Test. The lawns of the Old Boot Inn run down to a lovely

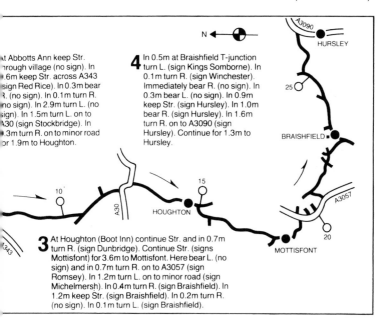

At Abbotts Ann keep Str.
through village (no sign). In
.6m keep Str. across A343
sign Red Rice). In 0.3m bear
R. (no sign). In 0.1m turn R.
no sign). In 2.9m turn L. (no
sign). In 1.5m turn L. on to
A30 (sign Stockbridge). In
.3m turn R. on to minor road
or 1.9m to Houghton.

4 In 0.5m at Braishfield T-junction
turn L. (sign Kings Somborne). In
0.1m turn R. (sign Winchester).
Immediately bear R. (no sign). In
0.3m bear L. (no sign). In 0.9m
keep Str. (sign Hursley). In 1.0m
bear R. (sign Hursley). In 1.6m
turn R. on to A3090 (sign
Hursley). Continue for 1.3m to
Hursley.

3 At Houghton (Boot Inn) continue Str. and in 0.7m
turn R. (sign Dunbridge). Continue Str. (signs
Mottisfont) for 3.6m to Mottisfont. Here bear L. (no
sign) and in 0.7m turn R. on to A3057 (sign
Romsey). In 1.2m turn L. on to minor road (sign
Michelmersh). In 0.4m turn R. (sign Braishfield). In
1.2m keep Str. (sign Braishfield). In 0.2m turn R.
(no sign). In 0.1m turn L. (sign Braishfield).

stretch of the river. The Test
provides some of the best trout
fishing in England. The
headquarters of the famous
Houghton Fishing Club are in
nearby Stockbridge, but the club
certainly made use of the Boot Inn,
where on the wall of the saloon
bar a member recorded his angling
experiences in the 1830s.
Boot Inn. T (0794) 388310. (C)

18c. In 1938 Rex Whistler (1905–
44) was commissioned to
decorate the saloon where murals
as celebrated as those to be seen
at the Tate Gallery are on display.
Mottisfont Abbey stands amid
spacious lawns, shaded by
magnificent cedar, oak and beech
trees above the River Test.

Mottisfont (Hants)

Mottisfont Abbey and the estate
of 2,000 acres was given to the
National Trust in 1957. This Tudor
mansion began as a
reconstruction of a 13c priory, a
priory which was demolished
apart from the nave wall of the
church that now forms the north
front of the abbey. Further
transformation took place in the

Hursley (Hants)

A gracious village where thatched
cottages and timber-framed
houses stand among trees and
meadows. To the west is Hursley
Park on the fringe of a glorious
beech wood and near to the
remains of Merdon Castle. The
castle, on the site of an Iron Age
stronghold, was built in the 12c.
All that now remains are the
gateway and well.

A peaceful scene at Buriton in Hampshire.

Thatched cottage in the village of Singleton.

The Route

Some problems exist in navigating from Otterbourne to Shawford. Signs here are indifferent and the road branches to the left before veering to the right and running beneath the motorway on a minor road into Shawford. Apart from a short stretch of road through Clanfield the roads are quiet, undulating through wooded countryside.

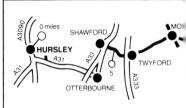

1 At Hursley turn L. on to A31 (sign Otterbourne). In 3.0m at Otterbourne turn L. on to A33 (sign Winchester). In 1.1m turn L. on A33 (sign Winchester). In 0.3m bear L. on to minor road (sign Twyford). In 0.1m bear R. on minor road (signs Shawford and Twyford). In 0.1m bear L. (sign Shawford) for 0.2m to Shawford. Continue Str. for 0.7m to Twyford.

Otterbourne (Hants)

Charlotte Yonge (1823–1901), the Victorian novelist, lived and wrote in this charming village of the Itchen Valley. Much of the income from her popular novels went to the new church here, and there is a cross in the chancel to her memory. Cranbury Hall and Park lie to the west of the village. Cranbury Hall was once the home of John Conduitt and here he entertained his friend Sir Isaac Newton during the later years of his life.

Shawford (Hants)

Though close to a motorway the village is a quiet place, sheltered by Shawford Down where there is a well-sited picnic area.

Twyford (Hants)

The village is associated with at least three famous names. It was at Twyford House that Benjamin Franklin (1706–90), American statesman and writer, stayed as a guest and wrote his autobiography. Alexander Pope (1688–1744), the British satirical poet, was schooled here at Seagers Buildings. A house that once stood by the River Itchen was the girlhood home of Maria Anne Fitzherbert, morganatic wife of the Prince of Wales, later George IV. She was believed to have married the Prince here in 1785.

Morestead (Hants)

A cross stands to the west of the village on Hazeley Down. This was placed in remembrance of soldiers stationed here during the First World War.

Corhampton (Hants)

On a hill above the village is a church that people come from far and wide to see. It is Hampshire's oldest church, all Saxon with the exception of the chancel wall. On the walls of the nave and chancel are tinted paintings believed to

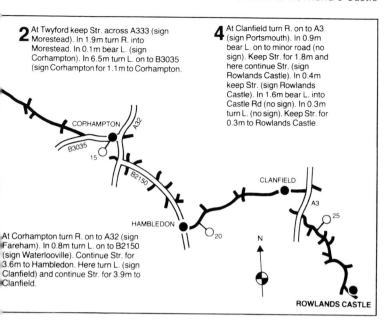

2 At Twyford keep Str. across A333 (sign Morestead). In 1.9m turn R. into Morestead. In 0.1m bear L. (sign Corhampton). In 6.5m turn L. on to B3035 (sign Corhampton for 1.1m to Corhampton.

4 At Clanfield turn R. on to A3 (sign Portsmouth). In 0.9m bear L. on to minor road (no sign). Keep Str. for 1.8m and here continue Str. (sign Rowlands Castle). In 0.4m keep Str. (sign Rowlands Castle). In 1.6m bear L. into Castle Rd (no sign). In 0.3m turn L. (no sign). Keep Str. for 0.3m to Rowlands Castle.

3 At Corhampton turn R. on to A32 (sign Fareham). In 0.8m turn L. on to B2150 (sign Waterlooville). Continue Str. for 3.6m to Hambledon. Here turn L. (sign Clanfield) and continue Str. for 3.9m to Clanfield.

date back to 1225 or even earlier. Below and across the meadows, less than a mile from Corhampton, is Meonstoke. Here is a church less ancient, but lying in a more beautiful setting, on the banks of the River Meon, surrounded by picturesque houses and garlanded in springtime with hosts of daffodils and tulips.

Hambledon (Hants)

The main street of the village is composed mainly of Georgian houses and cottages, among them a former coaching inn, the George Hotel. The short High Street leads from the George to the church, flanked by a number of old houses and shops, among them a butcher's shop with outward folding shutters which when opened form the counter. Hambledon's chief distinction, however, is its claim to be the

birthplace of village cricket. The ground of the original Hambledon Cricket Club lies some two miles further along the route on Broadhalfpenny Down. At a corner of the ground with its thatched pavilion is a monument engraved with a two stump wicket, a ball between the stumps. E.W. Swanton, the distinguished cricket writer, describes how, in the days when the ball passed between the stumps, arguments would arise and so a third stump was introduced. Opposite the ground is the 17c Bat and Ball Inn, once the clubhouse of the cricket club first formed in 1767 and later conqueror of an All England XI.

Rowland's Castle (Hants)

A large and sprawling village, the pleasant part of it standing around a spacious green.

The Route

The final few miles are by way of a peaceful B road which runs all the way into the centre of Chichester.

Funtington (Sussex)

A quiet village on the southern extremity of the Sussex Downs. Nearby in Stanstead Park is the Racton Monument, a tower that still serves as a landmark for ships entering Chichester Harbour.

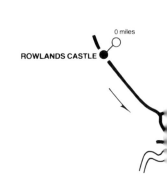

0 miles

ROWLANDS CASTLE

1 At Rowlands Castle bear R. under bridge Westbourne). In 2.0m turn L. on to B214 B2146 (signs Funtington) for 3.2m to Fu

The Bat and Ball Inn at Hambledon.

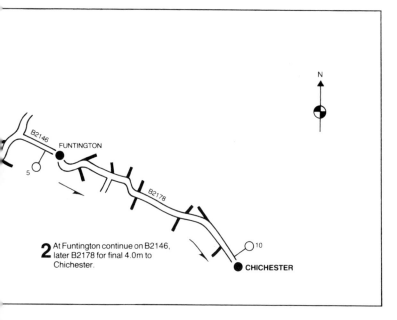

2 At Funtington continue on B2146, later B2178 for final 4.0m to Chichester.

6 East Anglia (South): Cambridgeshire, Essex, Suffolk

THE ROUTE runs momentarily into Hertfordshire at Barley. The great part of it, however, is confined to the counties of Cambridgeshire, Essex and Suffolk. To the north of Cambridge are the Fens, once marshland first drained by the Romans and now flat farmlands interspersed with countless waterways. This route, however, leads through the southern part of Cambridgeshire, hilly by comparison, with country roads that undulate between ridges and valleys, winding among little copses and quiet meadows. Highest point along the route is Chapel Hill, between Haslingfield and Barrington, with panoramic views as far as Ely a score of miles away.

At Wendens Ambo the route runs into Essex, low-lying like its East Anglian neighbours, but apart from a short stretch around industrialized Braintree, it is confined to delightful agricultural unspoilt countryside. Thaxted and Coggeshall could be described as either small towns or large villages, the former crammed with buildings of great historic interest, the latter graced by a charming little National Trust house beside a narrow street, Paycockes. Among many pretty Essex villages Great Bardfield is outstanding.

The county of Suffolk is reached at the delightful little town of

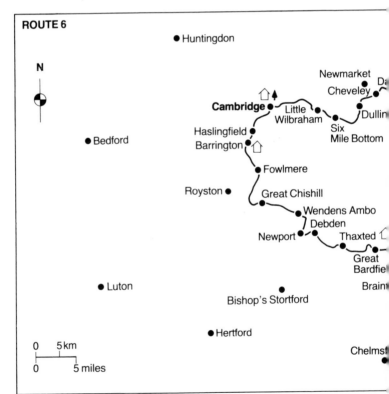

Bures on the River Stour. From here the road meanders northwards by the Stour Valley to Sudbury. In the first volume of *Through Britain on Country Roads* the route led through the Constable country of Dedham Vale. Here at Sudbury are memories of a painter of equal repute, Thomas Gainsborough, with his statue in the square and the house where he was born nearby.

After leaving Sudbury many quiet charming villages are encountered, none prettier perhaps than Monks Eleigh and Chelsworth on the River Brett, and Dalham to the extreme west of Suffolk near the border with Cambridgeshire.

All three counties possess vast acreages of wheat, barley and sugar beet, providing a depth of green landscape that contrasts with the vivid yellow of rape that is now also widely grown.

Cambridge

Many of the famous colleges back on to the gardens and lawns of the River Cam. This area, known as the Backs, alive in spring with crocuses and daffodils, the river spanned by graceful bridges, is the focal point of this lovely university city.

Cambridge was a place of importance long before the university was born. In the first century BC an Iron Age Belgic tribe settled here. Later came the Romans, the Saxons and the Normans, who under William the Conqueror built a castle as a base for fighting Hereward the Wake. The Castle Mound can be seen near Castle Street to the north of the city.

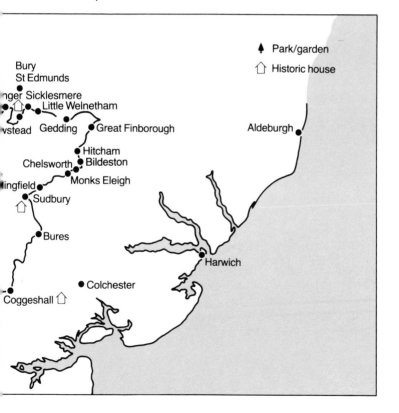

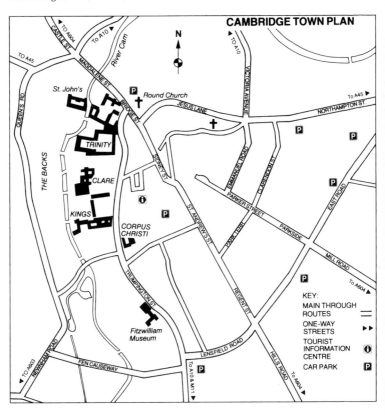

Oldest of the thirty-one colleges are Peterhouse (1280–84); Clare (1326) with beautiful gardens and the oldest surviving river bridge; Pembroke (1347) with a chapel that was Sir Christopher Wren's first building; Gonville and Caius (1348); Trinity Hall (1350); Corpus Christi (1352) with Old Court considered the best surviving medieval college court in Cambridge; and King's College (1441) with a chapel considered Cambridge's grandest building and famous for its choir and carol services. Among younger colleges are St John's (1511) with its magnificent gatehouse and Bridge of Sighs, and Trinity (1546) with the huge Great Court and the famous Wren library. Among churches to be seen are St Benet, oldest church in Cambridgeshire with a Saxon tower; the Round Church, one of only four round churches in England; and All Saints, with glass and decorations by Morris, Burne Jones and Madox Brown. Museums include the Fitzwilliam, displaying paintings, ceramics and armour, and the Scott Polar Research Institute. The Botanical Gardens contain a huge collection of plants in landscaped gardens and houses.

University Arms, Regent St. T (0223) 351241. (A)

Arundel House, 53 Chesterton Rd. T (0223) 67701. (B)

Tourist Office, Wheeler St. T (0223) 322640.

Suffolk Bridge over the River Brett at Chelsworth.

The Route

Shortly after leaving Haslingfield there is a superb view from Chapel Hill, encompassing the spires of Cambridge and scores of surrounding villages. From here the road runs southwards, briefly entering Hertfordshire near Barley, before turning to the east and entering the Cam Valley at Wendens Ambo, the first Essex village. Quiet traffic-free roads throughout.

Haslingfield (Cambs)

The village nestles beneath Chapel Hill. The church (left) lies amid lime trees, crowned by a 15c battlemented tower with magnificent windows and wooden spire. In the chancel are many monuments to the Wendy family, lords of the manor since the early 16c.

Barrington (Cambs)

A charming place with a large village green surrounded by orchards and cottages. At one end of the green is the gabled Barrington Hall, home of the Bendyshe (pronounced Bendish) family over centuries but now, unromantically, providing offices for a cement works. At the other end is the Church of All Saints. From the south door of the church there is a good view of the twenty-two-acre green, among the largest village greens in England. In the Bendyshe chapel are monuments to the Bendyshe family. In the ground floor of the tower the instructions are precise: 'Drinking, smoking and jesting forbidden to bell-ringers'. These were placed by the Victorian vicar, an eccentric character who was often seen around the village with his wife perched on the handlebars of his tricycle.

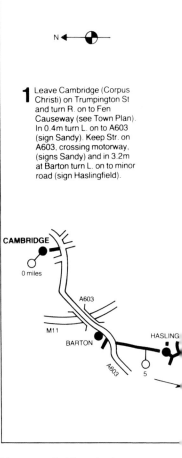

1 Leave Cambridge (Corpus Christi) on Trumpington St and turn R. on to Fen Causeway (see Town Plan). In 0.4m turn L. on to A603 (sign Sandy). Keep Str. on A603, crossing motorway, (signs Sandy) and in 3.2m at Barton turn L. on to minor road (sign Haslingfield).

Shepreth (Cambs)

The little village green and war memorial stand beneath lime trees. Nearby is an elegant Georgian house, Docwras Manor, the gardens of which are sometimes open to the public.

Fowlmere (Cambs)

The name, perhaps, originates from the days when men settled by the mere, or lake, which provided them with wildfowl to eat. It is surprising to find no less than four inns in what is now little more than a charming village. At one time, however, Fowlmere was an important staging post on the Cambridge to London route.

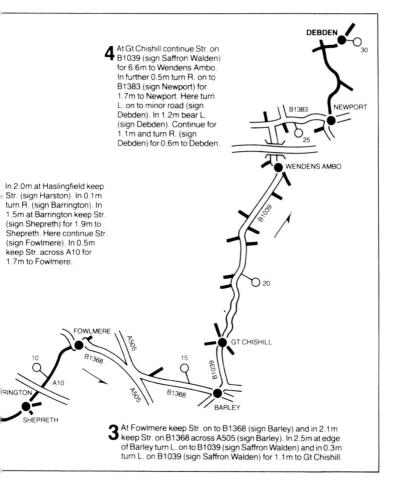

4 At Gt Chishill continue Str. on B1039 (sign Saffron Walden) for 6.6m to Wendens Ambo. In further 0.5m turn R. on to B1383 (sign Newport) for 1.7m to Newport. Here turn L. on to minor road (sign Debden). In 1.2m bear L. (sign Debden). Continue for 1.1m and turn R. (sign Debden) for 0.6m to Debden.

In 2.0m at Haslingfield keep Str. (sign Harston). In 0.1m turn R. (sign Barrington). In 1.5m at Barrington keep Str. (sign Shepreth) for 1.9m to Shepreth. Here continue Str. (sign Fowlmere). In 0.5m keep Str. across A10 for 1.7m to Fowlmere.

3 At Fowlmere keep Str. on to B1368 (sign Barley) and in 2.1m keep Str. on B1368 across A505 (sign Barley). In 2.5m at edge of Barley turn L. on to B1039 (sign Saffron Walden) and in 0.3m turn L. on B1039 (sign Saffron Walden) for 1.1m to Gt Chishill.

Great Chishill (Cambs)

Shortly before reaching the village is the Great Chishill post mill (right). This mill, built in 1819, was constructed using timbers from the mill of 1726 and has been designated an historic monument. It was last worked in 1951 and is open to the public. Picturesque thatched cottages stand near the church in the hilltop village of Great Chishill, a mile further along the road. A column above a garden in the churchyard remembers the fallen with the words:

> True love by Life, true love by Death is tried;
> Live then for England, we for England died.

Wendens Ambo (Essex)

The first of the Essex villages along the route and among the most charming. The River Cam flows to the east, the village name derived from the Saxon for 'winding valley'.

Newport (Essex)

The spacious and pleasant main street of this little town runs more or less parallel to the River Cam. Many of the houses that line the street are Georgian, some even older.

Debden (Essex)

A charming little village, tucked away among trees with the inn, village shop, playing fields and small pond as the central features.

The Route

The road narrows between Great Bardfield and Shalford. Apart from the short stretch of the A120 leaving Braintree, the country roads undulate through charming Essex countryside with very little traffic.

Thaxted (Essex)

The majestic church, standing on the hill-top with a 180-foot spire, dominates the village. A feature of historic interest is the chapel dedicated to John Ball, leader of the Peasants' Revolt and famed for his lines: 'When Adam delved and Eve span, Who was then the gentleman?' Near the church a path leads between a double row of almshouses to a windmill which contains a museum of local interest. Central point of the village is the timbered 14c guildhall. A narrow alley close to the guildhall is lined by a variety of ancient houses, among them Dick Turpin's Cottage, where the highwayman is said to have lived at one time. The 16c Recorder's House is now a restaurant and next door is a house where the composer Gustav Holst (1874–1934), lived between 1917 and 1925.

Swan Hotel, The Bullring.
T (0371) 830321. (C)

1 At Debden continue Str. through villa (no sign) and in 2.0m keep Str. (sign Thaxted) for 2.2m to Thaxted. Here R. on to B184 (no sign) and in 0.3m tu on to minor road (sign The Bardfields 0.6m fork R. (sign Gt Bardfield). Kee for 2.2m to Little Bardfield and here continue Str. for 1.4m to Gt Bardfiel

The impressive 14c guildhall in Thaxted.

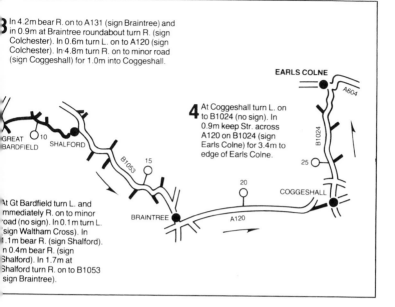

In 4.2m bear R. on to A131 (sign Braintree) and in 0.9m at Braintree roundabout turn R. (sign Colchester). In 0.6m turn L. on to A120 (sign Colchester). In 4.8m turn R. on to minor road (sign Coggeshall) for 1.0m into Coggeshall.

At Coggeshall turn L. on to B1024 (no sign). In 0.9m keep Str. across A120 on B1024 (sign Earls Colne) for 3.4m to edge of Earls Colne.

At Gt Bardfield turn L. and immediately R. on to minor road (no sign). In 0.1m turn L. (sign Waltham Cross). In 1.1m bear R. (sign Shalford). In 0.4m bear R. (sign Shalford). In 1.7m at Shalford turn R. on to B1053 (sign Braintree).

EARLS COLNE
A604
GREAT BARDFIELD
SHALFORD
B1053
BRAINTREE
A120
COGGESHALL
B1024

Little Bardfield (Essex)

The church of St Katherine is signed to the left, almost in the grounds of Bardfield Hall (now a hotel).

Great Bardfield (Essex)

A number of pleasant houses of historic interest are scattered around this charming village. The name most associated with Great Bardfield is that of William Bendlowes, Sergeant at Law and MP, who was born here and died in 1584 after founding a charity to help the poor and needy. The timber-framed Place House was the lawyer's home, bearing his initials and the date 1564. A tiny thatched cottage, occupied until 1958 when it became unfit for human habitation, was taken over by the Bendlowes Charity and converted into a cottage museum. Other buildings of interest include the 15c timbered Gobions and adjacent Town House; the White Hart Inn, also 15c and now a private house; and the Friends' Meeting House in the High Street.

Shalford (Essex)

The village has some pleasant houses that straggle for some length, woods to the south and the River Pant to the north and east.

Braintree (Essex)

The described route by-passes much of this industrial town.

Coggeshall (Essex)

A feature of this delightful small town is the National Trust-owned Paycockes, seen on the right when entering Coggeshall. Paycockes House was built in 1500 by a wealthy butcher, Thomas Paycocke. It is numbered among the most attractive half-timbered houses in East Anglia. Many of the timbers bear the original carpenter's marks. The upper storey bears the initials and trademark of Thomas Paycocke, being graced by five evenly-spaced oriel windows. Inside there is fine oak furniture, carved timber work and original fireplaces. *White Hart Hotel.* T (0376) 61654. (A)

111

The Route

Initially the road from Bures to Sudbury runs through the Stour Valley. From Monks Eleigh to Chesworth, lush meadows flank the River Brett. Quiet country roads throughout.

4 At Gt Finborough keep Str. and in 1.0m at One House turn L. on to minor road (sign Rattlesden). In 1.7m turn L. (sign Rattlesden) for 1.8m into Rattlesden.

3 In further 0.3m bear L. to B1115 (sign Stowmarket) for 1.0m to Chelsworth. Here keep (sign Bildeston) for 0.9m Bildeston. At Bildeston L. on B1115 (sign Stowmarket) and conti for 1.6m to Hitcham. He keep on B1115 for 5.1m Gt Finborough.

Bures (Suffolk)

A charming little town on the River Stour, marking the entry into Suffolk. The oldest part of the magnificent church is the flint tower (13c). The south chapel was built in 1514 as a memorial to the Waldegrave family. In addition to monuments to the Waldegraves is a wooden effigy to an unknown knight (*circa* 14c). Scattered around the town are a number of old timbered buildings. Among them and close to the church is a quaint little house, Maynscroft, now an antique shop.

Sudbury (Suffolk)

There is plenty of room to park in the spacious square of this one-time wealthy wool town. The wool merchants gave Sudbury three churches – St Peter's, All Saints, and St Gregory's. It is St Peter's church that stands in the square, no longer used for services but maintained by the redundant churches fund. The most famous son of Sudbury is the portrait and landscape painter Thomas Gainsborough (1727–88) and it was here that he started to paint while still at school. His statue stands in the square, an imposing figure in breeches and long coat, clasping a brush and palette.

Gainsborough House, where the artist was born, stands in a narrow street that leads from the square, a wrought iron figure over the doorway. The house is now listed as a historic building. Dotted around the town are many older buildings, timber-framed with overhanging storeys. There are several ancient inns. The grand fourteenth to sixteenth century church of St Gregory stands aloof from the town centre and is the burial place of Simon, 14c Archbishop of Canterbury.
Mill Hotel, Walnut Tree Lane. T (0787) 75544. (A)

Little Waldingfield (Suffolk)

The church (right of village) was built during the 14c on the site of a much earlier building. It has a fine pinnacled tower and is

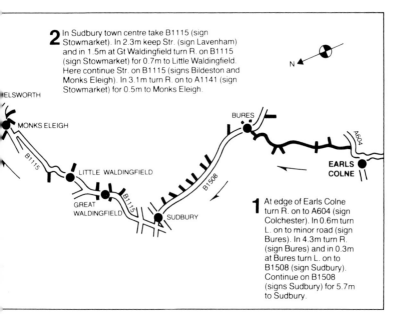

2 In Sudbury town centre take B1115 (sign Stowmarket). In 2.3m keep Str. (sign Lavenham) and in 1.5m at Gt Waldingfield turn R. on B1115 (sign Stowmarket) for 0.7m to Little Waldingfield. Here continue Str. on B1115 (signs Bildeston and Monks Eleigh). In 3.1m turn R. on to A1141 (sign Stowmarket) for 0.5m to Monks Eleigh.

1 At edge of Earls Colne turn R. on to A604 (sign Colchester). In 0.6m turn L. on to minor road (sign Bures). In 4.3m turn R. (sign Bures) and in 0.3m at Bures turn L. on to B1508 (sign Sudbury). Continue on B1508 (signs Sudbury) for 5.7m to Sudbury.

dedicated to St Lawrence, said to have been martyred by being burned to death on a gridiron.

Monks Eleigh (Suffolk)

A picturesque village with many thatched colour-washed cottages.

Chelsworth (Suffolk)

This must surely be one of Suffolk's most beautiful villages. A pleasant old inn, the Peacock, stands before the bridge over the River Brett. Charming thatched cottages as well as larger old houses lie along the river. The Church of All Saints is found in meadows across the stream, the tower and chancel dating from the 14c. In the church is a rare example of a village memorial to a single fallen soldier: 'The people of Chelsworth erected this tablet in proud memory of Charles Peck, who gave his life for his country in the Great War, aged 19'. Charles Peck was the only native of this small village to be killed in action.

Bildeston (Suffolk)

A pleasant little town with a number of old timbered buildings. Less busy than in former days, when it was famous for its cloth and blankets.

Great Finborough (Suffolk)

A chestnut tree stands on the small triangular green. From here a path, also shaded by chestnuts, leads to the church which was much restored a century ago.

The Route
*Pleasant country roads until
reaching the final stretch
into Cambridge.*

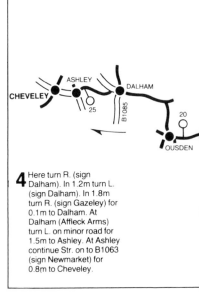

4 Here turn R. (sign
Dalham). In 1.2m turn L.
(sign Dalham). In 1.8m
turn R. (sign Gazeley) for
0.1m to Dalham. At
Dalham (Affleck Arms)
turn L. on minor road for
1.5m to Ashley. At Ashley
continue Str. on to B1063
(sign Newmarket) for
0.8m to Cheveley.

Gedding (Suffolk)

Parts of the moat which once
encircled the little Norman church
can be seen. Nearby is a fine Tudor
house, the tower gateway
approached by a bridge across the
moat.

Little Welnethan (Suffolk)

The church stands in a meadow,
shaded by many old trees.
Standing by the 13c tower there is
a magnificent view of the rolling
Suffolk countryside. Here, also, is
a turn of the century rake factory,
a factory still in use which invites
inspection of the fine traditional
wooden tools made from
machinery driven by belts and
overhead shafts.

Sicklesmere (Suffolk)

The village lies on the main Bury
to Sudbury road. The minor road
from here follows the River Lark.
Signed to the right, isolated
among fine trees and meadows, is
St Peter's Church, Nowton,
standing beneath a 14c tower and
containing a rich collection of
window pictures of Flemish glass.

Hawstead (Suffolk)

Entering the village (right) are
almshouses donated in 1811.
Hawstead, however, has a history
much older than the almshouses.
It is said that the plane and lime
trees which grace the road to Bury
were given by Francis Bacon to
his friend and lord of the manor

Robert Drury. Hawstead Place,
home of the Drury family and now
part of a farm, was visited by
Queen Elizabeth in 1578. Another
distinguished guest here was the
poet John Donne.

Horringer (Suffolk)

The village lies on the edge of the
lovely Ickworth Park and Ickworth
Hall, National Trust property.
Some maps indicate that the entry
road to the park at Horringer runs
directly past the hall to
Chevington. Unfortunately the
latter part of the road, beyond the
hall, is private and not motorable.
The indicated road to Chevington,
therefore, runs south from
Horringer, avoiding the park. The
one-mile diversion, however, is
rewarding. Ickworth Hall was
begun in the 1790s by Frederick
Augustus Hervey, fourth Earl of
Bristol. Standing among pines and
cedars, the focal point of the hall
is the huge central dome,
connected to flanking wings by
semi-circular corridors, the whole

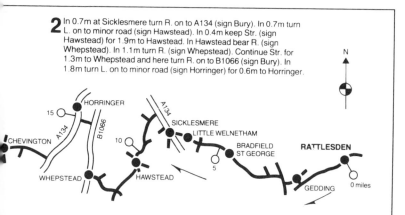

2 In 0.7m at Sicklesmere turn R. on to A134 (sign Bury). In 0.7m turn L. on to minor road (sign Hawstead). In 0.4m keep Str. (sign Hawstead) for 1.9m to Hawstead. In Hawstead bear R. (sign Whepstead). In 1.1m turn R. (sign Whepstead). Continue Str. for 1.3m to Whepstead and here turn R. on to B1066 (sign Bury). In 1.8m turn L. on to minor road (sign Horringer) for 0.6m to Horringer.

At Horringer note short diversion to R. for Ickworth. If NOT visiting Ickworth turn L. on to A143 (sign Haverhill). In 1.7m turn R. on to minor road (sign Chevington). In 1.5m at Chevington keep Str. (sign Hargrave). In 0.9m at Hargrave Green turn R. and in 0.1m turn L. (sign Ousden) for 1.4m to Ousden.

1 At Rattlesden continue Str. (signs Felsham) and in 2.0m turn R. (sign Gedding). In 0.1m at Gedding turn L. (sign Bradfield St George) and in 0.5m turn R. (sign Bradfield St George). Continue Str. for 2.1m to Bradfield St George and here keep Str. (sign Welnetham). Keep Str. (signs Welnetham and Sicklesmere for 1.9m to Little Welnetham.

structure almost 700 ft in length. Two friezes beneath the dome illustrate themes from Homer, the stories of the *Iliad* and the *Odyssey*. Among many treasures in the hall are paintings by Gainsborough and Reynolds, eighteenth and nineteenth century French and English furniture, and rare collections of silver. In the basement is a small restaurant and shop. Here brochures are available, indicating the Albana and Canal walks through the extensive park.

Ickworth Hall, one mile from Horringer.

Dalham (Suffolk)

Picturesque thatched cottages line the banks of the River Kennet in a secluded valley and little arched footbridges span the river to enhance the scene. The church and the hall, once the property of Cecil Rhodes, stand on a hill almost a mile from the village. The inn (below) enjoys a lovely setting in what is certainly one of Suffolk's most beautiful villages. *Affleck Arms.* T (0638) 79306. Restaurant and excellent bar meals. No accommodation.

Ashley (Cambs)

From Dalham the road crosses the River Kennet into Cambridgeshire. Ashley is quiet and spacious, its church seen on the left before entry, with a duck pond as the village's focal point.

Cheveley (Cambs)

The wooded Cheveley Park to the west was formerly owned by the Duke of Rutland. The war memorial outside the church shows a soldier with bowed head in a recess below a cross. In the porch of the church are precise details of the war records of all the villagers who took part in the First World War.

Dullingham (Cambs)

Fine meadows and trees surround the village and a grand sycamore stands at the church gates.

Six Mile Bottom (Cambs)

So called because it lies six miles from Newmarket at the junction of two main roads and the railway line.

3 Here continue Str. across A1304 and A11. In 2.4m turn L. (sign Gt Wilbraham). In 0.1m turn R. (sign Little Wilbraham). In 0.2m turn R. (sign Cambridge). In 0.1m turn L. (sign Cambridge). In 1.3m turn L. on to A1303 (sign Cambridge) and continue for final 4.0m to Cambridge.

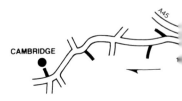

2 In 0.6m turn L. on to B1061 (sign Dullingham) and keep Str. for 0.7m into Dullingham. Here keep Str. and in 0.9m keep Str. on to B1052 (sign Balsham). In 0.9m turn R. on to minor road (sign Six Mile Bottom). Keep Str. for 3.4m to Six Mile Bottom.

Little Wilbraham (Cambs)

The final village before returning to the main road into Cambridge. Here was once a famous Saxon cemetery in which some 200 graves have been found.

Back at Cambridge, punting on the River Cam, from Trinity Bridge.

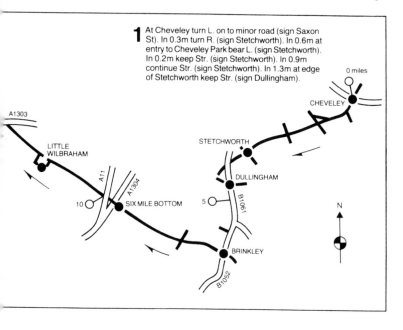

1 At Cheveley turn L. on to minor road (sign Saxon St). In 0.3m turn R. (sign Stetchworth). In 0.6m at entry to Cheveley Park bear L. (sign Stetchworth). In 0.2m keep Str. (sign Stetchworth). In 0.9m continue Str. (sign Stetchworth). In 1.3m at edge of Stetchworth keep Str. (sign Dullingham).

7 East Anglia (North): Suffolk, Norfolk

THE ROUTE starts from Bury St Edmunds in Suffolk. The greater part of it, however, is confined to Norfolk, a county of some 2,000 square miles bounded on the north and east by the Wash and the North Sea. Chief rivers are the Ouse, Yare, Bure and Waveney.

Norwich is the only industrial centre of importance and the county depends principally on the growth of oats, wheat, barley and beet. Turkeys and geese are reared for the London market. Tourists are attracted to the many coastal resorts, among them Great Yarmouth, Cromer, Sheringham and Hunstanton. The added tourist attraction, of course, is the Broads, a series of lakes and canals famous for wildlife and frequented for sailing, fishing and shooting.

The route described in *Through Britain on Country Roads* explored areas of the Norfolk coast as well as the Broads. This route, therefore, has been planned to cover the heart of Norfolk, an area less sophisticated and not as well known, yet offering a variety of charming towns and villages, places of general interest, and a view of the lovely city of Norwich.

After leaving Bury St Edmunds the road runs northwards through the King's Forest in Suffolk and later the Thetford and Swaffham forests. Across this area runs a prehistoric track and a Roman road. The prehistoric Icknield Way was the connection between Avebury in Wiltshire and Hunstanton in Norfolk, encompassed by the King's Forest. The Roman road, Peddars Way, ran from Colchester in Essex to Hunstanton, crossing this route between Swaffham and Sporle.

From this area the road runs north eastward to Aylsham, a pleasant small town eleven miles from the coast at Cromer. After leaving Aylsham the road follows the River Bure before veering south westward through Norwich, and then continues in much the same direction past some delightful villages on the return journey to Bury St Edmunds.

Two National Trust houses are passed, one at Oxborough, one at Blickling. Among other features of interest are the Brandon Country Park, the Iceni village at Cockley Cley and the Saxon cathedral at North Elmham. Outstanding among many picturesque villages are New Buckenham and Brooke.

Bury St Edmunds

In 869 AD King Edmund of East Anglia was martyred by the heathen Danes. Here he was buried; and the great Abbey Gate marks the entry to the Benedictine abbey founded in 1020 to protect and honour the shrine of a king who by now had become a national saint.

Abbey Gate, on the edge of a square named Angel Hill, leads to some glorious gardens where the monks once walked. A botanical guide to this extensive area is available in the town. Among many relics of the abbey are the Abbot's Bridge (*circa* 1211) across the River Lark; the chapter house where the remains of five of the abbots of St

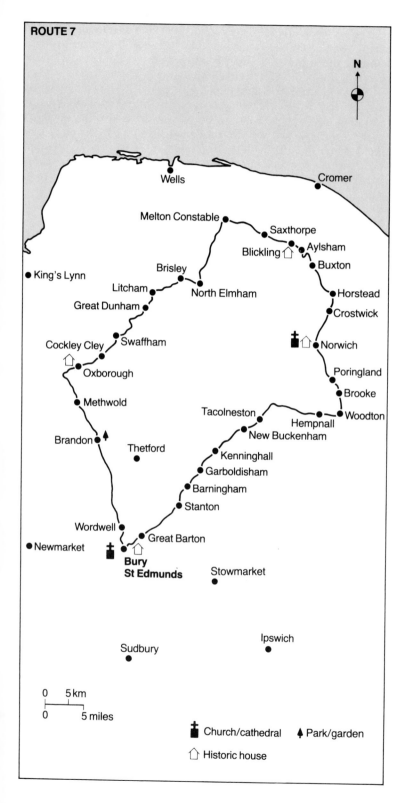

ROUTE 7

N

Wells

Cromer

Melton Constable

Saxthorpe

Blickling

Aylsham

Buxton

King's Lynn

Brisley

Litcham

North Elmham

Horstead

Great Dunham

Crostwick

Cockley Cley

Swaffham

Norwich

Oxborough

Poringland

Methwold

Brooke

Tacolneston

Woodton

Brandon

New Buckenham

Hempnall

Thetford

Kenninghall

Garboldisham

Barningham

Stanton

Wordwell

Great Barton

Newmarket

Bury
St Edmunds

Stowmarket

Sudbury

Ipswich

0   5 km

0   5 miles

✝ Church/cathedral   ♠ Park/garden

⌂ Historic house

Edmund were discovered; the west front, the largest surviving part of the abbey church; and the Norman tower, built as an entrance gate to the abbey church, now serving as the bell tower to the 16c Cathedral Church of St James. A century older than St James is St Mary's Church, burial place of Mary Tudor, sister of Henry VIII.

Among many other interesting buildings in this charming town are the Theatre Royal (National Trust), the only surviving Regency theatre in the provinces and the one chosen for the world première of *Charlie's Aunt* in 1892; the medieval guildhall with a doorway of 1250; the Athenaeum with its fine ballroom; and Moyses Hall, originally two Norman dwellings that have served a variety of purposes and now house a museum of local interest. Charles Dickens stayed at the Angel Hotel on Angel Hill, bringing it to fame in his *Pickwick Papers*. The town also embraces the Nutshell Inn, reputed to be the smallest inn in England.

Angel Hotel, Angel Hill. T (0284) 3926. (A)

Suffolk Hotel, Buttermarket. T (0284) 3995. (A)

Tourist Office, Northgate St. T (0284) 63233.

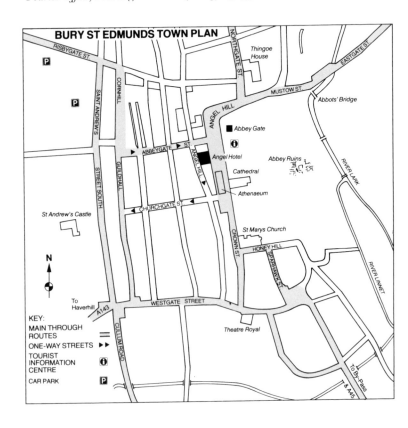

Bury St Edmunds: (opposite above) west front of the abbey; (below) The Nutshell, possibly the smallest inn in England.

The Route

From Bury St Edmunds to Methwold the straight road runs through wooded countryside. A short stretch from Methwold to the River Wissey is dull, but after crossing the river there is more delightful rural scenery.

4 Here turn L. (signs Newmarket and Swaffh and immediately R. at roundabout (sign Swaffham). In 0.4m at level crossing keep on B1106 (sign Stoke Ferry). In 5.8m at Methwold continue Str. on B1106 (sign Kir Lynn). In 3.4m keep Str. on to A134 (sign Downham Market). In 0.6m turn R. on to m road (sign Oxborough). In 0.6m bear R. (si Oxborough). Continue for 1.8m to Oxboro

Fornham St Martin
(Suffolk)

A busy little village, now almost a suburb of Bury St Edmunds. The little church (left) has a battlemented tower, chequered at the top with gargoyles.

Culford (Suffolk)

Off the immediate route and signed to the left is West Stow, a country park with a reconstructed Anglo-Saxon village and nature reserve. A diversion of only two to three miles.

Wordwell (Suffolk)

The secluded little church (left) is surrounded by farm buildings and lies at the extremity of an area sometimes known as Suffolk's Black Forest. The church, once used as a granary, is now preserved by the redundant churches fund. In a further three miles, in the heart of the King's Forest, a commemoration stone to mark the silver jubilee of King George V informs that: 'the Forestry Commission began in 1935 to afforest the King's Forest and to plant with beeches Queen Mary's Avenue'. This lovely

avenue follows the course of the Icknield Way, the prehistoric route from the south west to Norfolk.

Brandon (Suffolk)

Brandon Country Park (left) is signed just before reaching the town. The car park is approached between copper beeches. Here in 1974 some thirty-two acres of woodland were opened to the public. There are walks through an area populated by deer, squirrels, pheasants, jays and long-tail tits. In 1984 an information centre was sited in the car park. The most attractive part of the town is approached by the arched bridge across the River Ouse. Here on meadows by the river are some pleasant tea rooms. The old Ram Hotel and the modern Brandon House Hotel lie on opposite sides of the road, also close to the river. An inn in the town, the

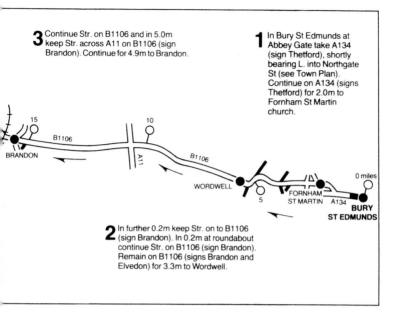

3 Continue Str. on B1106 and in 5.0m keep Str. across A11 on B1106 (sign Brandon). Continue for 4.9m to Brandon.

1 In Bury St Edmunds at Abbey Gate take A134 (sign Thetford), shortly bearing L. into Northgate St (see Town Plan). Continue on A134 (signs Thetford) for 2.0m to Fornham St Martin church.

2 In further 0.2m keep Str. on to B1106 (sign Brandon). In 0.2m at roundabout continue Str. on B1106 (sign Brandon). Remain on B1106 (signs Brandon and Elvedon) for 3.3m to Wordwell.

Flintknappers Arms, reminds that the centuries-old trade of flint-knapping flourished here until recent times.
Brandon House Hotel.
T (0842) 810771. (B)
Ram Hotel. T (0842) 810275. (C)

Methwold (Norfolk)

Much modern building has sprung up here.

Oxborough (Norfolk)

The Bedingfield Arms, named after the lords of the manor, and the church of St John the Evangelist stand together in this remote village. In the chapel of the church is a model of the church as it was before disaster struck one summer's day in 1948, when the spire collapsed, pulling down the tower and destroying the nave roof. Today the chancel and chapel are approached through the roofless nave which serves as a turfed forecourt. In the chapel there is a magnificent screen and monuments to the Bedingfields. Among the monuments is one to Sir Henry Bedingfield (1510–83), guardian of Princess Elizabeth when imprisoned by Queen Mary in the Tower of London. The history of Oxborough Hall relates entirely to the Bedingfield family, dating from 1482 when Sir Edmund Bedingfield began the building. The hall, now owned by the National Trust, is built round a courtyard, with battlements, patterned chimneys and stepped gables. Its glory is the gateway, flanked by two turrets seven storeys high. Much internal restoration to the hall took place in Victorian times. The King's Room in the gatehouse, however, remains much as it was when Henry VII slept there in 1487.

The Route

*Wooded countryside
between Cockley Cley and
Swaffham. The road
narrows and winds from
here to Litcham. From here
by way of the Nar Valley.
Pleasant countryside
despite some unattractive
building around Mileham.*

2 At Swaffham town centre turn R. (sign Norwich). In 1.8m at roundabout turn R. on to A47 (sign Norwich). In 0.6m turn L. on to minor road (sign Sporle) for 1.0m to Sporle.

OXBOROUGH   5   **SWAFFHAM**

0 miles   **COCKLEY CLEY**

1 At Oxborough continue Str. on minor road (signs Cockley Cley) for 3.7m to Cockley Cley. Here continue Str. (sign Swaffham) for 2.8m and turn R. (sign Town Centre). In 0.1m turn L. for 0.2m to town centre.

Cockley Cley (Norfolk)

At one time this small village
contained four manors and three
churches. Today nothing remains
of St Peter's Church, but St Mary's
Chapel, after serving a variety of
roles, has been restored. All Saints
Church, reconstructed in 1866, is
still graced by a fine 11c round
tower. Next to the church is an inn,
The Twenty Church Wardens,
reminding that Cockley Cley is one
of ten parishes, presuming two
wardens to each parish. On the
banks of the River Gadden is a
replica of the village of the Iceni
people, inhabitants of Norfolk
before 60 A.D. Cockley Cley Hall
is a red-brick building in the
Italianate style.

Swaffham (Norfolk)

There is a spacious square here,
the centre dominated by the
market cross, a rotunda with eight
columns that support a dome
topped by a statue of Ceres, in
Roman mythology the goddess of
agriculture. The market square is
surrounded by a variety of
pleasant shops and inns.
Dominating the town is the fine
tower of the church of St Peter and
St Paul. The names Petyr and
Pawle are carved on the parapet
stones. The glory of the church is
the hammer-beam chestnut roof,
the ends of the beams being
adorned by angels with outspread
wings.
George Hotel. Station Rd.
T (0760) 21238. (B)

Sporle (Norfolk)

The cottages here are approached
by footbridges across the little
stream.

Great Dunham (Norfolk)

Stands to the south of the valley
of the Nar in an area of some 2,000
acres of farmland. A rectangle of
lime trees enclose the church of
St Andrew at the end of the village.
The church with its rough flint
walls stands beneath a square
central tower, a building which
began in Saxon times, from which
period traces remain.

Litcham (Norfolk)

In 1636 most of this compact
village on the River Nar was
destroyed by fire. The inn faces a
little village green.

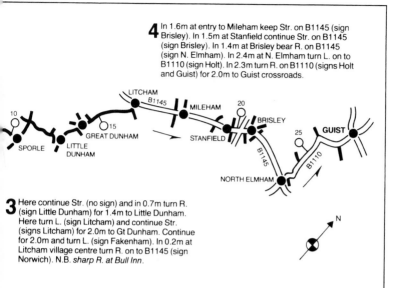

4 In 1.6m at entry to Mileham keep Str. on B1145 (sign Brisley). In 1.5m at Stanfield continue Str. on B1145 (sign Brisley). In 1.4m at Brisley bear R. on B1145 (sign N. Elmham). In 2.4m at N. Elmham turn L. on to B1110 (sign Holt). In 2.3m turn R. on B1110 (signs Holt and Guist) for 2.0m to Guist crossroads.

3 Here continue Str. (no sign) and in 0.7m turn R. (sign Little Dunham) for 1.4m to Little Dunham. Here turn L. (sign Litcham) and continue Str. (signs Litcham) for 2.0m to Gt Dunham. Continue for 2.0m and turn L. (sign Fakenham). In 0.2m at Litcham village centre turn R. on to B1145 (sign Norwich). N.B. *sharp R. at Bull Inn*.

Brisley (Norfolk)

The soaring tower of the church overshadows the village. In the nave is a brass coat of arms marking the grave of John Taverner. John's son, Richard, was born here in 1505, an eccentric character who was licensed to preach throughout England though never ordained. He translated the Bible into English.

Market Cross and church tower at Swaffham.

North Elmham (Norfolk)

By the crossroads in the centre of the village is the King's Head Inn (good bar snacks available). But the real interest begins on leaving the village. Here (signed right) is St Mary's Church and the Anglo-Saxon cathedral. The church has a grand square tower erected in three stages. A feature of the tower is the porch, the doorway carved with flowers and dragons. The walls of the ruined Saxon Cathedral, six feet high in places, define a building first used as a cathedral in the 10th and 11th centuries. In about 1388 the

Remains of the Anglo-Saxon Cathedral at North Elmham.

cathedral was appropriated by the despicable Bishop Despenser. Turning the building into a country seat or hunting lodge, the Bishop surrounded it with inner and outer moats, scattering the bones of the interred to the winds. After Despenser's death his home was abandoned. Among remains unearthed from the site were drinking horns, reminders of bibulous nights spent during the Bishop's tenure. The ruins are now in the care of the Department of the Environment.

The Route

*Quiet country road after
leaving Melton Constable.
Road signing in Aylsham
was poor. From Aylsham to
Horstead the road follows
the Bure Valley, then across
heathland to Crostwick and
beyond.*

Melton Constable
(Norfolk)

The name sounds enticing. But
there is disappointment here in the
shape of some very ugly building.

Saxthorpe (Norfolk)

The church stands by the
crossroads of this busy village by
the River Bure. It is believed to
have been built by the vicar, Peter
Page, in the late 15c. His initials
can be seen carved on benches in
the church.

Blickling (Norfolk)

An entrancing village, dominated
by the huge and gracious Blickling
Hall (National Trust). From the
main road there is a good frontal
view of the hall, looking across
lawns and gardens to the
prominent red-brick facade of one
of the loveliest Jacobean halls in
England. The tallest structure is
the central cupola and clock
tower, flanked by mullion
windows, gables and chimney
stacks with tall square towers at
each corner. Blickling Hall was
built between 1619 and 1625 by
Sir Henry Hobart, Lord Chief
Justice to James I. Many
furnished rooms are on view,
among them the Long Gallery,
123 ft in length. The gardens have
massive yew hedges, colourful
flower beds, borders and lawns.

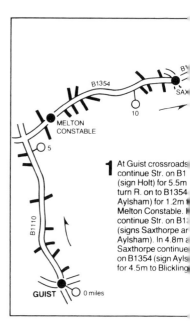

B1354
SAX
MELTON
CONSTABLE
10
5
B1110
GUIST 0 miles

1 At Guist crossroads
continue Str. on B1
(sign Holt) for 5.5m
turn R. on to B1354
Aylsham) for 1.2m
Melton Constable.
continue Str. on B1
(signs Saxthorpe an
Aylsham). In 4.8m
Saxthorpe continue
on B1354 (sign Ayls
for 4.5m to Blickling

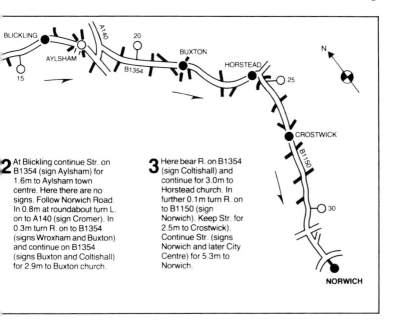

2 At Blickling continue Str. on B1354 (sign Aylsham) for 1.6m to Aylsham town centre. Here there are no signs. Follow Norwich Road. In 0.8m at roundabout turn L. on to A140 (sign Cromer). In 0.3m turn R. on to B1354 (signs Wroxham and Buxton) and continue on B1354 (signs Buxton and Coltishall) for 2.9m to Buxton church.

3 Here bear R. on B1354 (sign Coltishall) and continue for 3.0m to Horstead church. In further 0.1m turn R. on to B1150 (sign Norwich). Keep Str. for 2.5m to Crostwick). Continue Str. (signs Norwich and later City Centre) for 5.3m to Norwich.

Blickling Hall, an outstanding Jacobean house set in beautiful gardens.

129

In the park is a mile-long lake. St Andrew's Church overlooks the neighbouring Hall from a rise known as Church Hill. Monuments include those to the Boleyn family, ancestors of Anne Boleyn. Among them is an earlier Anne Boleyn, buried here aged three years, eleven months and thirteen days on 1 October 1479.

Aylsham (Norfolk)

The small market town has a little square, sometimes providing parking problems. Around the square are a number of mellow red-brick Georgian houses. Centuries ago Aylsham was famous for its production of linen. Much later, in the 18c, a spring to the south of the town yielded water said to be good for asthma, and Aylsham became something of a spa resort. A narrow road from the square leads to the church with its square tower and spire. The church is believed to have been first built by John of Gaunt, Duke of Lancaster, in 1372, who sited it to overlook the Bure Valley, a countryside once called the Garden of Norfolk.

Buxton (Norfolk)

The church (left) stands by a small triangular green.

Horstead (Norfolk)

The church enjoys a peaceful position on meadows that stretch to the River Bure. The neighbouring vicarage is now a conference hall. The long tithe barn at the edge of the churchyard has been modernized and is used for local activity. The picturesque mill by the river was burned down in 1963.

Crostwick (Norfolk)

The church is hard to find. It lies beyond the village, approached by a rough track across a common of bramble and bracken and finally an avenue of limes. Built in the 15c it appears, today, to be in danger of collapse.

Norwich (Norfolk)

The route runs through the heart of this ancient city. The beginnings are Tombland, once a Saxon market place. From here two medieval gateways lead to the Norman cathedral, founded in 1069 with its fine decorated cloisters. To the west of the cathedral is Elm Hill, a medieval street lit by lanterns at night, with the civic halls St Andrew's and Blackfriars, once monastery churches. Overlooking the market place is the Norman castle, now a museum with a large art collection. Among many famous people associated with Norwich are Lord Nelson (1758–1805) who went to school here; Elizabeth Fry (1780–1845), philanthropist and prison reformer, who lived at Gurney Court in Magdalen St; and Nurse Cavell (1865–1915), executed by the Germans for helping Allied prisoners of war to escape, who lies buried near the cathedral walls.

Hotel Norwich, Boundary Rd. T (0603) 410431. (A)
Castle Hotel, Castle Meadow. T (0603) 611511. (B)
Tourist Office, Tombland. T (0603) 666071.

Norwich Cathedral, as seen from Cloister Walk.

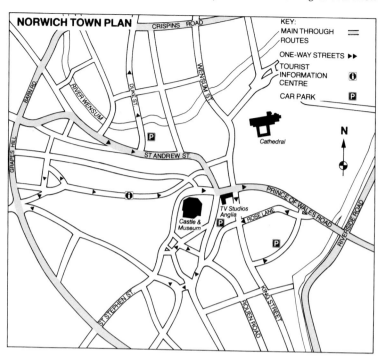

NORWICH TOWN PLAN

KEY:
MAIN THROUGH ROUTES
ONE-WAY STREETS
TOURIST INFORMATION CENTRE
CAR PARK

CRISPINS ROAD
WENSUM ST
DUKE ST
BARN RD
RIVER WENSUM
GRAPES HILL
ST ANDREW ST.
Cathedral
N
PRINCE OF WALES ROAD
TV Studios Anglia
ROSE LANE
Castle & Museum
RIVERSIDE ROAD
ST STEPHEN ST
KING STREET
ROUEN ROAD

The Route

Soon after leaving the suburbs of Norwich the road quietens through charming rural scenery. Between Banham and Kenninghall is a small zoo. (left).

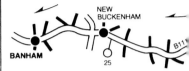

4 Here continue on B1113 (signs New Buckenham for 5.2m to New Buckenham. At New Buckenham bear L. on B1113 (sign Banham) for 2.4m to Banham.

3 Here continue Str. on B1135 (sign Hapton). In 2.5m cross A140 (sign Hapton). Continue for 2.4m to Hapton. Here keep Str. (sign Wymondham) and in 1.0m turn L. on to B1113 (sign New Buckenham) for 1.0m to Tacolneston church.

Poringland (Norfolk)

A dormitory village for Norwich.

Brooke (Norfolk)

In sharp contrast to Poringland, this is a charming little village – though to appreciate it there is need to turn left off the route, looping round pleasant greens and the tree-shaded duck pond. Here are picturesque thatched cottages and the Lamb Inn. Further still along the road is the Norman church with a round tower.

Woodton (Norfolk)

The road by-passes the centre of the village past some attractive old farmhouses.

Hempnall (Norfolk)

To the right of the route is a busy little square with a pleasant inn. Like many Norfolk inns this is called the Lord Nelson, reminding that the Admiral was born in Norfolk, though many miles away at Burnham Thorpe.

Tacolneston (Norfolk)

The church stands outside the village before reaching it (right). It dates from the 13c and its separation from the present village is explained by the Black Death of 1349 when houses near the church were abandoned. Within the church are monuments to the Browne family who lived at Sparkes, the moat of this house surviving in a field near the church. Later monuments are to the Warren family who lived at Old Hall, opposite the church. Several other gracious old houses can be seen as the village is approached. Here amid wooded scenery is the delightful old Pelican Inn. To the west is Tacolneston Hall in a fine park.

New Buckenham (Norfolk)

One of Norfolk's most picturesque villages. Focal point is the large tree-clad village green with a market house from where extends a handsome line of cottages. The upper floor of the market house is supported by wooden pillars. At one time it was planned to make use of this building as a museum, but this idea has not materialized. A number of Georgian houses stand around the green of the old

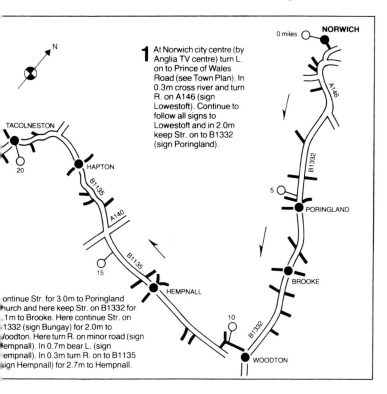

1 At Norwich city centre (by Anglia TV centre) turn L. on to Prince of Wales Road (see Town Plan). In 0.3m cross river and turn R. on A146 (sign Lowestoft). Continue to follow all signs to Lowestoft and in 2.0m keep Str. on to B1332 (sign Poringland).

ontinue Str. for 3.0m to Poringland hurch and here keep Str. on B1332 for .1m to Brooke. Here continue Str. on 1332 (sign Bungay) for 2.0m to /oodton. Here turn R. on minor road (sign lempnall). In 0.7m bear L. (sign empnall). In 0.3m turn R. on to B1135 sign Hempnall) for 2.7m to Hempnall.

market place. The remainder of New Buckenham is made up of streets laid out in a grid pattern. The streets have conventional names such as King Street and Queen Street, but there is a strangely named Boosey Walk with a picturesque thatched cottage dated 1731.

Banham (Norfolk)

Stately limes fringe the rectangular green in front of the church. There are many old houses and timbered cottages, some with thatched roofs and overhanging storeys. The church, 14c, has a splendid tower with gargoyles.

The wooden pillars of the market house, New Buckenham.

The route

*Quiet country roads apart
from the final stretch of the
A143 into Bury St
Edmunds.*

Kenninghall (Norfolk)

A spacious village with a large
square. Here there is an inn and
thatched cottages with dormer
windows. The church with its 15c
tower lies to the left. At the
extremity of Kenninghall there is a
large green.

Garboldisham (Norfolk)

There is a lovely approach to the
village, with woods shading old
houses set among meadows in the
valley of the Little Ouse. The
centre of Garboldisham lies at the
junction of several roads, but here
are some greens with an inn and
the 13–15c flint church beneath a
perpendicular tower.

Barningham (Suffolk)

A cluster of pretty whitewashed
thatched cottages stands to the
right of the road. The rest of the
housing is modern. The flint
church dates from the 14c.

Stanton (Suffolk)

Beyond the village a track climbs
the hill (right) to the lost church
of St John. The track leads by
ancient tombstones, sad and
neglected, to the church which
stands roofless beneath its defiant
tower in a place of lofty solitude.
Nearby, however, is a well-tended
cemetery still in use.

Great Barton (Suffolk)

The church lies up a lane through
fields a mile or more from the
village (signed left). It serves a
large and scattered parish. Barton,

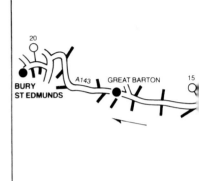

2 Here keep Str. across A1066 on to B1111 (sign
St Edmunds) for 2.0m to Hopton. Here continu
B1111 (sign Bury) for 2.2m to Barningham. Con
Str. on B1111 and in 1.9m at Stanton turn R. o
A143 (sign Bury). Remain on A143 (signs Bury
Gt Barton) for 6.2m to Great Barton. Here keep
on A143 (signs Bury) for 2.5m to Bury St Edmu

we are told, deserves the title Great
because the area of the parish is
larger than the Borough of Bury St
Edmunds. The church is one of
very few in the country dedicated
to the Holy Innocents, the little
Jewish boys massacred by Herod.
The hall of the lords of the manor,
the Bunburys, was burned down
in 1914 but monuments to the
family remain in the church. One
of these is to Sir Henry Bunbury
(1778–1860) who was given the
unenviable task of informing
Napoleon of his exile to St Helena.
Sir Henry's uncle, Sir Thomas, is
buried in Barton Park. His fame is
due to his ownership of the first
winner of the Derby in 1780,
Diomed. It is said that had not Sir
Thomas lost the toss of a coin with
Lord Derby the famous race
would have been called the
Bunbury.

*Back at Bury St Edmunds, the
Norman Gate Tower next to the
Cathedral Church of St James.*

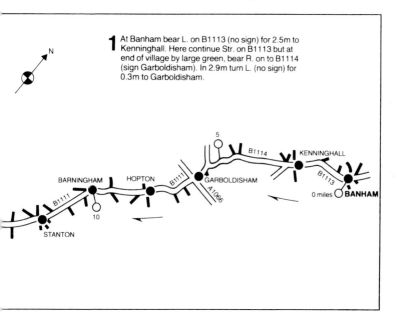

1 At Banham bear L. on B1113 (no sign) for 2.5m to Kenninghall. Here continue Str. on B1113 but at end of village by large green, bear R. on to B1114 (sign Garboldisham). In 2.9m turn L. (no sign) for 0.3m to Garboldisham.

8 South Wales

THIS ROUTE of 150 miles is confined almost entirely to the lovely border counties of Gwent and Powys. There are two exceptions. The road north from Pandy through Clodock, Longtown and Craswall has edged across the border, and these three villages, despite their Welsh atmosphere, are located in the county of Hereford and Worcester. Later, when taking the Head of the Valleys road, the route touches momentarily into Glamorgan.

Apart from its natural beauty this part of Wales has much to offer in both history and legend. The road passes many of the castles occupied by the Norman barons, castles initiated by William the Conqueror to subdue the hostile Welsh. It was not until 1282 that Edward I established English rule over all Wales but, ironically, the destruction of many of these castles took place during the Civil War, after siege by the Parliamentarians on a country that had by now become a Royalist stronghold.

If history abounds so does legend. At Trellech, for example, the official explanation for the three massive stones is that they date from the Bronze Age, dragged there on logs and placed either as marker stones, seasonal information, or for religious ceremony. The legendary explanation is quite different, telling that the stones were thrown by a giant from a hill twelve miles away.

Initially the road from Chepstow to Monmouth runs parallel to the busy A road in the Wye Valley beneath, offering superb views on every side. From Monmouth the little road follows the River Monnow through enchanting countryside. Here is the immediate Wales/England border and as the road runs to the east of the Monnow before crossing it there is a brief encroachment of a few yards into England. This border aspect is emphasized when passing an interesting fortified farmhouse, one of very few buildings seen along this stretch.

The road continues north westward past the delightful villages of Skenfrith and Grosmont with their castles, later following the general line of the border to the east of the Brecon Beacons until reaching Hay-on-Wye. Hay-on-Wye and Builth Wells are small peaceful towns, the latter marking the northern extremity of the route which now turns southward through the Honddu Valley to Brecon.

From Brecon there is more spectacular scenery, the road running south through the Brecon Beacons National Park until reaching the Head of the Valleys road near Merthyr Tydfil. From here, inevitably, the A road to Abergavenny has to be taken.

Beyond Abergavenny the road meanders through more traffic-free unspoilt countryside, passing White Castle and Raglan Castle, the latter a well-preserved ruin despite a massive Parliamentarian onslaught. Usk is a pleasant little town in which to pause, though little remains of the castle. From Usk the B road runs directly to Chepstow, with very little traffic encountered along the way.

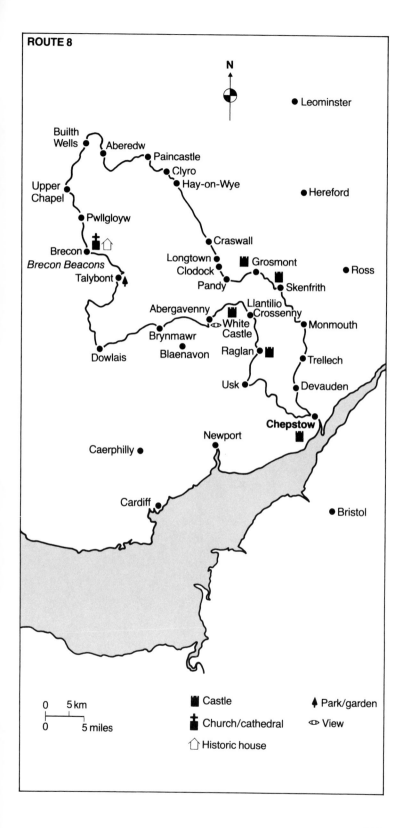

ROUTE 8

N

Leominster

Builth Wells
Aberedw
Paincastle
Clyro
Hay-on-Wye
Upper Chapel
Hereford
Pwllgloyw
Brecon
Brecon Beacons
Craswall
Longtown
Clodock
Grosmont
Ross
Talybont
Pandy
Skenfrith
Abergavenny
Llantilio Crossenny
White Castle
Monmouth
Brynmawr
Blaenavon
Raglan
Trellech
Dowlais
Usk
Devauden
Chepstow
Newport
Caerphilly
Cardiff
Bristol

0   5 km
0   5 miles

Castle
Park/garden
Church/cathedral
View
Historic house

Chepstow

The town is only a few minutes drive from the Severn Bridge, making it an ideal starting point for this tour. Though now a popular tourist and shopping centre, the town held markets over centuries, hence its name (Cheap-stowe, or market place).

The route starts at Town Gate, built in the late 13c and used as a collection point for market tolls. There is a section of the portwall to be seen here, a defensive wall which looped round the south of Chepstow from the castle to the river.

The castle site offers fine views of the River Wye and the wooded hills beyond. In common with many castles along the route, Chepstow Castle was first built as a Norman stronghold for the subjugation of Wales. The castle controlled the road into South Wales, often depending upon the river for its supplies. Extensions were made in the 12th and 13th centuries; but it was not until the Civil War that the castle came under serious attack, a plaque recording the gallant and bloody fight waged by the Royalists before final surrender to the Ironsides. Despite the onslaught, the castle was kept in some state of repair. The huge round Marten Tower is named after Henry Marten, a signatory to the death warrant of Charles i, who was imprisoned here for twenty years.

In Chepstow Museum many aspects of local history and social life are on display. Finally, before leaving the town, the road passes the entry to Chepstow race course, set in charming surroundings where the Welsh Grand National is held annually.

Beaufort Hotel,
Beaufort Square,
St Mary St.
T (029 12) 2497 (B)

George Hotel,
Moor St.
T (029 12) 5363. (A)

Castle View,
16 Bridge St.
T (029 12) 70349. (B)

Tourist Office,
High St.
T (029 12) 3772
(summer only).

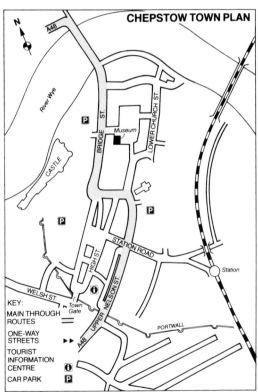

CHEPSTOW TOWN PLAN

KEY:
MAIN THROUGH ROUTES
ONE-WAY STREETS
TOURIST INFORMATION CENTRE
CAR PARK

Brecon Beacons National Park.

The Route

The B road from Chepstow to Monmouth runs along a ridge of hills, offering superb views. The road is almost traffic-free as it runs parallel to the alternative route, the busy A road in the Wye Valley. After leaving Monmouth the minor road is very narrow but enjoys magnificent pastoral scenery along the banks of the River Monnow.

3 At Agincourt Square, Monmouth, keep Str. and 0.2m at traffic lights turn L. on to A466 (sign Hereford). In 0.1m bear L. on to minor road (sign Monnow Mill and Osbarton). Keep Str. for 4.0m a at T-junction turn L. (no sign) and cross river. In 0.5m turn R. (sign Skenfrith) for 2.6m to Skenfri

Itton (Gwent)

The small church is signed (left).

Devauden (Gwent)

A mixture of buildings, some old, some new, make up this hillside village. The Wolvesnewton Model Farm Folk Museum is signed from here (two miles to the left). The farm was built by the Duke of Beaufort, *circa* 1790. It includes a massive cruciform barn and is listed as a County Treasure.

Llanishen (Gwent)

The inn (left) was built by a Huguenot in the 17c.
Carpenters Arms.
T (0600) 860405. (C)
Accommodation in double or single rooms with bathrooms en suite.

Trellech (Gwent)

On the right of the road before entering the village are three upright stones known as Harold's Stones. No connection with King Harold, however, as they date back 3,500 years to the Bronze Age. In the thirteenth and fourteenth centuries Trellech (sometimes spelt Trelleck) was one of the larger towns of South Wales. Later fire, pillage and plague reduced Trellech to what it is today – a charming small village. The children of Trellech school have compiled an excellent history trail (on sale in the village), listing thirty-two interesting features of Trellech.

Monmouth (Gwent)

Entry to the town is by way of the Monnow Bridge Gateway, built in the 13c astride the bridge over the River Monnow, the only remaining fortified bridge gate in Great Britain. The broad main street with many Georgian houses culminates in the old market place, Agincourt Square. Dominating the square is the Shire Hall, built in 1724 on the site of an Elizabethan market hall. Here in a recess is the statue of Henry V,

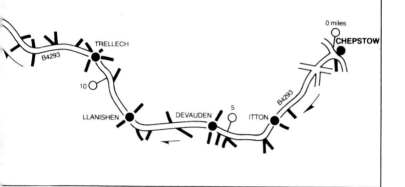

At Llanishen continue Str. (signs Monmouth and Trellech) for 2.2m to Trellech. Here keep Str. (signs Monmouth) and in 4.4m bear R. (sign Monmouth). In 0.9m turn R. (sign Town Centre) for 0.4m to Monmouth town centre.

1 At Chepstow Town Gate take Welsh St (see Town Plan). In 0.7m at roundabout keep Str. on to B4293 (signs Devauden and Itton). Keep Str. for 2.4m to Itton and here continue Str. for 2.4m to Devauden. Here bear L. on B4293 (sign Llanishen) and continue Str. (signs Llanishen and Trellech) for 3.0m to Llanishen.

born in Monmouth Castle in 1387; and below the statue is a bust of the Hon. C. S. Rolls, pioneer of flying and one half of the original Rolls Royce partnership. The nearby Beaufort Arms is an old coaching inn where Lord Nelson stayed when he visited the town. In the Monmouth Museum, Market Hall, there is a Nelson collection where the Admiral's fighting sword is a prized exhibit. The Parliamentarians destroyed Monmouth Castle, first built in 1071, but in 1673 the third Marquess of Worcester built Great Castle House in order, it is said, that his daughter-in-law might have her first child as near as possible to the birthplace of Henry V.
King's Head Hotel, Agincourt Square. T (0600) 2177. (A)

Skenfrith (Gwent)

Skenfrith Castle stands in a blissful setting between the church and swift-flowing river. The castle was built in the early 13c by Hubert de Burgh and is noted for its round tower keep and well-preserved curtain walls. Older parts of St Bridget's church date from 1207, probably also built by de Burgh. Among many treasures here is John Morgan's tomb, the tomb of the last governor of the three castles – Grosmont, Skenfrith, and White Castle. Near the tomb is the Morgan pew, carved in the Jacobean style. Behind a curtain in the north aisle is a glass case. This contains the Skenfrith Cope, an example of English embroidery of the 15c.
Priory Motel. T (0600) 84210. (B) There is a tendency to associate motels with motorways. There can surely be no motel with a quieter and more pleasant aspect than this. Next to the comfortable bedrooms there is an excellent small restaurant. Highly recommended.

The Route

The road from Grosmont follows the course of the River Monnow all the way to its source at Craswall. The road is narrow in places but almost traffic-free. To the west are the Brecon Beacons and from a field past the inn at Craswall (right) is a superb southward view of the Monnow Valley. The road from Hay to Paincastle, also narrow, is rather less interesting.

At Hay turn R. on to B4350 (sign Hereford) and in (L. on to B4350 (sign Hereford). In 0.2m turn L. on t (sign Clyro) and cross R. Wye. In 1.2m at Clyro k across A438 on to minor road (sign Paincastle). I turn L. (sign Paincastle). In 0.4m turn L. (sign Pai and continue (signs Paincastle) for 3.8m to Painc

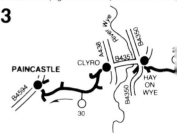

Grosmont (Gwent)

In common with Skenfrith Castle, Grosmont Castle was built by Hubert de Burgh. Unlike Skenfrith, however, it stands on a hill (right), taking its name from the French 'gros mont' (big hill). There are fine views from the remains which include two round towers and an octagonal chimney.

Pandy (Gwent)

The minor road crosses the busy A465 here, avoiding the village. At this junction, however, is the pleasant Old Pandy Inn, offering accommodation and good bar meals.
Old Pandy Inn. T (0873) 890208.

Clodock (Hereford and Worcs)

The church of Sant Clydawg is named after a crown prince, the son of King Ewias, who was murdered in the fifth century. The church occupies a lovely position on the river, the towering Brecon Beacons to the west.

Longtown (Hereford and Worcs)

A charming village which as the name implies straggles for some length until reaching the village

Ruins of Grosmont Castle.

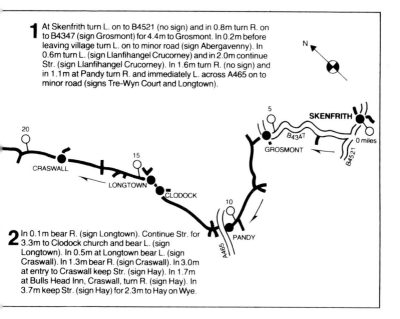

1 At Skenfrith turn L. on to B4521 (no sign) and in 0.8m turn R. on to B4347 (sign Grosmont) for 4.4m to Grosmont. In 0.2m before leaving village turn L. on to minor road (sign Abergavenny). In 0.6m turn L. (sign Llanfihangel Crucorney) and in 2.0m continue Str. (sign Llanfihangel Crucorney). In 1.6m turn R. (no sign) and in 1.1m at Pandy turn R. and immediately L. across A465 on to minor road (signs Tre-Wyn Court and Longtown).

2 In 0.1m bear R. (sign Longtown). Continue Str. for 3.3m to Clodock church and bear L. (sign Longtown). In 0.5m at Longtown bear L. (sign Craswall). In 1.3m bear R. (sign Craswall). In 3.0m at entry to Craswall keep Str. (sign Hay). In 1.7m at Bulls Head Inn, Craswall, turn R. (sign Hay). In 3.7m keep Str. (sign Hay) for 2.3m to Hay on Wye.

shop (left). Here is St Peter's church, dating from the 13c and once the private chapel of the Norman lords who occupied Longtown Castle. Later it became the chapel of ease to the parish church at Clodock. Today, however, it is in a derelict condition awaiting reconstruction as a private house. The ruins of the castle lie nearby.

Craswall (Hereford and Worcs)

A handful of farm buildings culminate at the Old Bull Inn. The ruins of Craswall Priory lie in the Monnow Valley, approachable on foot by way of a steep path that leads to the right after passing the inn.

Hay-on-Wye (Powys)

A maze of narrow streets criss-cross the centre of this hill town. The Norman gateway and tower of the 11c castle stand in the heart

of Hay-on-Wye, adjoining an Elizabethan house now privately owned. A feature of the town is the multiplicity of second-hand bookshops, the largest shop a converted cinema, making Hay a mecca for book lovers.
Old Black Lion, Lion St.
T (0497) 820841. (C)

Clyro (Powys)

The village lies across the River Wye. All that remains of the castle is the moat and small mound.

Paincastle (Powys)

Henry III once held court at the castle here; but, like Clyro Castle, the remains are minimal. They can be approached past a farm to the north of the road and stand forlornly beneath the Begwyn hills. There is a nice inn in the village.
Maesllwch Arms. T (049 75) 279. (C) Accommodation and restaurant.

The Route

The B4567 runs parallel to the busier A470, through pleasant woods on the other side of the river. From Builth Wells the road rises before descending through the picturesque Honddu Valley into Brecon.

Aberedw (Powys)

Stands at a point of great beauty above the River Wye, the river joined here by a tributary that cascades down through a narrow gorge. Above the village, a mile away, is Llewellyn's Cave where Prince Llewellyn, the last native Prince of Wales, sheltered on the night before his treacherous murder in 1282.

Builth Wells (Powys)

There is good fishing at this small spa town where the Rivers Wye and Irfon meet. By the side of the Wye and overlooked by a medieval bridge is the Groe, a pleasant expanse of green in use as a public recreation ground. The town is composed of solid grey stone buildings, all of them built since the great fire that took place here at the end of the 17c.
Lion Hotel, Broad St.
T (0982) 553670. (C)

Upper Chapel (Powys)

From Builth Wells the road has risen high, crossing moors in sharp contrast to the earlier valley scenery. Some military ranges lie to the right, with barely a building to be seen apart from the lonely little Cwm Owen Inn (right).

2 At Builth Wells turn L. and immediately R. on to B4520 (signs Upper Chapel). Continue on B4520 and in 7.5m keep Str. on B4520 (sign Brecon) for 0.4m to Upper Chapel. Here continue Str. on B4520 for 3.8m to Lower Chapel.

3 At Lower Chapel re on B4520 for 1.5m Pwllgloyw. Here ke Str. for 3.5m to Bre Cathedral and from continue for further to town centre.

Arrival at Upper Chapel, therefore, marks the first real sign of habitation and from here the road joins the River Honddu, descending into the lovely Honddu Valley.

Lower Chapel (Powys)

The little chapel lies to the right of the road. The valley has narrowed here with beech woods clinging to the hills on both sides of this small hamlet.

Pwllgloyw (Powys)

No inn was detected at either Upper or Lower Chapel. Here, however, is a delightful 17c inn,

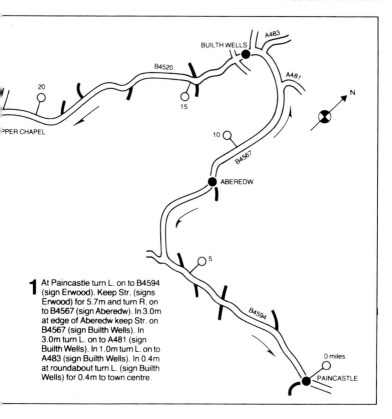

1 At Paincastle turn L. on to B4594 (sign Erwood). Keep Str. (signs Erwood) for 5.7m and turn R. on to B4567 (sign Aberedw). In 3.0m at edge of Aberedw keep Str. on B4567 (sign Builth Wells). In 3.0m turn L. on to A481 (sign Builth Wells). In 1.0m turn L. on to A483 (sign Builth Wells). In 0.4m at roundabout turn L. (sign Builth Wells) for 0.4m to town centre.

broad-fronted with quaint old bars and small restaurant. Opposite the inn is a lawn on the banks of the Honddu.
Camden Arms. T (087 489) 282. (C)

Brecon (Powys)

The town's Welsh name, Aberhonddu, tells that it stands at the junction of the Honddu with the Usk. First sight of Brecon is the grand cathedral (left). Once a priory of Norman foundation, the church saw much restoration over the centuries, in particular by Sir Gilbert Scott in two stages from 1862–74. In 1923 this one-time parish church was chosen as the cathedral for the Diocese of Swansea and Brecon. The pride of the cathedral is the Early English chancel and the St Keynes and Harvard Chapels. The ruins of the Norman castle lie close to the Castle Hotel. There are many interesting old buildings, among them the Sarah Siddons, formerly the Shoulder of Mutton, where the actress Sarah Siddons was born in 1755; and Boleyn House, still owned by the descendants of Ann Boleyn.
Castle of Brecon Hotel, The Avenue. T (0874) 2551. (A)

The Route

Initially runs through the heart of the National Park. The final few miles along the A465, though dreary, provide the only link to the east.

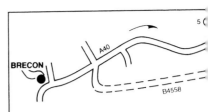

Talybont (Powys)

The Brecon Beacons National Park occupies an area of 519 square miles and embraces some of the finest scenery in Britain. The chosen route from Talybont to Dowlais runs more or less due south through the heart of the park. To the east of the route the busier main roads to Abergavenny run parallel to the River Usk, with the Black Mountains further east still. This latter area was chosen in *Through Britain on Country Roads*. Past the village of Talybont the road narrows and leads to a car park (left) on the northern extremity of the lovely Talybont Reservoir, overlooked by pine-clad hills. Some details of the National Park are displayed in the car park.

1 At Brecon (Tourist Information Centre) keep Str. (s Abergavenny). In 1.4m at roundabout bear R. on ƚ A40 (sign Abergavenny). In 5.1m bear R. on to mi road (sign Talybont). In 0.7m turn R. (sign Pencell and in 0.2m at Talybont turn L. (sign Torpantau). Continue for 1.3m to Talybont Reservoir car park (ƚ

2 Here continue Str. on minor road. In 4.3m keep Str. sign) for 1.6m to Taf Fechan Forest car park. In 0 bear L. (sign Pontsticill). In 0.9m at T-junction turn (sign Pontsticill). In 1.8m turn L. (sign Merthyr Tyd In 0.4m turn R. (sign Mountain Railway). In 0.4m ke Str. (no sign). In 1.4m turn L. (sign Dowlais).

The 'Big Pit' Mining Museum at Blaenavon.

Fechan Forest (Powys)

There are no dwellings along the route which passes between the reservoir and moors and forest. Upon entering the Taf Fechan forest there is another well-sited car park, to the immediate north of the Pentwyn and Pontsticill Reservoirs. From here the road runs south, passing both reservoirs until reaching Dowlais.

Dowlais (Glamorgan)

A mining village and a suburb of Merthyr Tydfil. With the Brecon

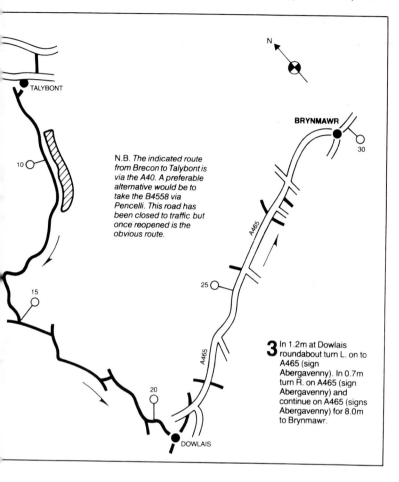

N.B. *The indicated route from Brecon to Talybont is via the A40. A preferable alternative would be to take the B4558 via Pencelli. This road has been closed to traffic but once reopened is the obvious route.*

3 In 1.2m at Dowlais roundabout turn L. on to A465 (sign Abergavenny). In 0.7m turn R. on A465 (sign Abergavenny) and continue on A465 (signs Abergavenny) for 8.0m to Brynmawr.

Beacons to the north and the Valleys to the south, the only route to Abergavenny is along the busy A465. This road, known as the Head of the Valleys road, provides entry to the coal-mining valleys, among them the Rhymney and Sirhowy Valleys and the famous Ebbw Vale, areas which often surprise with their charm.

Brynmawr (Glamorgan)

From here the chosen route runs as directly as possible to Abergavenny. There is, however, an interesting alternative. This means turning right at Brynmawr onto the B4248 for five miles to Blaenavon. Here is a fascinating mining museum with both a surface display and an underground tour. This tour is conducted by ex-miners, starting with a thrilling ride in the pit cage down the 300-ft shaft. The two distinct underground routes are illuminated only by cap lamps.

The Route

The minor road, very narrow in parts, runs through charming rural scenery all the way from the Abergavenny road to Raglan. The road from Raglan to Usk, also unclassified, is straighter and broader. The final stretch along the B4235 from Usk to Chepstow presents some good views. A little-populated area that culminates at the woods near Chepstow.

1 At Brynmawr continue on A465 for 8.0m to Abergavenny. Here take A465 (sign Hereford) and in 0.6m at edge of town turn R. on to B4521 (sign Skenfrith). Keep Str. on B4521 (signs Skenfrith). In 6.1m turn R. on to minor road (sign White Castle). In 0.7m continue Str. (sign White Castle) for 0.2m to White Castle. N.B. *Castle signed here down cul de sac.*

Abergavenny (Gwent)

This popular touring and holiday centre occupies a pleasant position at a point where the Rivers Usk and Gavenny meet. The two oldest structures are the castle ruins and the parish church. The castle ruins comprise two towers, a gateway and wall; the surrounds include the castle mound laid out as a public park with flower beds, grassy walks and sports facilities. There is a splendid view of the Blorenge Cairn (1833 ft) to the south west. The Abergavenny and District Museum stands within the castle grounds. Among over 600 exhibits are bronze age tools, Roman coins, and Tudor and Queen Anne furniture. The parish church of St Mary was the priory church of the 12c Benedictine monastery. Although the church has been much restored it retains many ancient features. There is a fine Victorian market hall, a spacious building with gracious iron pillars. *Angel Hotel*, Cross St. T (0873) 7121. (A) *Llanwenarth Arms*, Brecon Rd.

T (0873) 810550. This hotel lies a little out of the town centre in a pleasant position on the river.

White Castle (Gwent)

Oldest of the Three Castles (the other two, Skenfrith and Grosmont, seen earlier on the route), White Castle was built in 1180 and is perhaps the best preserved of the three. Entry is by way of a wooden bridge across a steep moat leading to the castle towers. At one time the castle walls were covered in white plaster, giving the castle its name. It is said that Hitler's deputy, Rudolph Hess, once fed swans here in the castle moat. White Castle lies directly on the Offa's Dyke Path, the earthwork along the Welsh border attributed to the Anglo-Saxon King Offa, King of Mercia in 757 AD.

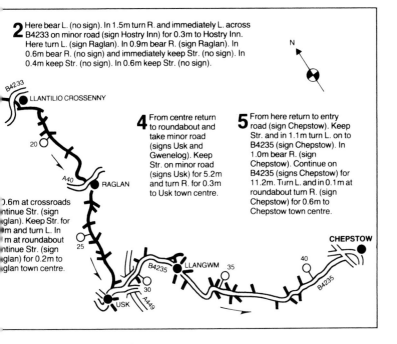

2 Here bear L. (no sign). In 1.5m turn R. and immediately L. across B4233 on minor road (sign Hostry Inn) for 0.3m to Hostry Inn. Here turn L. (sign Raglan). In 0.9m bear R. (sign Raglan). In 0.6m bear R. (no sign) and immediately keep Str. (no sign). In 0.4m keep Str. (no sign). In 0.6m keep Str. (no sign).

N

B4233

LLANTILIO CROSSENNY

20

A40 RAGLAN

4 From centre return to roundabout and take minor road (signs Usk and Gwenelog). Keep Str. on minor road (signs Usk) for 5.2m and turn R. for 0.3m to Usk town centre.

5 From here return to entry road (sign Chepstow). Keep Str. and in 1.1m turn L. on to B4235 (sign Chepstow). In 1.0m bear R. (sign Chepstow). Continue on B4235 (signs Chepstow) for 11.2m. Turn L. and in 0.1m at roundabout turn R. (sign Chepstow) for 0.6m to Chepstow town centre.

0.6m at crossroads ntinue Str. (sign glan). Keep Str. for m and turn L. In m at roundabout ntinue Str. (sign glan) for 0.2m to glan town centre.

25

CHEPSTOW

40

B4235 LLANGWM 35

30

USK A449

B4235

Llantilio Crossenny
(Gwent)

Immediately outside the village in remote and charming scenery is the little Hostry Inn, stone built and dating from 1459. The inn bears the arms of David Gam, the Welsh squire who is said to have saved the life of his friend Henry V at Agincourt. The home of the Gam family, Old Court, has been demolished.

Raglan (Gwent)

The central points of the little town are the church and pleasant hotel. Within the church is the Beaufort Chapel, resting place of William Somerset, third Earl of Worcester, who had done much to enrich his home at Raglan Castle in Elizabethan times. The castle is perched on a hill, separated from Raglan by the main road. The Great Tower still stands prominently despite Parliament's order to 'slight' the castle after its capture by Fairfax in 1646. After the Roundhead army departed the 'slighted' castle provided free building materials for the neighbourhood.
Beaufort Arms Hotel.
T (0291) 690412. (A)

Usk (Gwent)

Enjoys a charming position on the River Usk, a popular centre for angling as the name of the hotel suggests. There is a spacious square with the 19c clock tower as the focal point. Two pleasant inns, together with other colour-washed shops and houses, face each other across the square.
Three Salmons Hotel, Bridge St. T (029 13) 2133. (B)

9 Gloucestershire, Avon

IN VOLUME I of *Through Britain on Country Roads* the route ran through the heart of the Cotswolds, by way of many of the better known villages. This new route has been planned to visit some of the less frequented villages in the south west Cotswolds, the southern extremity at Marshfield (Avon), the northern at Bisley (Glos). The link between these extremities runs from Pucklechurch to Berkeley in the Severn Valley, a less scenic area but one which allows the sight of two historic small towns, Thornbury and Berkeley.

The route passes all five of the 'quiet churches of the Thames Head villages' – Coates, Tarlton and Rodmarton at the start, Frampton Mansell and Sapperton at the conclusion.

The first town of any size is Tetbury, once a wealthy wool town, where many of the wool merchants' houses look much as they did 300 years ago, giving meaning to the description of Tetbury as an architectural gem. Later, on the extreme western edge of the Cotswolds, is the breath-taking viewpoint from the Somerset monument above Hawkesbury.

Horton Court (National Trust) deserves a visit, as does the little town of Marshfield and the marvellous house and deer park at

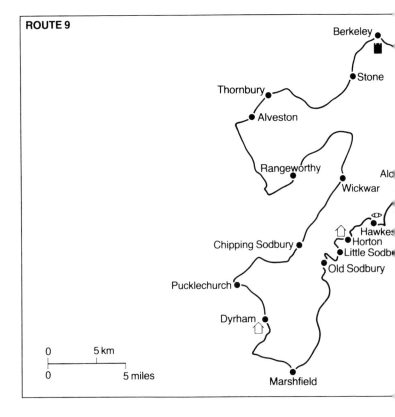

ROUTE 9

Berkeley
Stone
Thornbury
Alveston
Rangeworthy
Ald
Wickwar
Hawkes
Horton
Chipping Sodbury
Little Sodb
Old Sodbury
Pucklechurch
Dyrham
Marshfield

0   5 km
0   5 miles

Dyrham (also National Trust). Gloucestershire has no more historic or better preserved castle than at Berkeley, scene of the murder of Edward II.

The hills above Uley contain prehistoric burial grounds of the Stone Age as well as offering superb panoramic views. The villages of Bisley and Sapperton, both picturesque and interesting in their different ways, conclude a tour through much unspoilt and unfrequented countryside.

Cirencester

Known as the capital of the Cotswolds, Cirencester has a variety of attractions, making it an ideal starting point for the tour. The parish church of St John the Baptist, one of the great wool churches of the Cotswolds, lies near the market place. Cirencester Park comes right into the heart of the town, 3,000 acres with woodland walks open to the public. In the Corinium Museum are displays of Romano-British antiquities, mosaics, sculptures and period reconstructions. The Roman amphitheatre is a grass-covered arena which conjures up visions of displays that took place here in Roman times. A group of Victorian stone buildings in the centre of the town, originally a brewery, have been converted into workshops, a gallery, shop and coffee house. The buildings are run by the Cirencester Workshop Trust, a non-profit making venture run as an educational project.

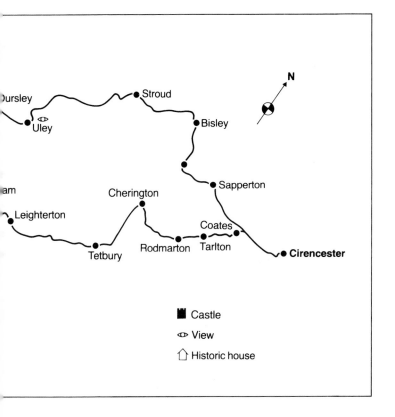

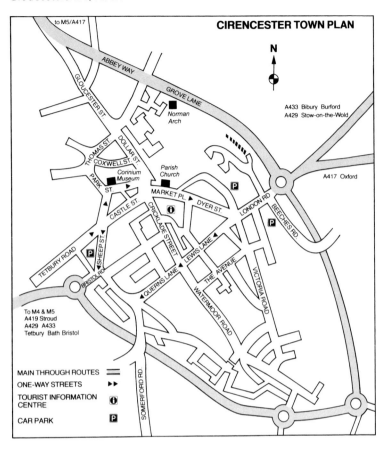

Fleece Hotel, Market Place. T (0285) 68507. (A)
Corinium Court Hotel, Gloucester St. T (0285) 69711. (B)
White Lion Inn, Gloucester St. T (0285) 4053. (C)
Tourist Office, Corn Hall. T (0285) 4180.

Market day in Cirencester.

The Route

*Traffic-free minor roads
throughout, though they
are never unduly narrow.*

Coates (Glos)

Together with Tarlton and
Rodmarton this quiet place is
numbered among the Thames
Head villages. The maps show
that the source of the River
Thames emerges at a point some
two miles south of Coates and a
mile east of Tarlton. St Matthew's
Church dates from 1068, though
it was much restored in the 19c.
After leaving Coates but before
arrival at Tarlton note a sign 'Inn'
(right). It is worth taking the rough
wooded track to the secluded
Tunnel House Inn on the edge of
the Bathurst Estate. Here, below
the inn, note the stone portico
above the canal which has run
underground for two miles from
Sapperton before emerging here.
The canal tunnel was opened in
1792, the barges propelled
through the tunnel by the legs of
labourers lying on their backs
(there is no tow path). The horses
and donkeys were luckier. They
were stabled here while the men
returned on foot to the Sapperton
doss house, now the inn.
Tunnel House Inn.
T (028 577) 280. Good bar meals.
No accommodation.

Tarlton (Glos)

St Oswald's church has been
associated with the manor of
Tarlton since 1226. By the 19c it
was being used as a farm store,
but in 1875 it was restored.

Rodmarton (Glos)

The church lies to the right of an
elm-shaded green. St Peter's is
among the loveliest of the Thames

3 Here keep Str. and in 0.1m at village green
bear L. (sign Tetbury). Continue to follow
minor road (all signs Tetbury) for 2.9m and
turn R. on to A433 (no sign) for 1.0m to
Tetbury. Here bear R. on to A4135 (sign
Dursley). In 0.6m turn L. on to minor road
(sign Leighterton) and in 2.4m at
crossroads keep Str. (sign Leighterton)
for 1.9m to Leighterton.

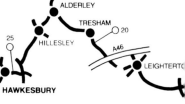

4 Keep Str. for 0.6m and turn L. on to A46 (sign
Bath). In 0.9m turn R. on to minor road (sign
Tresham) for 1.2m to Tresham. Here
continue Str. (no sign) for 1.5m to Alderley
and at T-junction turn L. (sign Hillesley) for
0.8m to Hillesley. Keep Str. through village
(no signs) and in 1.6m turn R. (sign
Hawkesbury) for 0.5m to Hawkesbury church.

Head village churches, dating
from Saxon times with a Celtic
cross and standing beneath a fine
broached spire of the 14c.

Tetbury (Glos)

Although the direct route avoids
the centre of Tetbury it is worth
pausing in this delightful market
town. In particular note the
pillared market house in the heart
of the town, once the hub of wool
trading which first made Tetbury
prosperous. From the market
place Chipping Lane leads to the
Chipping, the original market, the
Chipping Steps descending past
charming stepped houses.
Snooty Fox Hotel, Market Place.
T (0666) 52436. (A)

Leighterton (Glos)

The church is approached past a
line of stone cottages to the left of
the pleasant inn. It stands beneath
an ancient tower, timbered belfry
and oak spire, the churchyard
shaded by yew trees.
Royal Oak Inn. T (066 689) 250.
No accommodation.

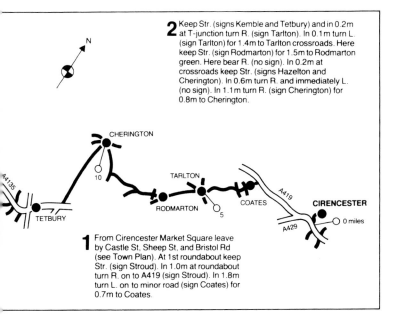

2 Keep Str. (signs Kemble and Tetbury) and in 0.2m at T-junction turn R. (sign Tarlton). In 0.1m turn L. (sign Tarlton) for 1.4m to Tarlton crossroads. Here keep Str. (sign Rodmarton) for 1.5m to Rodmarton green. Here bear R. (no sign). In 0.2m at crossroads keep Str. (signs Hazelton and Cherington). In 0.6m turn R. and immediately L. (no sign). In 1.1m turn R. (sign Cherington) for 0.8m to Cherington.

1 From Cirencester Market Square leave by Castle St, Sheep St, and Bristol Rd (see Town Plan). At 1st roundabout keep Str. (sign Stroud). In 1.0m at roundabout turn R. on to A419 (sign Stroud). In 1.8m turn L. on to minor road (sign Coates) for 0.7m to Coates.

Alderley (Glos)

After passing the hilltop village of Tresham the road descends to this little village in a wooded vale. The church with its battlemented tower stands by an Elizabethan house (now a school).

Hawkesbury (Avon)

There are superb views along the road to Hawkesbury, none finer than the view from the top of the towering monument (left). The monument is to the memory of Lord Edward Somerset who served at Waterloo. Details of his service are displayed inside the door of the tower. From here 144 spiral steps lead to the platform – not a place for those who have no head for heights. Nor is the ascent one for the claustrophobic as the darkness of the tower staircase is relieved only by the occasional slit window. Shortly after passing the monument the road descends sharply to St Mary's church in a charming secluded setting.

Hawkesbury, monument to Lord Edward Somerset.

The Route

*The road is narrow between
Horton and the Sodburys.
Thereafter pleasant and
straightforward apart from
the short stretch between
Chipping Sodbury and
Wickwar, where there are
quarries.*

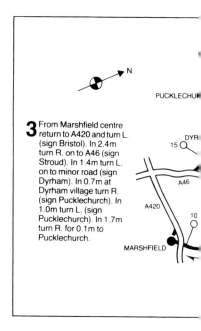

3 From Marshfield centre
return to A420 and turn L.
(sign Bristol). In 2.4m
turn R. on to A46 (sign
Stroud). In 1.4m turn L.
on to minor road (sign
Dyrham). In 0.7m at
Dyrham village turn R.
(sign Pucklechurch). In
1.0m turn L. (sign
Pucklechurch). In 1.7m
turn R. for 0.1m to
Pucklechurch.

Horton Court (Avon)

A typical Cotswold manor house
with a Norman hall and an unusual
Perpendicular ambulatory
detached from the house. The
National Trust owns the house
together with 146 acres of
surrounding farmland.

Little Sodbury (Avon)

The gabled 15c manor house was
the home of Sir John Walshe,
King's Champion at the
coronation of Henry VIII. William
Tyndale, English translator of the
Bible, stayed here as tutor to Sir
John's children before his flight to
Worms and subsequent
execution.

Old Sodbury (Avon)

The route touches the edge of this
main road village. The pleasant
modernized hotel became famous
when Queen Elizabeth II was
stranded here during a violent
snowstorm.
Cross Hands Hotel.
T (0454) 313000. (A)

Marshfield (Avon)

This delightful small town stands
to the south of the Cotswolds,
some 600 ft above sea level and
said by some to be the coldest
spot in England. Marshfield, once
an important market town and
coaching station, used to boast no
less than thirteen inns. Today
there are three old inns, among
them the 17c Crown Inn with a
Mummer's Bar, so called because
every Boxing Day the Marshfield
Mummers perform a traditional
English folk dance. The cellar
under the Mummer's Bar is
believed to have been the town
jail, while the restaurant was a
butcher's shop. Detached from
the High Street is the small market
square, flanked by Marshfield
House and small picturesque
cottages whose names convey
their original functions, among
them the Old Inn, Bakehouse
Cottage and Saddler's Cottage.
Nearby is the church, its tall
pinnacled tower and golden
weather vane dominating the full
length of the High Street.
Crown Inn. T (022 124) 346.
Restaurant. No accommodation.

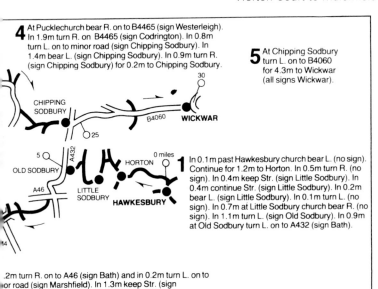

4 At Pucklechurch bear R. on to B4465 (sign Westerleigh). In 1.9m turn R. on B4465 (sign Codrington). In 0.8m turn L. on to minor road (sign Chipping Sodbury). In 1.4m bear L. (sign Chipping Sodbury). In 0.9m turn R. (sign Chipping Sodbury) for 0.2m to Chipping Sodbury.

5 At Chipping Sodbury turn L. on to B4060 for 4.3m to Wickwar (all signs Wickwar).

1 In 0.1m past Hawkesbury church bear L. (no sign). Continue for 1.2m to Horton. In 0.5m turn R. (no sign). In 0.4m keep Str. (sign Little Sodbury). In 0.4m continue Str. (sign Little Sodbury). In 0.2m bear L. (sign Little Sodbury). In 0.1m turn L. (no sign). In 0.7m at Little Sodbury church bear R. (no sign). In 1.1m turn L. (sign Old Sodbury). In 0.9m at Old Sodbury turn L. on to A432 (sign Bath).

.2m turn R. on to A46 (sign Bath) and in 0.2m turn L. on to or road (sign Marshfield). In 1.3m keep Str. (sign rshfield). In 0.2m turn L. (sign Marshfield). Keep Str. (signs rshfield) and in 3.6m keep Str. across A420 into Marshfield.

The 17c Crown Inn at Marshfield.

Dyrham (Avon)

Although the road runs through the village the entry to Dyrham Park is from the main Bath/Stroud road, a few hundred yards past the turning onto the minor road. This 17c house (National Trust) has fine panelling, tapestries and furniture of the Dutch style. William Blathwayt, builder of Dyrham Park, habitually accompanied William III to Holland in his capacity as Secretary of State, hence the Dutch influence. The house is surrounded by 263 acres of parkland with a herd of fallow deer. Refreshments are served in the Orangery.

Pucklechurch (Avon)

A large busy village. Two oaks stand like sentries by the gate to the church with its sturdy pinnacled tower.

Chipping Sodbury (Avon)

The broad main street of gabled houses leads to the 16c cross. Outside the Baptist church is a bust of Andrew Foxwell, 'Musician, Philanthropist and Friend'. The parish church lies along the route on the Wickwar Road with a huge pinnacled tower and strange gargoyles. Above the 14c doorway stands the figure of Christ between the two Saint Johns.

Dyrham Park, built of local Cotswold stone.

Chipping Sodbury High Street.

The Route

*This section of the route,
though passing towns of
great interest and beauty, is
dull by comparison with the
remaining sections.*

Rangeworthy (Avon)

Although much restored in the 16c
much of the little church is of
Norman origin. Among many
features of interest are the carved
Elizabethan chair and a chest of
much the same age. The chest was
removed from the barn of
Rangeworthy Court, the site of an
earlier manor house and home of
the widow of Piers Gaveston,
favourite of Edward II who was
executed by the barons.

Thornbury (Avon)

This busy little town with many
picturesque houses is famous for
its magnificent church and historic
castle. The two buildings stand
side by side, aloof from the town
centre. The builder of the castle
(now a hotel) was Edward
Stafford, Duke of Buckingham,
intent upon endowing the parish
with a 'perpetual college, with
dean, sub-dean, eight secular
priests, four clerks and eight
choristers'. The dream was never
realized due to his execution on
Tower Hill in 1521. There is a good
view of the castle from the wall of
the churchyard. Entry is confined
to hotel customers.
Thornbury Castle Hotel.
T (0454) 412647. (A)

Berkeley (Glos)

The castle, built as a fortress and
dominated by its Norman keep,
was first established to protect the
surrounding vale from intrusion
by marauders across the River
Severn. Berkeley Castle was

1 At Wickwar turn L. on to
B4059 (sign Charfield).
In 2.1m turn L. on to
B4058 (sign Bristol). In
4.5m at Rangeworthy
keep Str. on B4058 and
in 1.4m turn R. on
B4058 (sign Bristol). In
0.4m turn R. on to B4059
(sign Thornbury). Keep
Str. on B4059, later
B4427 (signs Thornbury)
and in 4.0m at
Rudgeway turn R. on to
A38 (sign Thornbury). In
1.0m at Alveston turn L.
on to B4061 (sign
Thornbury) for 1.3m to
Thornbury.

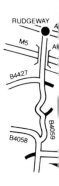

begun in 1117 by the family of that
name, and descendants of the
Berkeleys have lived here ever
since. Within the austere
battlemented walls are gracious
rooms, among them the huge
Great Hall with a timbered 14c
roof; drawing rooms with 18c gilt
furniture; and the morning room,
once a chapel, where around the
roof timbers is a 14c translation of
the Book of Revelation. The
darkest moment in the history of
the castle came in 1327, for here
was the scene of the torture and
brutal murder of Edward II,
instigated by his wife and her lover
Earl Mortimer. In the centre of the
town, next to the church, is the
Jenner Museum, former home of
Edward Jenner who originated
vaccination in 1796 as protection
against smallpox. In the garden is
the Temple of Vaccinia, the hut
where Jenner often vaccinated his
patients. Within the church is the
Jenner family tomb.
Berkeley Arms. T (0453) 810291.
(B)
Old Schoolhouse.
T (0453) 811711. (B)

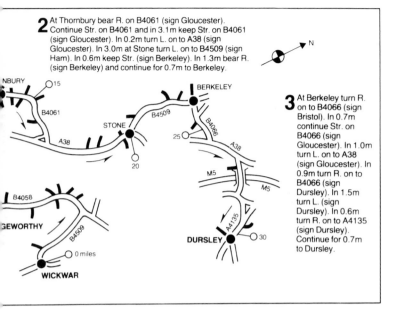

2 At Thornbury bear R. on B4061 (sign Gloucester). Continue Str. on B4061 and in 3.1m keep Str. on B4061 (sign Gloucester). In 0.2m turn L. on to A38 (sign Gloucester). In 3.0m at Stone turn L. on to B4509 (sign Ham). In 0.6m keep Str. (sign Berkeley). In 1.3m bear R. (sign Berkeley) and continue for 0.7m to Berkeley.

3 At Berkeley turn R. on to B4066 (sign Bristol). In 0.7m continue Str. on B4066 (sign Gloucester). In 1.0m turn L. on to A38 (sign Gloucester). In 0.9m turn R. on to B4066 (sign Dursley). In 1.5m turn L. (sign Dursley). In 0.6m turn R. on to A4135 (sign Dursley). Continue for 0.7m to Dursley.

The Great Hall of Berkeley Castle, with its 14c timbered roof.

The Route

Magnificent views from Uley to Stroud. Roads very narrow from Bisley to Sapperton. Before entering Bisley a sign points (right) to Lypiatt Park, the house where the conspirators in the Gunpowder Plot took refuge.

Uley (Glos)

The pretty village nestles beneath wooded hills. After leaving it the road ascends sharply through Coaley Wood to Coaley Peak. Here (left) is a car park with a glorious view of the Forest of Dean to the north and the Severn Valley to the west. At another car park, less close to the edge of the ridge, a notice describes the variety of butterfly and plant life found in these thirteen acres of National Trust land on the Cotswold escarpment. But there is more than this. A site plan indicates the various prehistoric burial grounds. Among these is the famous Uley Barrow, a long barrow of the Stone Age which was opened in the early 19c to reveal some thirty skeletons.

Stroud (Glos)

The road climbs from the Frome Valley to the heart of this town of narrow streets. Stroud is a centre of woollen manufacture that takes place in the surrounding mills.

Bisley (Glos)

A busy little village of narrow streets, possibly the reason for the sign 'Bisley Village Only', despite the fact that the road does continue directly east. In any case it would be a pity to miss this charming spot. At the point of entry is the Bear Inn, originally the Court House with an upper storey supported by pillars. Next to the inn is the old village lock-up.

1 In Dursley bear L. on A4135 (sign Tetbury). In 0.3m turn L. on to B4066 (signs Stroud and Uley) for 2.0m to Uley. Here continue Str. on B4066 (signs Stroud) for 6.5m and turn L. on to A419(A46) for 1.4m to Stroud town centre.

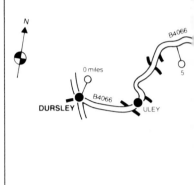

Nearby is the church, the school and Over Court, a fine stone house granted to Elizabeth I as part of her estate before she became Queen. Much of the ancient church was restored by Thomas Keeble, brother of the famous religious poet John Keeble. Thomas Keeble was vicar here for forty-six years, instituting the ceremony of well dressing, an occasion more generally associated with Derbyshire villages.

Sapperton (Glos)

The hillside village overlooks the wooded 'Golden Valley' where the autumnal tints are best seen from the churchyard. Many of Sapperton's houses were designed and built by Ernest Gimson and Ernest and Sidney Barnsley, architects of the William Morris school of international repute. All three men are buried here, their graves beneath yew trees by the church path. Across the 'Golden Valley' is Daneway House (14c) where Gimson had his workshops.

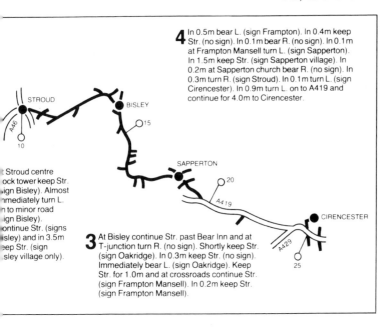

4 In 0.5m bear L. (sign Frampton). In 0.4m keep Str. (no sign). In 0.1m bear R. (no sign). In 0.1m at Frampton Mansell turn L. (sign Sapperton). In 1.5m keep Str. (sign Sapperton village). In 0.2m at Sapperton church bear R. (no sign). In 0.3m turn R. (sign Stroud). In 0.1m turn L. (sign Cirencester). In 0.9m turn L. on to A419 and continue for 4.0m to Cirencester.

Stroud centre
ock tower keep Str.
ign Bisley). Almost
mediately turn L.
n to minor road
ign Bisley).
ontinue Str. (signs
sley) and in 3.5m
eep Str. (sign
sley village only).

3 At Bisley continue Str. past Bear Inn and at T-junction turn R. (no sign). Shortly keep Str. (sign Oakridge). In 0.3m keep Str. (no sign). Immediately bear L. (sign Oakridge). Keep Str. for 1.0m and at crossroads continue Str. (sign Frampton Mansell). In 0.2m keep Str. (sign Frampton Mansell).

A row of quaint terraced cottages in Bisley.

THE THIRD largest county of England and, in the eyes of many, one of the most beautiful. The county is renowned for its dairy produce and its cider. Initially the route starts through the South Hams, the name coming from the Old English word for meadowland. At first it follows the coastline. Although designated as an A road it is narrower than most B roads in other parts of the country; fortunately there are numerous passing places. After some grand coastal views the road turns inland, eventually crossing the heart of the Dartmoor National Park from south to north.

The Dartmoor National Park consists of high granite moorland together with farmed valleys, wooded hillsides and occasional market towns and villages sheltering in the folds. Altogether the National Park covers 365 square miles, of which 146 square miles are open moorland known as the Dartmouth Common. Here, on unfenced roads, cattle and sheep wander as well as the world famous Dartmoor ponies, a breed first recorded in 1012.

Dartmoor abounds with tors, rocky heights from which there are often splendid views – none finer, perhaps, than the view from Combestone Tor above Hexworthy. Close to the road between Chagford and Widdon Down is a neolithic burial chamber, Spinsters Rock, some 4,000 years old and just one of many ancient monuments and enclosures that abound hereabouts.

Much of the later history of the Moor relates to the Civil War. Chagford and Moretonhampstead, for example, were once bitter rivals, the former siding with the King and the latter with Cromwell. North of the Moor at Great Torrington, a Royalist stronghold, some 200 Cavaliers were imprisoned in the church by Sir Thomas Fairfax and perished in a huge explosion.

Much land and many coastal and inland features of Devon have been preserved by the National Trust. Large tracts of woodland around Holne and Bovey Tracey are typical of the areas that the Trust tends to preserve. National Trust buildings which lie along the route include Drogo Castle, Bradley Manor and Compton Castle. Most minor roads in Devon are narrow, usually winding beneath high hedges. This does not make motoring easy and the height of the hedges often obscures the view of the lovely pastoral scenery. Most of this route avoids these roads as far as possible, but inevitably some have to be taken. Very often some of Devon's most beautiful towns and villages can only be approached by minor roads. It would certainly be a pity to miss villages such as Holne, North Bovey and Manaton because of difficulties encountered in reaching them.

Dartmouth

Daniel Defoe in his *Tour through the whole Island of Great Britain* (1724) describes Dartmouth thus:

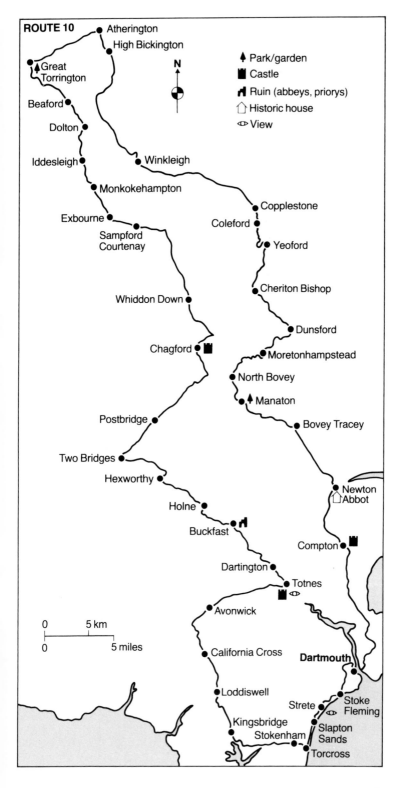

Dartmouth, a town of note, seated at the mouth of the River Dart, and where it enters into the seas at a very narrow, but safe, entrance. The opening into Dartmouth Harbour is not broad, but the channel deep enough for the biggest ships in the royal navy; the sides of the entrances are high mounded with rocks; without which just at the first narrowing of the passage, stands a good strong fort without a platform of guns, which commands the port.

Having described the harbour, Defoe turns to the town:

Round the west side of this basin, or harbour in a kind of semi-circle, lies the town of Dartmouth, a very large and populous town, though but meanly built, and standing on the side of a steep hill; yet the quay is large, and the street before it spacious.

Although Defoe's description of the street before the quay as 'spacious' is correct, many of the town's streets are narrow as they climb from the quayside. In fact Dartmouth can only be appreciated on foot. Among interesting old houses by the quay is the Royal Castle Hotel, an enlargement of two 16c houses that were re-fronted and heightened in the last century.

The most famous group of houses is the Butterwalk, Duke Street, built *circa* 1635. The houses have fronts carved in wood and stone, the ground floors used for business purposes with a projecting colonnade over the pavement. In the parlour of No 12 Duke St the ceiling depicts the descent of Christ through twenty-eight generations of kings and prophets from Jesse.

Dartmouth Castle faces Kingswear Castle across the narrow estuary, the two castles linked by chains in times of war to hold off enemy ships. Built in 1481, this was the first castle designed for artillery and guns were mounted here during World War Two. On a slope of the hill above the town is the broad-fronted Royal Naval College, used for training naval cadets since 1905.

Royal Castle Hotel, The Quay. T (080 43) 2397. (B)
Royle House, Mount Boone. T (080 43) 3649. (B)
Tourist Office, Royal Avenue Gardens. T (080 43) 4224 (summer only).

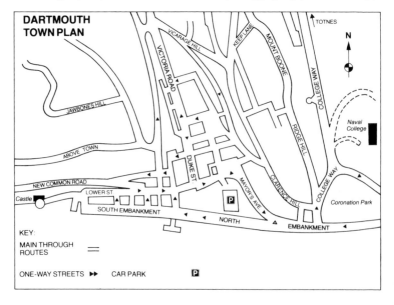

DARTMOUTH
TOWN PLAN

KEY:
MAIN THROUGH ROUTES —
ONE-WAY STREETS ▸▸   CAR PARK 🅿

Dartmoor National Park, an area of outstanding beauty.

Some of the charming shopfronts in Dartmouth's famous Butterwalk.

The Route

There are magnificent coastal views from Strete as the road descends to the sea. On the right, separated from the sea by a narrow shingle bank, are freshwater lakes known as leys which enhance this lovely stretch of coastline. From Torcross the road runs inland towards the Dartmouth National Park.

Stoke Fleming (Devon)

Stoke Fleming and Strete are attractive villages of narrow streets, both villages standing high on the cliffs above Start Bay. The road beyond Stoke Fleming drops to the sea at Blackpool Cove where there is a broad sheltered sandy beach. Beyond Strete is Start Bay car park and picnic site above Pilchard Cove.

Slapton (Devon)

On the beach at Slapton Sands is a monument, a granite obelisk erected by the Americans 'as a lasting tribute to the people of South Hams'. This tribute was well earned. In 1943 not only Slapton but a number of surrounding coastal and inland villages were evacuated to allow the US forces to train here for the Normandy landings. In all some 3,000 people and 180 farms with their livestock were affected. Slapton village lies a mile inland and is worth the diversion. A notable feature is the tall tower, known as the chantry, all that remains of a college founded in 1372 by Sir Guy de Brian, standard bearer to Edward III. The chantry dominates the village and church.

5 Continue Str. on B3196 (signs S. Brent) and in 2.5m turn R. on to B3210 (sign Avonwick and Totnes) for 2.0m to Avonwick.

4 Continue Str. on B3196 (signs Wrangton) and in 2.3m at Coldharbour Cross keep Str. (sign Wrangton). In 0.5m at California Cross bear R. (sign S. Brent) and in 0.1m keep Str. (sign S. Brent).

3 At Kingsbridge continue Str. through High Street (*NB.* do not divert round ring road). In 0.3m at town centre keep Str. onto B3196 (sign Lodiswell). In 1.3m at Sorley Cross continue Str. (sign Lodiswell) for 1.8m to Lodiswell. Here, at inn, bear L. (no sign) and in 0.3m keep Str. (signs Wrangton and Exeter).

Blackpool Sands, part of Devon's dramatic coastline.

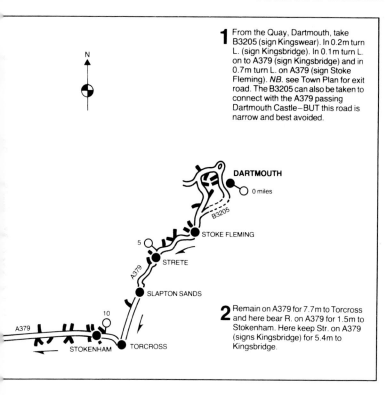

N

1 From the Quay, Dartmouth, take B3205 (sign Kingswear). In 0.2m turn L. (sign Kingsbridge). In 0.1m turn L. on to A379 (sign Kingsbridge) and in 0.7m turn L. on A379 (sign Stoke Fleming). *NB.* see Town Plan for exit road. The B3205 can also be taken to connect with the A379 passing Dartmouth Castle—BUT this road is narrow and best avoided.

DARTMOUTH

0 miles

B3205

STOKE FLEMING

5

STRETE

A379

SLAPTON SANDS

10

A379

STOKENHAM TORCROSS

2 Remain on A379 for 7.7m to Torcross and here bear R. on A379 for 1.5m to Stokenham. Here keep Str. on A379 (signs Kingsbridge) for 5.4m to Kingsbridge.

Torcross (Devon)

A further reminder of the US wartime presence here is the Sherman tank in the car park. In 1984 the tank was recovered a mile out at sea in sixty ft of water; it had lain there since 1944 when an accident dislodged it from its landing craft.

Stokenham (Devon)

The best of this pretty village is seen by walking along the narrow lane between the church and Church House Inn. Here a crescent of thatched cottages, many bedecked with climbing plants and window boxes, looks across the fields to the church. Among the cottages is the picturesque Tradesmen's Arms.

Kingsbridge (Devon)

This busy little market town occupies a delightful position at the head of a tidal estuary. Kingsbridge is known as the capital of the South Hams, the southernmost part of South Devon, bounded by the Dartmoor National Park and the sea. From the colourful quayside the steep main street climbs past shops with slate-hung frontages, narrow passages diverging in every direction. The Cookworthy Museum in Fore St displays a history of the area.
Crabshell Motor Lodge.
T (0548) 3301. All the bedrooms and the dining room overlook the estuary. Highly recommended. (B)

Loddiswell (Devon)

Loddiswell vineyard was established in 1977. It lies to the left of the road between Loddiswell and California Cross, offering one-and-a-half hour guided tours and walkabouts.

169

Inset: looking along the estuary towards Kingsbridge.

Main picture: Stokenham, a picturesque row of thatched cottages, including The Tradesmen's Arms.

The Route

The stretch of A road from Totnes to Buckfast is rather dull. Very narrow hedged roads from Buckfast to Holne. From here the road ascends to the wild and spectacular scenery of the Dartmouth National Park. The Venford Reservoir (left) was built at the beginning of the century, supplying Paignton with its water. There are superb views on both sides of the road, particularly the view of the Dart Valley from Combestone Tor (right) before descending to Hexworthy.

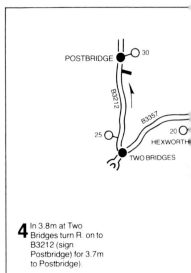

4 In 3.8m at Two Bridges turn R. on to B3212 (sign Postbridge) for 3.7m to Postbridge).

Totnes (Devon)

It is possible to take the A385 to Dartington, avoiding the town centre. This would be a pity as there is a great deal to see in this fine old market town. The English antiquary William Camden (1551–1623) described Totnes as a 'little town hanging from east to west on the side of a hill'. It is certainly worth wandering up the hill by way of Fore St, passing beneath the East Gate that spans the road and separates Fore St and High St. Here a house built in 1575 contains the Elizabethan Museum, worth visiting to see a good example of a rich merchant's house of the period as well as the varied exhibits. At the top of the town, near North Gate, are the well-preserved ruins of Totnes Castle with marvellous views across the Dart Valley.
Royal Seven Stars Hotel.
T (0803) 862125. (A)

Dartington (Devon)

Dartington Hall was once the palace of the Duke of Exeter (14c). Now an arts centre, it stands amid beautiful gardens with a medieval tilt yard and baronial hall. The thatched Cott Inn dates from the 14c.

Buckfast (Devon)

Buckfast Abbey occupies a superb position on the banks of the River Dart. The site of what was once a Saxon abbey was bought by French monks of the Benedictine order who between 1906 and 1983 rebuilt the abbey church.

Holne (Devon)

This tiny village is where Charles Kingsley (1819–75), Anglican divine and author, was born. The charming Church House Inn, first built in 1320, is said to have housed Oliver Cromwell during the Civil War.
Church House Inn T (036 43) 208. Restaurant. Bar Snacks. No accommodation.

Dartington Hall, now an Arts Centre.

2 Continue on A384 (signs Buckfastleigh) and in 4.3m keep Str. over bridge across A38. In 0.2m turn R. on to minor road (sign Buckfast). In 0.4m at Buckfast Abbey turn L. (sign Buckfast). In 0.1m keep Str. (sign Holne). In 0.4m turn R. (sign Holne). In 0.1m bear R. (sign Holne). In 0.2m bear L. (sign Holne). In 0.4m turn R. (sign Holne) for 1.0m to Holne

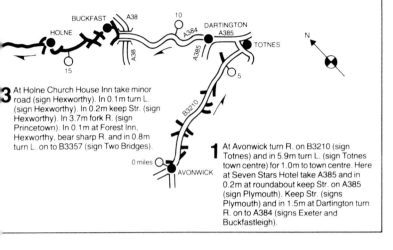

3 At Holne Church House Inn take minor road (sign Hexworthy). In 0.1m turn L. (sign Hexworthy). In 0.2m keep Str. (sign Hexworthy). In 3.7m fork R. (sign Princetown). In 0.1m at Forest Inn, Hexworthy, bear sharp R. and in 0.8m turn L. on to B3357 (sign Two Bridges).

1 At Avonwick turn R. on B3210 (sign Totnes) and in 5.9m turn L. (sign Totnes town centre) for 1.0m to town centre. Here at Seven Stars Hotel take A385 and in 0.2m at roundabout keep Str. on A385 (sign Plymouth). Keep Str. (signs Plymouth) and in 1.5m at Dartington turn R. on to A384 (signs Exeter and Buckfastleigh).

Hexworthy (Devon)

Here is the delightful Forest Inn, very much a sheltered haven after descending sharply from the rugged moors above. The inn is a centre for anglers and horse riders. In addition it is a meeting place for letter box walkers, ramblers who search the moors for the 1,000 or more boxes hidden there, using their orienteering skills to find the boxes where they leave evidence of their visit.
Forest Inn. T (036 43) 211. (C) Accommodation. Restaurant. Bar Food.

Two Bridges (Devon)

The River Cowsic joins the West Dart here, the two bridges being the main road bridge and the turnpike bridge near the hotel.

Postbridge (Devon)

The village is said to have been so named because the post road from Exeter to Cornwall once crossed the ancient bridge here. This fine example of a clapper bridge can be seen to the right of the road. It is built with flat granite slabs laid across stone piers, its design allowing heavily laden packhorses to cross because there are no sides to interfere with the loads.

Holne Bridge over the River Dart.

The ancient clapper bridge at Postbridge.

The Route

The entry and exit roads from Chagford are narrow. The road runs almost due north from Chagford to Great Torrington, nearly traffic-free in contrast to the busier A386 which runs parallel to it.

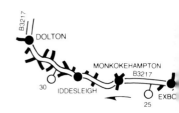

5 At Iddesleigh continue Str. on B3217 (sign Dolton) for 1.5m to Dowland. Here continue Str. (sign Dolton). in 0.5m at crossroads turn R. on B3217 (no sign) for 0.8m to Dolton.

4 In 2.1m turn R. on to B3217 into Exbourne village and keep Str. on B3217 for 2.9m to Monkokehampton. Here continue Str. (sign Iddesleigh) and in 0.2m turn L. (sign Iddesleigh) for 2.1m to Iddesleigh.

Warren House Inn
(Devon)

This isolated inn (left) was once the rendezvous for tin miners who worked the Vitifer mines to the south. The whole area to the left of the road is a maze of gulleys and mines from tin working days, at their height in the mid-19c. Traces of buildings, wheel pits and shafts can still be seen in the area. The inn today is a pleasant place to visit, especially to check if the legend that the fire in the bar has been kept burning for more than 100 years remains true.

Chagford (Devon)

This small market town nestles beneath Meldon Hill to the south, while to the south west is Fernworthy Forest and Reservoir and to the north west the village of Gidleigh where prehistoric remains exist. The narrow main street of Chagford leads into the market square and nearby church and inn. Two miles to the north east (along the route between Chagford and Whiddon Down) is the National Trust-owned Castle Drogo, built during the reign of King George V and historically the latest of the Trust's houses. This granite castle, built by Sir Edwin Lutyens, stands at over 900 ft, overlooking the wooded gorge of the River Teign with fine views of Dartmoor.
Mill End Hotel, Sandy Park T (064 73) 2282. (A) (Two miles north on the A382, near Castle Drogo).

Sampford Courtenay
(Devon)

A delightful huddle of whitewashed stone thatched cottages including the 16c New Inn (right). It is not surprising that the village with its well-kept gardens and bright window boxes holds national awards in village competitions. The lord of the manor until his execution in 1539 was Henry Courtenay, Marquis of Exeter. After his death the manor was acquired by the present owners, the Provost and Fellows of King's College, Cambridge.

Iddesleigh (Devon)

Charming thatched cottages and an inn stand around a small village

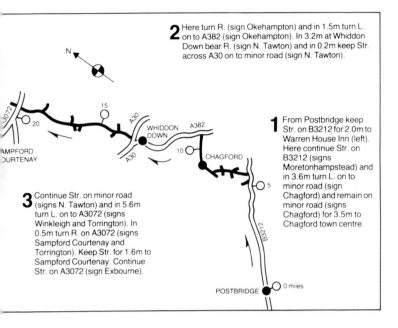

2 Here turn R. (sign Okehampton) and in 1.5m turn L. on to A382 (sign Okehampton). In 3.2m at Whiddon Down bear R. (sign N. Tawton) and in 0.2m keep Str. across A30 on to minor road (sign N. Tawton).

1 From Postbridge keep Str. on B3212 for 2.0m to Warren House Inn (left). Here continue Str. on B3212 (signs Moretonhampstead) and in 3.6m turn L. on to minor road (sign Chagford) and remain on minor road (signs Chagford) for 3.5m to Chagford town centre.

3 Continue Str. on minor road (signs N. Tawton) and in 5.6m turn L. on to A3072 (signs Winkleigh and Torrington). In 0.5m turn R. on A3072 (signs Sampford Courtenay and Torrington). Keep Str. for 1.6m to Sampford Courtenay. Continue Str. on A3072 (sign Exbourne).

green. Iddesleigh was once the home of the John Peel of the west country, for the vicar here, the Rev. 'Jack' Russell, started his pack in 1827 and became the pioneer of fox hunting in mid-Devon.

Dolton (Devon)

Yet another secluded village of thatched houses and pubs. The church is renowned for its font, a composition of two separate Saxon crosses.

Warren House Inn.

The Route

Almost entirely confined to good B roads, by Devon's standards straight and not unduly narrow. The road undulates approaching Atherington, as steep as 1 in 4 at one point.

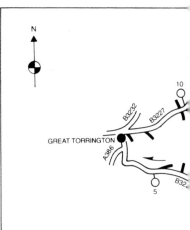

1 In 0.1 m at end of Dolton turn L. on to minor road (sign Beaford). In 1.8m at Torches Corner turn L. on to B3220 (sign Torrington). In 0.3m at Beaford keep Str. on B3220 (signs Torrington) for 4.5m and bear R. on to A386 for 1.0m to Great Torrington.

Great Torrington
(Devon)

There are marvellous views from the well laid out car park of this hilltop town. Barely a trace remains of the castle, its site now occupied by a bowling green which has existed here for a century or more. In the square is the town hall, a Victorian fountain, and the gabled Black Horse Inn (15c). Leading from the square is the Pannier Market, with antique iron gates and the market house at the entrance. The hall and gallery above the market archway, once the town hall, now serve as a library. The market way leads past a variety of small shops, linking the market square with Castle Hill. An interesting building to the north of the square is the mellow brick 18c Palmer House, named after John Palmer who married into the family of Sir Joshua Reynolds. The artist and his friend Dr Samuel Johnson stayed here in 1752. The parish church of St Michael and All Angels was rebuilt in 1651 after its destruction during the Civil War. Before entering Great Torrington the Rosemoor Garden is signed, worth visiting for its astonishing variety of plants.

Castle Hill Hotel, South St. T (0805) 22339. (B) Good views from this well-run hotel.

Atherington (Devon)

A hillside village where thatched and slate-roofed cottages cluster around the church. The tiny green is dwarfed by a giant chestnut tree. The pride of the church (*circa* 1150) is the carved oak screen and rood loft, the only one in Devon.

High Bickington (Devon)

It is worth pausing here to see the heart of the village which lies off the road (right). High Bickington

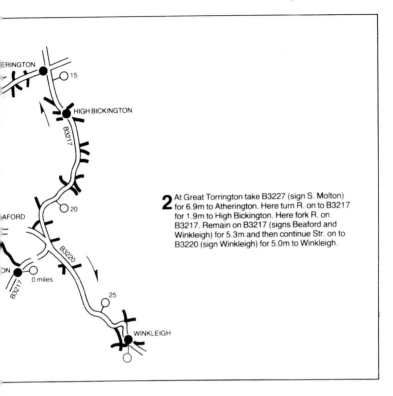

2 At Great Torrington take B3227 (sign S. Molton) for 6.9m to Atherington. Here turn R. on to B3217 for 1.9m to High Bickington. Here fork R. on B3217. Remain on B3217 (signs Beaford and Winkleigh) for 5.3m and then continue Str. on to B3220 (sign Winkleigh) for 5.0m to Winkleigh.

is aptly named for it stands some 600 ft above sea level and on clear days the 15c church tower can be seen from Exmoor twenty miles away. The church is approached by way of the school and there are fine views from the churchyard. St Mary's Church is renowned for its pew-ends, some seventy-eight intricately carved panels.

Winkleigh (Devon)

Is signed to the right of the road and must be numbered among Devon's prettiest villages. The centre is rectangular in shape, delightful cottages and shops facing each other at close quarters, among them the picturesque Kings Arms (below). From the centre of Winkleigh there is a maze of narrow streets and stepped paths, the church a focal point among them. In the churchyard can be seen the roofs of the pretty thatched cottages that line the edge of the yard. Among these, to the south east, is the old Church House, built in 1536 for a cost of £28 14s 4d, and now converted into two private residences.

Kings Arms. T (083 783) 384. Restaurant. Good bar food. Holiday apartment.

The Route

*Roads very narrow between
Copplestone and Dunsford.
The same applies between
Moretonhampstead and
Manaton.*

Copplestone (Devon)

The route avoids the centre of this
large village on the A377 – from
here running through typical
Devon lanes, narrow with high
hedges.

Coleford (Devon)

A fascinating little huddle of stone
and timbered cottages, far from the
beaten track.

Cheriton Bishop (Devon)

The village straggles along the
busy A30 across which the route
runs. The older parts of Cheriton
Bishop stand round the church
half a mile away.

Dunsford (Devon)

This typical Devon village situated
above the River Teign has many
whitewashed and thatched
cottages, granite houses, and a
church that overlooks the whole
romantic scene. After leaving
Dunsford the road descends
sharply to Steps Bridge across the
Teign, a host of daffodils to be
seen in the spring.

Moretonhampstead
(Devon)

This small country town has been
described as the gateway to
Dartmoor. There are many ancient
buildings. The central square is
dominated by two listed buildings,

1 At Winkleigh continue on B3220
(sign Exeter). In 8.3m turn R.
on to A377 (sign Exeter) for 2.0m
to Copplestone. Here turn R.
(sign Okehampton). In 0.1m bear
L. and immediately turn L. on to
minor road (sign Colebrooke). In
1.1m at Coleford keep Str. (sign
Colebrooke). In 0.4m keep Str.
(no sign) and in 0.3m turn L. (sign
Yeoford). Continue Str. and in
1.2m turn L. (sign Yeoford).

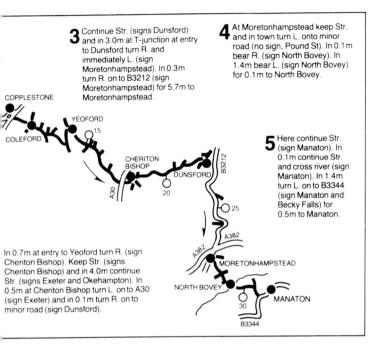

3 Continue Str. (signs Dunsford) and in 3.0m at T-junction at entry to Dunsford turn R. and immediately L. (sign Moretonhampstead). In 0.3m turn R. on to B3212 (sign Moretonhampstead) for 5.7m to Moretonhampstead.

4 At Moretonhampstead keep Str. and in town turn L. onto minor road (no sign, Pound St). In 0.1m bear R. (sign North Bovey). In 1.4m bear L. (sign North Bovey) for 0.1m to North Bovey.

5 Here continue Str. (sign Manaton). In 0.1m continue Str. and cross river (sign Manaton). In 1.4m turn L. on to B3344 (sign Manaton and Becky Falls) for 0.5m to Manaton.

In 0.7m at entry to Yeoford turn R. (sign Cheriton Bishop). Keep Str. (signs Cheriton Bishop) and in 4.0m continue Str. (signs Exeter and Okehampton). In 0.5m at Cheriton Bishop turn L. on to A30 (sign Exeter) and in 0.1m turn R. on to minor road (sign Dunsford).

the White Horse Inn (1682) and the White Hart Hotel, where coaches once stopped on the Exeter to Princetown route. From the square four historic streets radiate – Fore, Ford, Court and Cross Streets. A building of particular interest is the thatched courthouse, in use as a magistrate's court until 1847. In Cross St are the almshouses, (National Trust), granite buildings with mullioned windows built in 1637.

White Hart Hotel. T (0647) 40406. (B)

Whitewashed and thatched cottages at Dunsford.

North Bovey (Devon)

In this isolated village, only approachable by twisting lanes, solid whitewashed thatched cottages cluster round the pretty oak tree green. The Ring of Bells Inn, one of the oldest structures, is set back from the green down a narrow lane. On the green is an ancient granite cross, recovered from the moors in 1829 where it had been used as a boundary marker. Near to the green is a house with a gabled porch dated 1728. There are fine views from the churchyard, the path from here descending sharply to a lovely stretch of the River Bovey. *Ring of Bells Inn.* T (064 74) 375. (C) Accommodation. Excellent menus. Highly recommended.

Manaton (Devon)

Most of this pretty village lies to the left of the road, the church and huge green standing side by side. A mile beyond the village (right) is the car park for the Becky Falls, a noted beauty spot of the River Bovey set in 50 acres of woodland.

North Bovey, on the edge of Dartmoor.

Moretonhampstead, the 'gateway to Dartmoor'.

The Route

The final stages of the route mean, inevitably, leaving the minor roads and heading for Kingswear by way of the busy and rather dull A road that serves the seaside resorts of Torquay, Paignton and Brixham.

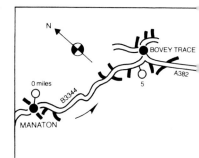

Bovey Tracey (Devon)

The route by-passes the centre of this large village. Sir William Tracey added his name to Bovey when the village came into his possession in the 12c. Sir William is said to have been one of the assassins of Thomas à Becket, building a church here and dedicating it to the Saint as a form of atonement.

Edgemoor Hotel, Haytor Road. T (0626) 832466. (C)

1 At Manaton keep Str. on B3344 (signs Becky Falls and Bovey Tracey) for 1.0m to Becky Falls (right). Here keep Str. (signs Bovey Tracey) and in 4.3m turn R. on to A382 (sign Newton Abbot). In 2.0m keep Str. across A38 (sign Newton Abbot).

Thatched inn at Bovey Tracey.

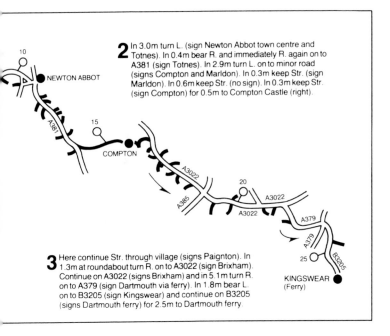

2 In 3.0m turn L. (sign Newton Abbot town centre and Totnes). In 0.4m bear R. and immediately R. again on to A381 (sign Totnes). In 2.9m turn L. on to minor road (signs Compton and Marldon). In 0.3m keep Str. (sign Marldon). In 0.6m keep Str. (no sign). In 0.3m keep Str. (sign Compton) for 0.5m to Compton Castle (right).

3 Here continue Str. through village (signs Paignton). In 1.3m at roundabout turn R. on to A3022 (sign Brixham). Continue on A3022 (signs Brixham) and in 5.1m turn R. on to A379 (sign Dartmouth via ferry). In 1.8m bear L. on to B3205 (sign Kingswear) and continue on B3205 (signs Dartmouth ferry) for 2.5m to Dartmouth ferry.

Newton Abbot (Devon)

This busy market town, the largest along the route, now has some sprawling suburbs. In the centre, however, are some interesting buildings, in particular Forde House, a Tudor manor house where Charles I came in 1625. A later visitor was William of Orange who occupied a bedroom here after leaving Brixham on his way to London. On the western fringe of the town is the National Trust-owned Bradley Manor, lying low in the Lemon Valley beneath steep wooded slopes. Its surviving 15c east wing provides one of the best examples of domestic Gothic architecture in the West Country. Another feature is the 15c chapel.
Globe Hotel, Courtenay St.
T (0626) 4106. (A)
Queens Hotel, Queen St.
T (0626) 63133. (B)

Compton (Devon)

Compton Castle stands to the right of the road before entering the village. This fortified manor house was built in three stages – 1340, 1450, and 1520. Throughout this period the owners were the Gilbert family, among them the three half-brothers of Sir Walter Raleigh, all of whom spent their childhood here. In the early 16c French raids were frequent, hence the need for the fortifications found here. In 1800 the Gilbert estates were sold. In 1930, however, Commander Walter Raleigh Gilbert bought them back, restoring the house and great hall before handing over the property to the National Trust in 1951.

Kingswear (Devon)

There is a frequent car and passenger ferry service across the Dart estuary, connecting this colourful village with the larger town of Dartmouth. The parish church is among several in Devon dedicated to Saint Thomas à Becket. It stands on a mound overlooking the estuary, rebuilt in 1847 but retaining its 12c tower.

11　Derbyshire, Staffordshire, Cheshire

THE ROUTE of only ninety-five miles is shorter than others in the guide, running through the heart of the Peak District National Park, an area which is best explored by leaving the car and taking to one's feet. This 35,000-acre park, Britain's first National Park, is managed in three estates, High Peak, South Peak, and Longshaw – areas protected by the National Trust and confined to the counties of Derbyshire and Staffordshire.

The River Dove, forty-five miles in length, rises at Axe Edge and acts as the boundary between Derbyshire and Staffordshire. Its loveliest stretch, Dovedale, a gorge that runs from Milldale southward to Thorpe, can only be seen on foot. 'Was you ever in Dovedale?' wrote Byron, 'I assure you there are things in Derbyshire as noble as in Greece or Switzerland.'

Milldale makes an excellent starting point from which to explore the river made famous by Izaak Walton and Charles Cotton in their *Compleat Angler* (1653). After leaving Milldale the road winds through the Manifold Valley where the car park at Wetton Mill makes a good venue for foot excursions. Along the route there is a good view of Thor's Cave, its mouth 40 ft high and the most spectacular of the many rocky clefts and tors to be seen in this area.

From the Manifold Valley the road runs northwards to the delightful market town of Longnor, re-entering Derbyshire briefly and crossing Axe Edge Moor before straying across the Cheshire border to reach England's second highest inn, the Cat and Fiddle. It is worth pausing at the handsome spa town of Buxton (several good hotels) before veering north eastward to Bradwell, the most northerly village of this route. Bradwell, incidentally, lies to the immediate south of Castleton and the Vale of Edale, lovely areas of the High Peak explored in Volume I of *Through Britain on Country Roads*.

There are marvellous views after leaving Great Hucklow, a famous gliding centre. The Longshaw Estate has an information office, and is an area best seen on foot.

From Longshaw the road runs almost due south by way of Baslow (hotels) and glorious Chatsworth Park. Haddon Hall, one of the best examples of a medieval home to be found in England, is worth the short diversion from Rowsley, while a little further south, less than a mile off the route, is Winster with its National Trust Market House.

Finally, no mention of Derbyshire villages is complete without reference to the ceremony of well dressing. The first village to institute this annual floral festival was Tissington, a brief westward diversion from the route between Ashbourne and Parwich. But many other small towns and villages along the route still preserve a custom that possibly originated in pagan times.

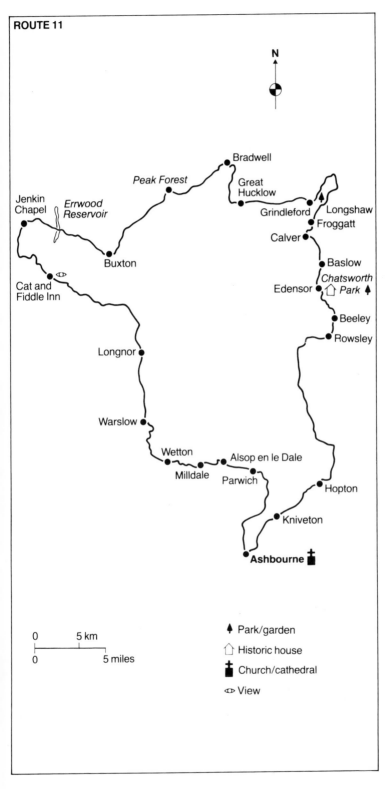

ROUTE 11

N

Bradwell

Peak Forest

Great Hucklow

Grindleford

Longshaw

Froggatt

Jenkin Chapel

Errwood Reservoir

Calver

Buxton

Baslow

Cat and Fiddle Inn

Chatsworth

Edensor ⌂ Park ♠

Beeley

Rowsley

Longnor

Warslow

Wetton

Alsop en le Dale

Milldale

Parwich

Hopton

Kniveton

Ashbourne ✝

0   5 km

0   5 miles

♠ Park/garden

⌂ Historic house

✝ Church/cathedral

⊂⊃ View

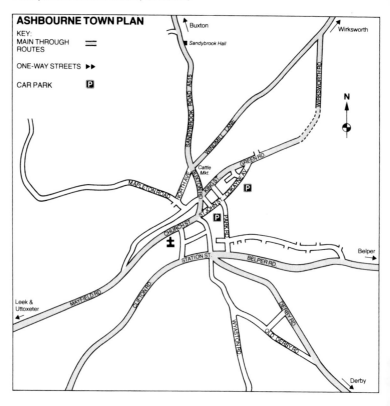

ASHBOURNE TOWN PLAN

KEY:
MAIN THROUGH ROUTES
ONE-WAY STREETS
CAR PARK

Ashbourne

'Oakbourne, that pretty town within sight of the blue hills . . .' wrote Mary Ann Evans (1819–90) under her pseudonym George Eliot in *Adam Bede*, Oakbourne being the fictitious representation of this market town, nestling beneath the great hills of the Peak District National Park.

Some of the most interesting buildings lie near the cathedral-like church, a church aloof from the centre of Ashbourne with a soaring 212-ft spire that dominates the town, justifying the title 'Pride of the Peak'.

Almost opposite the church is the former grammar school, built in 1585 by a charter of Elizabeth I and visited by Elizabeth II 400 years later. Opposite the grammar school is the town house once occupied by Dr John Taylor, frequent host to Dr Samuel Johnson and James Boswell. Nearby are the picturesque Owfield Almshouses (1640) and Pegge's Almshouses (1669) fronted by a neat garden area.

In 1777 James Boswell described the church of St Oswald as 'the largest and most luminous that I have seen in any town of the same size'. Within the church are monuments to the Bradburys, the Cokaynes, and the Boothbys. The most famous and touching of these monuments is the white figure of six-year-old Penelope Boothby, set in marble with the moving inscription:

She was in form and intellect most exquisite,
The unfortunate parents ventured their all
on this frail bark, and the wreck was total.

Penelope was the daughter of Sir Brooke Boothby and Lady Susannah, parents so stricken that as the inscription implies they parted after their small daughter's burial.

Details of Ashbourne's traditional game of football played each Shrove Tuesday and Ash Wednesday are displayed in the Green Man and Black's Head Hotel, its inn sign straddling the High Street. The game, which is played between points three miles apart and often lasts from 2 pm to dusk, is allowed the title of Royal Shrovetide Football due to the fact that H.R.H. The Prince of Wales kicked off in 1928. Near the Green Man is the Ashbourne Gingerbread Shop, one of the places where the famous Ashbourne gingerbread can be purchased. *Green Man and Black's Head Hotel.* T (0335) 43861. (A)

Ashbourne, view from the church towards the 16c former grammar school.

A beautiful part of the Peak District National Park, near Castleton.

The Route

Unspoilt country roads throughout. The road descending from Wetton is narrow, single track with passing places. There are a number of cattle grids on the moors beyond Longnor and great care is needed to avoid wandering sheep, particularly during the lambing season.

Parwich (Derbyshire)

This remote village nestles beneath wooded hills, a cluster of limestone cottages grouped round two greens and watered by a little stream. At the heart of Parwich is the Church of St Peter, rebuilt in Victorian times but with Norman relics. Among these are the west door, surmounted by strange intricate carvings that include serpents, a boar, a stag and a wolf. The terraced gardens of Parwich House above the village are occasionally open to the public.

Alsop en le Dale
(Derbyshire)

The village lies barely a mile from the Staffordshire border, offering glorious views of grassy hills from the churchyard. The church with its low square tower stands next to Church Farm, opposite the gabled manor house that until a century ago was the home of the Alsops.

Milldale (Staffs)

There is an information centre at a barn in this enchanting hamlet. The car park lies beyond Milldale (right) and from here it is but a short stroll back to Viators Bridge, a medieval packhorse bridge preserved by the National Trust, with a view of the sparkling stream

3 At Royal Oak Inn, Wetton, keep Str. (sign Butterton). In 1.2m bear R. (no sign). In 0.3m Wetton Mill continue Str. (sign Warslow). In after passing through tunnel bear R. (sign H End). In 0.7m turn L. (sign Warslow). In 0.4m edge of Warslow turn R. onto B5053 (sign Longnor). In 0.2m keep Str. on B5053 (sign Buxton) and continue Str. for 4.0m to Longn

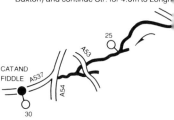

4 At Longnor continue Str. on B5053 (sign Bux 1.8m turn L. on to minor road (sign Dalehead 2.7m keep Str. (sign Axe Edge Moor). In 1.5m Str. across A53 (no sign). In 1.4m turn R. ont (no sign). In 0.1m turn L. on to A537 (sign Macclesfield) for 1.5m to Cat and Fiddle Inn.

The little hamlet of Milldale.

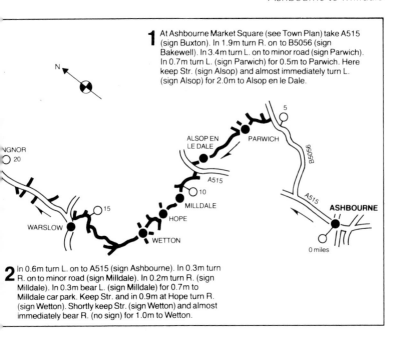

1 At Ashbourne Market Square (see Town Plan) take A515 (sign Buxton). In 1.9m turn R. on to B5056 (sign Bakewell). In 3.4m turn L. on to minor road (sign Parwich). In 0.7m turn L. (sign Parwich) for 0.5m to Parwich. Here keep Str. (sign Alsop) and almost immediately turn L. (sign Alsop) for 2.0m to Alsop en le Dale.

2 In 0.6m turn L. on to A515 (sign Ashbourne). In 0.3m turn R. on to minor road (sign Milldale). In 0.2m turn R. (sign Milldale). In 0.3m bear L. (sign Milldale) for 0.7m to Milldale car park. Keep Str. and in 0.9m at Hope turn R. (sign Wetton). Shortly keep Str. (sign Wetton) and almost immediately bear R. (no sign) for 1.0m to Wetton.

that has been described vividly in Walton's *Compleat Angler*. A notice by the bridge indicates a walk of breath-taking beauty along the footpath by the Dove.

Wetton (Staffs)

The road from this hillside village descends into the Manifold Valley. Wetton Mill (beyond the village, right), a corn mill until 1857, stands near a packhorse bridge rebuilt in 1807 by the Duke of Devonshire for horses carrying copper from Ecton mine. At a point near here the River Manifold disappears underground, re-emerging at Ilam a few miles to the south. Parts of the Manifold and Hamps Valleys are preserved by the National Trust, valleys overlooked by caves, gorges and rocky precipices of exceptional beauty. Among many outstanding features is Beeston Tor (south of Wetton) where Saxon coins and jewellery were discovered in a cave in 1924. The single-track Leek and Manifold Railway, used primarily for carrying milk, operated in the valley until 1934.

Picturesque view of the Manifold Valley.

Although the rails have gone the track bed now provides a popular route for cyclists and ramblers.

Longnor (Staffs)

Set in pastoral country this is a spacious village, the cobbled market square bordered by the Crewe and Harpur Arms that faces the town hall of 1837. A notice here tells of former tolls raised by the lord of the manor. A seller's stall cost four pence, buyers of a horse were charged four pence but those of a pig only one penny.

Crewe and Harpur Arms.
T (029 883) 205. (C)

Cat and Fiddle Inn
(Cheshire)

There are magnificent panoramic views from here, and from the nearby Axe Edge Ridge it is claimed that areas as far apart as Snowdonia and Lincoln have been seen. The inn, at 1,690 ft above sea level, is the second highest inn in England, second only to the inn at Tan Hill in Yorkshire.

Longnor, a village of cobbled roads and old stone cottages.

The Route

*Narrow and steep after
leaving the Cat and Fiddle.
A little dull for a few miles
past Buxton. From Peak
Forest the road runs through
the isolated Bradwell Moor.
Splendid views beyond
Great Hucklow.*

Jenkin Chapel (Cheshire)

After leaving the A road the narrow
minor road descends sharply past
a reservoir (left) where there is a
car park with fine views. The
isolated little chapel further along
the road was consecrated in 1733,
standing somewhat forlornly a
mile from the Derbyshire border
and the Goyt Forest.

Errwood Reservoir
(Derbyshire)

The road passes directly between
the Fernilee and Errwood
Reservoirs, the latter a popular
venue for sailing boats.

Buxton (Derbyshire)

Standing some 1,000 ft above sea
level, this spa town of the River
Wye is said to be the highest
market town in England. In the
late 18c the fifth Duke of
Devonshire commissioned John
Carr, the Yorkshire architect, to
develop this sleepy old town as a
popular resort. The Crescent, built
between 1780 and 1786 at a cost
of £120,000, is a curved three
storey building with a span of 200
feet and embraces 378 windows.
Other features of the town include

the Pump Room, presented to
Buxton by the seventh Duke of
Devonshire in 1894; the Royal
Hospital, originally built as stables
and with a dome among the
biggest in Europe; and the
twentieth century opera house
where an annual music and drama
festival takes place.
Leewood Hotel, Manchester
Road. T (0298) 3002. (A)
Grove Hotel, Grove Parade.
T (0298) 3804. (C)

Peak Forest (Derbyshire)

This stone-built village lies in what
was once the hunting ground of
kings. The church has an unusual
dedication to King Charles the
Martyr. A mile to the north is Eldon
Hill (1,543 ft) with the famous
Eldon Hole, a chasm some 180 ft
deep and once known as the

---

2 At Buxton town centre turn L. (signs Matlock and
Chapel en le Frith). In 0.2m bear L. on to A6 (sign
Stockport). In 1.6m turn R. on to minor road (sign
Peak Dale). Continue Str. for 1.7m to Smalldale
and here keep Str. (sign Peak Forest). In 1.1m
turn L. (sign Peak Forest) for 0.7m to Peak Forest

1 At Cat and Fiddle Inn continue
Str. on A537 and in 2.7m turn
R. on to minor road (sign Goyt
Valley). In 1.7m turn R. (sign
Saltersford). In 0.7m bear R.
(sign Goyt Valley). In 0.7m
keep Str. (sign Buxton). In
1.5m at Errwood Reservoir
turn L. (sign Buxton). In 1.6m
turn R. on to A5002 (no sign)
for 2.3m to Buxton.

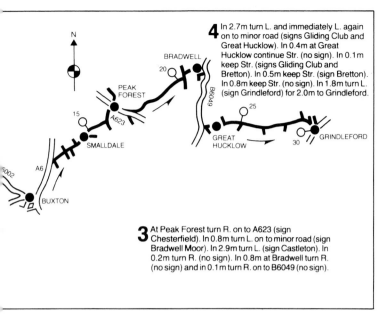

4 In 2.7m turn L. and immediately L. again on to minor road (signs Gliding Club and Great Hucklow). In 0.4m at Great Hucklow continue Str. (no sign). In 0.1m keep Str. (signs Gliding Club and Bretton). In 0.5m keep Str. (sign Bretton). In 0.8m keep Str. (no sign). In 1.8m turn L. (sign Grindleford) for 2.0m to Grindleford.

3 At Peak Forest turn R. on to A623 (sign Chesterfield). In 0.8m turn L. on to minor road (sign Bradwell Moor). In 2.9m turn L. (sign Castleton). In 0.2m turn R. (no sign). In 0.8m at Bradwell turn R. (no sign) and in 0.1m turn R. on to B6049 (no sign).

'bottomless pit'. The historian Thomas Hobbes (1588–1679) recounted how he rolled stones into the hole which 'dropped to the depths of hell'.

Bradwell (Derbyshire)

Although there has been some recent building the older part of Bradwell stands on the hillside around the 16c Bowling Green Inn. At the foot of the hill there are some further pleasant grey stone buildings around the Church of St Barnabas. Further along the route, a mile away, is Hazelbadge Hall, a 16c farmhouse said to be among the oldest in Derbyshire.

Great Hucklow
(Derbyshire)

A delightful hilltop village, above which on Camp Hill is the

Derbyshire and Lancashire Gliding Club where world gliding championships have been held. Great Hucklow was renowned for many years for its Village Players, a theatrical group formed by L. du Garde Peach, the playwright and producer. Unfortunately the group has now been disbanded.

Grindleford (Derbyshire)

A spacious village set in the heart of the Derwent Dale.
Maynard Arms. T (0433) 30321. (A)

The Route

*Unspoilt almost traffic-free
country throughout most of
this section. There are two
possible short diversions off
the route. The first is a visit
to Winster (only a mile off
the B5056), a charming
village with a National
Trust-preserved Market
House. The second is a half-
mile diversion beyond
Rowsley to Haddon Hall,
seat of the Duke of Rutland,
a medieval home with a
romantic history.*

2 In 0.2m turn R. back on to B6054 (sign
Calver). In 0.6m turn L. on to B6001 (sign
Bakewell) and in 0.2m at Calver turn L. on to
A623 (sign Chesterfield) for 2.2m to Baslow.

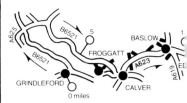

1 In Grindleford turn R. (no sign) and in 0.1m turn
on to B6521 (sign Sheffield). In 2.4m turn R. on
A625 (sign Sheffield) and in 0.1m turn R. on to B
(sign Dronfield). In 0.7m turn R. on to B6054 (s
Calver). In 2.3m turn R. on to minor road (sign
Froggatt). In 0.4m at Froggatt continue Str. (no

Longshaw Estate
(Derbyshire)

The Estate, signed off the route,
occupies some 1,500 acres of
open moorland, woodland and
farms described by a 17c traveller
as 'a strange, mountainous, misty,
moorish, rocky, wild country'. The
area is owned by the National
Trust with spectacular views from
Millstone Edge overlooking
Hathersage. Here also is Padley
Grove with its ancient oak
woodland, and Longshaw Wood
with a nearby inn that was the
Whitcross of Charlotte Bronte's
novel, the inn where Jane Eyre
was set down after her flight. It
seems hard to believe that this
lovely and remote part of the
Derwent Valley lies only eight
miles from the centre of Sheffield.

Froggatt (Derbyshire)

The short diversion the route takes
from the B road is worth while.
Here picturesque houses and
gardens nestle among trees above
the River Derwent by a 17c bridge.

Baslow (Derbyshire)

The large village lies in two
distinct parts. The smaller part,
Goose Green, comprises a tree-
shaded triangular green and the
stone-built Devonshire Arms.
Behind this inn a cluster of
thatched cottages huddle around
the bridge across the stream. A
footpath here is signed to
Chatsworth Park. In the main part
of Baslow two bridges cross the
river. The newer of these bridges
carries the main road traffic,
diverting it from the village street
which runs parallel to the river
towards the old packhorse bridge,
a graceful three-arched bridge
with a tiny stone structure, once a
shelter for toll collectors.
Cavendish Hotel.
T (024 688) 2311. (A)
Wheatsheaf Hotel.
T (024 688) 2240. (C)

Edensor (Derbyshire)

This estate village stands at the
threshold of Chatsworth Park,

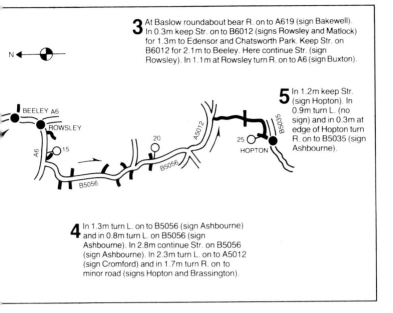

3 At Baslow roundabout bear R. on to A619 (sign Bakewell). In 0.3m keep Str. on to B6012 (signs Rowsley and Matlock) for 1.3m to Edensor and Chatsworth Park. Keep Str. on B6012 for 2.1m to Beeley. Here continue Str. (sign Rowsley). In 1.1m at Rowsley turn R. on to A6 (sign Buxton).

5 In 1.2m keep Str. (sign Hopton). In 0.9m turn L. (no sign) and in 0.3m at edge of Hopton turn R. on to B5035 (sign Ashbourne).

4 In 1.3m turn L. on to B5056 (sign Ashbourne) and in 0.8m turn L. on B5056 (sign Ashbourne). In 2.8m continue Str. on B5056 (sign Ashbourne). In 2.3m turn L. on to A5012 (sign Cromford) and in 1.7m turn R. on to minor road (signs Hopton and Brassington).

ancestral home of the Cavendish family and the Dukes of Devonshire. Grouped at random along the lower slopes of a hill, a jumble of houses of every shape and style emerges. Swiss chalet-type buildings mingle with others in the Italian style amid a complex pattern of irregular roofs and chimneys, turrets and

Edensor, looking towards St Peter's Church.

The Devonshire Arms at Beeley.

battlements. At the top end of the sloping churchyard of St Peter's Church, designed by Sir Gilbert Scott, a stone commemorates the visit of U.S. President John F. Kennedy to his sister's grave. Across the road from Edensor is Chatsworth Park, on the western edge of the old Sherwood Forest, designed by Capability Brown for the fourth Duke of Devonshire (1720–64). This magnificent deer park is graced by oaks 1,000 years old, the largest with a girth of 28 ft 10 ins at chest height. In addition to copses scattered about the park are sky-line woods, shaped to follow the highest contours of the hills that embrace the park. Chatsworth House (signed left) is built in the Palladian style on a rising slope above the River Derwent. The house is open to the public on specified occasions, with rare collections of paintings, sculptures, and furniture among the many treasures. At the Farmyard, Chatsworth, representative animals and birds from the estate include a pedigree shire horse, a mountain pony from the Tyrol, Jacob sheep and rare breeds of poultry, turkeys and geese.

Beeley (Derbyshire)

Cupped beneath the hills and woods of the Chatsworth estate is the Norman church, standing by lime trees and a huge yew. Clustering around the church are stone-built houses and the Devonshire Arms.

Rowsley (Derbyshire)

Perhaps the most picturesque building is the Peacock Hotel, 17c with gables and mullioned windows, an arbour of roses and stone peacock above the porch. *Peacock Hotel.* T (0629) 733518. (A)

Hopton (Derbyshire)

The road passes the end of this little village, famous for its lords of the manor, the Gells. Nearby signs point the way to the Via Gellia, a lovely wooded valley road to the north of Hopton named after the Gell family.

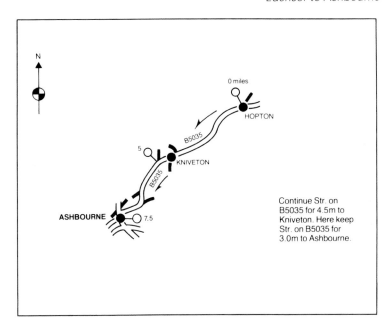

The Route

Only three further miles to Melton Mowbray.

Kniveton (Derbyshire)

The little church with its squat tower and short spire (left) stands in fields above the village. At the church gate a huge sycamore almost overshadows the church and below it is a wooded vale and bubbling stream. Further along the road grey stone houses and a pleasant inn stand in a complex pattern of winding lanes and streams. At the inn, incidentally, the fund-raising effort for 1987 was geared towards the purchase of a sonic hearing aid for a little girl, deaf from birth, who it was hoped could be helped to recover with this latest equipment.

12 Leicestershire, Lincolnshire, Northamptonshire

ALMOST EVERYWHERE along this 120-mile route the road undulates through gentle sparsely populated pastoral countryside. The road rarely reaches great heights yet the scenery is never dull, with copses and streams abounding.

The route begins and ends in Leicestershire, once a county of some 800 square miles but larger now since it embraces the former small county of Rutland. Early along the route is Buckminster, one of Leicestershire's prettiest villages, the road then intruding into Lincolnshire at Woolsthorpe Manor, birthplace of Sir Isaac Newton. The road now runs southward, parallel to the River Glen and rising to another picturesque village, Castle Bytham, before descending to the enchanting hamlet of Holywell. The intrusion into Lincolnshire is short-lived because on reaching the villages of Ketton and Edith Weston the road has returned to Rutland, now Leicestershire.

Uppingham and the charming village of Lyddington are also part of Leicestershire, but on reaching Gretton the road crosses into Northamptonshire and the northern part of the Rockingham Forest. Originally the hunting ground of the Norman kings, Rockingham Forest extends from the Welland Valley to the River Nene further south, an area where much woodland has survived together with rich farmlands, busy market towns and stone-built villages. Three historic houses lie within the boundaries of Rockingham Forest – Kirby Hall, Deene Park, and Boughton House, all deserving a visit. Wadenhoe must be among Northamptonshire's most charming villages, and at nearby Lilford Park the variety of animals includes Highland cattle, wallabies, and an aviary with one of the largest collections of owls in the country.

At Geddington is one of the three remaining Eleanor Crosses. On reaching Desborough, a main road town of little attraction, the road runs northward by way of the charming villages of Medbourne, Horninghold and Hallaton. From here gentle pastoral scenery almost all the way back to Melton Mowbray.

Melton Mowbray

This market town has associations with fox hunting, the territories of the famous Belvoir, Quorn and Cottesmore Hunts all adjoining at the colourful market square. Unfortunately some of the older houses of the square are today being demolished. Among the casualties is a former coaching inn with a swan porch that until very recently graced the scene.

Apart from fox hunting, Melton is renowned for pork pies that originated here more than a century ago, possibly as snacks for local huntsmen. The rich pasture lands around the town are renowned for Stilton cheese, a name reserved for cheese that must be produced in this particular area.

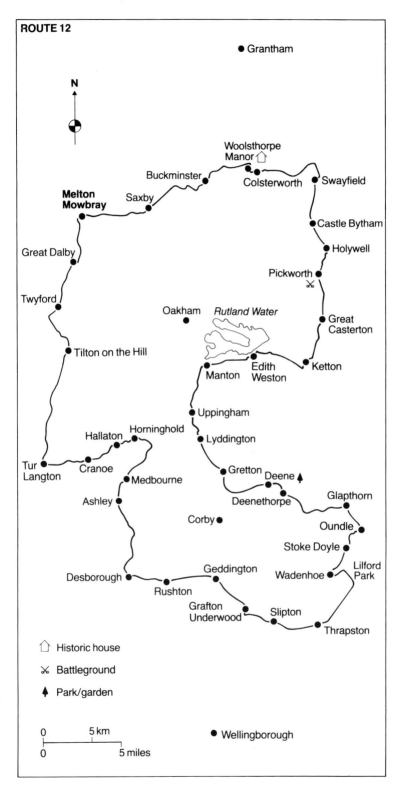

ROUTE 12

N

Grantham

Woolsthorpe Manor ⌂

Buckminster

Colsterworth

Swayfield

Melton Mowbray

Saxby

Castle Bytham

Holywell

Great Dalby

Pickworth ✂

Twyford

Oakham

Rutland Water

Great Casterton

Tilton on the Hill

Manton

Edith Weston

Ketton

Uppingham

Lyddington

Hallaton

Horninghold

Tur Langton

Cranoe

Gretton

Deene ♠

Glapthorn

Medbourne

Deenethorpe

Ashley

Corby

Oundle

Stoke Doyle

Desborough

Rushton

Geddington

Wadenhoe

Lilford Park

Grafton Underwood

Slipton

Thrapston

⌂ Historic house

✂ Battleground

♠ Park/garden

0   5 km

0   5 miles

Wellingborough

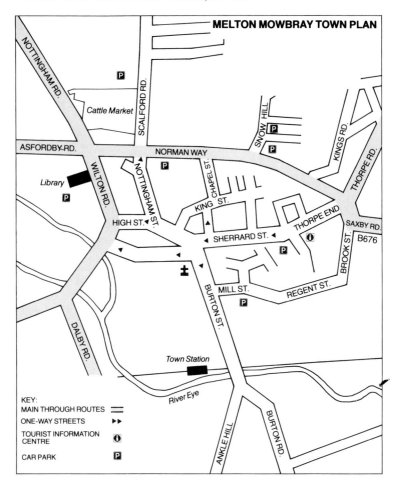

Notable buildings in Burton Street, the road from Oakham, include the Harborough Hotel with its Georgian frontage; Anne of Cleves House, a property given by Henry VIII to his discarded queen, which now serves as a restaurant; and Bede House, an elegant stone building of 1640 to house twelve deserving old people.

At the extreme end of Burton Street, central to the town, is the grand cathedral-like Church of St Mary the Virgin, dating from 1170 and the largest church in the county.

The High Street contains a number of Georgian buildings and culminates at the Egerton Lodge Memorial Gardens. Here at the entrance to the gardens is the Bread and Alms Door, a relic preserved from a demolished building where, as the name implies, bread was once issued to the poor of the town. Egerton Lodge was once the home of the Earl of Wilton and famous visitors have included Benjamin Disraeli, the Duke of Wellington and Edward VII when he was Prince of Wales.

Harborough Hotel, Burton Street. T (0664) 60121. (B)
Kings Head, Nottingham Street. T (0664) 62110. (C)
Tourist Office, Milton Carnegie Museum, Thorpe End, T (0664) 69946.

Country road along the Lincolnshire Wolds.

Anne of Cleves House, Melton Mowbray.

The Route

*The road undulates through
the heart of the
Leicestershire and
Lincolnshire Wolds.*

Saxby (Leics)

The village was once a Saxon
settlement. Skeletons of men and
horses found here can be seen at
Bede House Museum in Melton
Mowbray. Today the church and
most of the village buildings are
hidden behind tall trees on a knoll
to the left of the road.

Buckminster (Leics)

First sight of this lovely village that
straggles along a high point of the
Wolds is a spacious lawn and
houses of red-brick. Next in view
is a line of picturesque terraced
cottages with dormer windows
(right). The most glorious aspect,
however, is the large shaded
green that leads to the church with
its Norman tower. In the
churchyard is a strange railed-off
gabled stone building. This is the
mausoleum of the Earls of Dysart.

Colsterworth (Lincs)

Immediately before reaching this
large village the route leads to
Woolsthorpe Manor, birthplace of
Sir Isaac Newton in 1642. This
National Trust-owned stone
house with mullioned windows
was the place to which the
philosopher returned in 1665. In
the orchard is the descendant of
the apple tree which is said to
have inspired Newton's law of
gravitation. Over the front door of
the manor is the Newton coat of
arms, and on an inside wall a
tablet records Alexander Pope's
famous couplet:

1 In Melton Mowbray take B676, Saxby
Road (see Town Plan) for 4.3m to Saxby.
Here continue on B676 (sign Garthorpe).
Remain on B676 (signs Garthorpe and
Buckminster) for 5.2m to Buckminster.
Here keep Str. on to minor road (sign
Skillington). In 1.4m turn R. (sign
Colsterworth). In 0.6m keep Str. (sign
Woolsthorpe). In 1.1m turn R. (sign
Woolsthorpe Manor) and in 0.1m turn R.
(sign Woolsthorpe Manor) for 0.1m to
Woolsthorpe Manor.

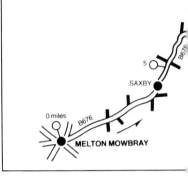

Nature and Nature's laws lay hid in
night;
God said, Let Newton be! and all
was light.

Swayfield (Lincs)

A small cluster of grey stone
buildings stands above the River
Glen and ample fields. The church
with its battlemented tower is
found along a lane (left) at the
entrance to the village.

Castle Bytham (Lincs)

This charming village rises in tiers
to the church on the hilltop,
overlooking woods to the west
and a little stream which joins the
River Glen to the east. All that
remains of the Norman castle are
the earthworks. Among
surrounding features are Monkery
Woods, named after the Saxon
owner of the castle at the time of
the Norman invasion.

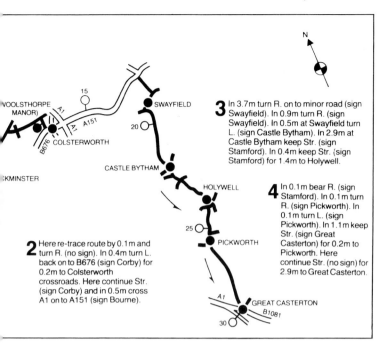

3 In 3.7m turn R. on to minor road (sign Swayfield). In 0.9m turn R. (sign Swayfield). In 0.5m at Swayfield turn L. (sign Castle Bytham). In 2.9m at Castle Bytham keep Str. (sign Stamford). In 0.4m keep Str. (sign Stamford) for 1.4m to Holywell.

4 In 0.1m bear R. (sign Stamford). In 0.1m turn R. (sign Pickworth). In 0.1m turn L. (sign Pickworth). In 1.1m keep Str. (sign Great Casterton) for 0.2m to Pickworth. Here continue Str. (no sign) for 2.9m to Great Casterton.

2 Here re-trace route by 0.1m and turn R. (no sign). In 0.4m turn L. back on to B676 (sign Corby) for 0.2m to Colsterworth crossroads. Here continue Str. (sign Corby) and in 0.5m cross A1 on to A151 (sign Bourne).

The ruins of Pickworth church.

Holywell (Lincs)

The road dips suddenly to this enchanting hollow close to the border with Leicestershire. It is worth pausing at the bridge for a view of the lake.

Pickworth (Leics)

Two miles to the south west, along the A1, a clump of oaks, known as the Bloody Oaks, was the scene of the Battle of Losecoat Field (1470), a battle of the Wars of the Roses during which Pickworth church was destroyed together with most of the original buildings. The 14c arch of the church remains on the hilltop.

The Route

Initially through the quiet roads of the former county of Rutland. Later the road returns to the counties of Leicestershire and Northamptonshire by way of several picturesque villages.

Ketton (Leics)

First sight of this one-time Rutland main road village is not impressive, a cement works dominating the scene. But first sights can be misleading. Ketton is in every way a beautiful village, Ketton stone providing building material not only here but in places as distant as the Tower of London and Exeter Cathedral. The best way to see Ketton is to park by the village shop and Victorian drinking fountain (left). From here a narrow footpath (entry marked by a No Cycling sign) leads by way of picturesque stone cottages to the church with its imposing 13c tower and 14c spire – a church described by the antiquary James Wright as being 'formed in the shape of a little cathedral as if intended for an epitome of its mother Lincoln'.

Edith Weston (Leics)

The village lies above the eastern shore of Rutland Water. It is best to park the car at the Wheatsheaf Inn (right) to see the bulk of the village which lies behind the inn. Edith Weston is a village of stone cottages, some thatched and others slate-roofed. The focal point is Well Cross, around which, grouped in a U-shape, is a cluster of cottages. Well Cross is so called because the little green contains an ancient well, now covered and acting as the support for the stem of the village cross. From here King Edward's Way leads to the church, a remainder of the origin of the

2 In 1.7m keep Str. (sign Edith Weston) and in at edge of Edith Weston turn L. (sign Edith Weston). In 0.4m turn R. (sign Manton). In 3 Manton keep Str. (sign Uppingham). In 0.1 L. on to A6003 (sign Uppingham) and contin for 3.2m (signs Uppingham) to Uppingham.

3 At Uppingham continue Str. on A6003 (sign Kettering). In 0.6m turn L. on to minor road (sign Lyddington). In 0.6m bear R. (sign Lyddington) for 0.7m to Lyddington. Here keep Str. (sign Gretton). In 1.1m keep Str. (sign Gretton). In further 1.1m turn L. (sign Gretton) for 0.3m to Gretton.

village name, for it was Edward the Confessor who gave much of this part of Rutland to his wife, Edith. From the churchyard of the limestone church there is a good view of Rutland Water.

Uppingham (Leics)

Though only a small town, Uppingham used to be the second largest centre in the former county of Rutland. A great part of the town comprises the famous public school, a small school when first founded in 1584 and only developed to its present size some 250 years later by an enterprising head master, Edward Thring. The school's museum recalls its history. In the school chapel is a bust of Edward Thring in white marble.
Falcon Hotel, High Street.
T (0572) 823525. (A)
Central Hotel, High Street West.
T (0572) 822352. (C)

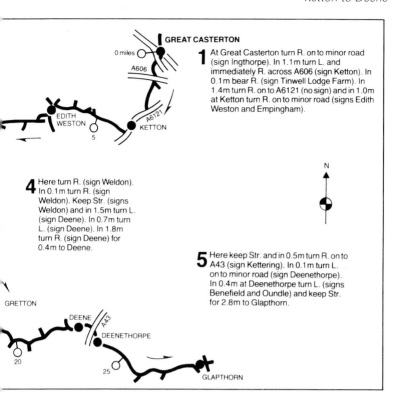

1 At Great Casterton turn R. on to minor road (sign Ingthorpe). In 1.1m turn L. and immediately R. across A606 (sign Ketton). In 0.1m bear R. (sign Tinwell Lodge Farm). In 1.4m turn R. on to A6121 (no sign) and in 1.0m at Ketton turn R. on to minor road (signs Edith Weston and Empingham).

4 Here turn R. (sign Weldon). In 0.1m turn R. (sign Weldon). Keep Str. (signs Weldon) and in 1.5m turn L. (sign Deene). In 0.7m turn L. (sign Deene). In 1.8m turn R. (sign Deene) for 0.4m to Deene.

5 Here keep Str. and in 0.5m turn R. on to A43 (sign Kettering). In 0.1m turn L. on to minor road (sign Deenethorpe). In 0.4m at Deenethorpe turn L. (signs Benefield and Oundle) and keep Str. for 2.8m to Glapthorn.

Lyddington (Leics)

The building of great interest in this village of iron-stone cottages is Bede House. This long two-storey building by the churchyard was first established in 1200 as a manorial retreat for the Bishops of Lincoln. It is classified as an ancient monument. Centuries later Bede House was converted into almshouses, the ground floor partitioned into a number of small rooms to accommodate a warden, twelve men and two women. Across the lawns of Bede House a public path leads beneath a look-out tower known as the Bishop's Eye.
Marquess of Exeter Hotel.
T (0572) 822477. (A)

Gretton (Northants)

Stocks, a whipping post and a maypole stand on the green by the church of this hill-top village. On the green also is a well-tended war memorial, an obelisk above a curved stone wall and platform giving the names of men of the village who fell in two world wars.

Kirby Hall (Northants)

The Hall is signed (left) after leaving Gretton. This is a partly renovated ruin of an Elizabethan stone mansion built in 1570.

Deene (Northants)

On the right is Deene Park, home of the Brudenell family since 1514 and that of the seventh Earl of Cardigan who led the Charge of the Light Brigade. Both house and gardens are on occasions open to the public. Across fields at the end of the small village (right) is the Church of St Mary, surprisingly large with a handsome tower.

The Route

There is a lovely stretch of the River Nene, much favoured by artists, between Wadenhoe and Lilford Park. From here the road by-passes the delightful villages of Aldwincle and Titchmarsh, both worth a short diversion.
Geddington lies to the south of the Rockingham Forest.

Oundle (Northants)

This busy little town lies within a curve of the River Nene. At present a by-pass is being constructed to relieve the congestion. Many of the buildings are the property of the public school, a foundation of the Worshipful Company of Grocers with 700 pupils. The glory of Oundle is the Church of St Peter with its imposing 17c spire, a landmark for miles around. Other notable buildings include the town hall in the centre of the market place; the timber-framed Talbot Hotel in New Street; Berrystead, a late 17c town house in North Street; and the Rodolphe Stahl Theatre in West Street. A market continues to be held here each Thursday, the market bell tolling at midday.
Talbot Hotel, New Street.
T (0832) 73621. (A)

Wadenhoe (Northants)

Ask any Oundle citizen which is Northamptonshire's prettiest village and the answer, invariably, is nearby Wadenhoe. This village of delightful stone cottages, many thatched, clusters above the banks of the River Nene. A cul-de-sac leads to the King's Head Inn which has a lovely garden bordering the willow-lined river. A footpath from here rises sharply

5 Continue Str. (signs Desborough) for 1.4m to Rushton and here turn R. (sign Desborough) for 2.4m to Desborough.

4 At Geddington keep Str. (no sign) and in 0.2m keep Str. across A43 (signs Newton and Great Oakley). In 1.0m keep Str. (sign Rushton). In 1.2m turn L. on to A6003 (sign Kettering) and in 0.3m turn R., looping back on to A6003 (sign Desborough). In 0.4m turn L. on to minor road (sign Desborough).

across the fields to the hilltop, site of the parish church with is rare saddleback roof. From this lonely little church the spires of the churches of Aldwincle can be seen, as well as a lovely stretch of river that flows by the old water-mill below. Other interesting structures of the village include a house with a polygonal end, once the toll house; and a fine round dovecote in a farmyard at the centre of Wadenhoe.

Lilford Park (Northants)

The entrance to the park is signed (left). Its 240 acres contain a wide selection of farm animals and birds. There are picnic meadows and children's farm and adventure playgrounds.

Grafton Underwood (Northants)

A bubbling stream flanks the

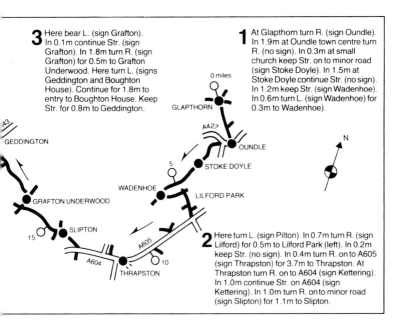

3 Here bear L. (sign Grafton). In 0.1m continue Str. (sign Grafton). In 1.8m turn R. (sign Grafton) for 0.5m to Grafton Underwood. Here turn L. (signs Geddington and Boughton House). Continue for 1.8m to entry to Boughton House. Keep Str. for 0.8m to Geddington.

1 At Glapthorn turn R. (sign Oundle). In 1.9m at Oundle town centre turn R. (no sign). In 0.3m at small church keep Str. on to minor road (sign Stoke Doyle). In 1.5m at Stoke Doyle continue Str. (no sign). In 1.2m keep Str. (sign Wadenhoe). In 0.6m turn L. (sign Wadenhoe) for 0.3m to Wadenhoe.

2 Here turn L. (sign Pilton). In 0.7m turn R. (sign Lilford) for 0.5m to Lilford Park (left). In 0.2m keep Str. (no sign). In 0.4m turn R. on to A605 (sign Thrapston) for 3.7m to Thrapston. At Thrapston turn R. on to A604 (sign Kettering). In 1.0m continue Str. on A604 (sign Kettering). In 1.0m turn R. on to minor road (sign Slipton) for 1.1m to Slipton.

pretty cottages here. Half a mile beyond the village (right) is the memorial to the 384th Bombardment Group of the U.S. Air Force who flew from the airfield here between 1943 and 1945. The proud granite monument stands by the former airfield which is now rich in wheat and barley.

Boughton House
(Northants)

This home of the Dukes of Buccleuch and their Montagu ancestors since 1528 is signed to the left. Begun as a monastery, Boughton grew around seven courtyards until the French-style addition of 1695. The house, set in a 350-acre park, has outstanding collections of paintings, furniture and porcelain. Many of the rooms have painted ceilings and there is an interesting armoury.

Geddington (Northants)

The stone and thatched cottages of the village lie on either side of the River Ise, joined by a narrow four-arched medieval bridge. Here is one of the three remaining Eleanor Crosses built by Edward I to mark the resting place of the body of his wife, Queen Eleanor, brought from Hardby to Westminster for burial.

Rushton (Northants)

Golden stone cottages and the parish church stand above the large village cricket ground. Rushton Hall, now a school for the blind, was formerly the home of the Tresham family, among them Sir Francis Tresham, a conspirator in the Gunpowder Plot of 1605. Half a mile beyond the village (left) is the strange Triangular Lodge, built by Sir Thomas Tresham in 1593 to symbolize the Trinity.

The Route

*The road undulates through
rich agricultural land, the
landscape never dull
because it is enlivened with
scattered copses, the skyline
often comprising gently
wooded hills.*

Stoke Albany (Northants)

The greater part of the village
stands on the hillside. At the foot
of the hill is a spacious green with
war memorial, encircled by the
village hall, manor house and
church.

Medbourne (Leics)

The route has now returned to
Leicestershire. First sight of this
lovely village is the Nevill Arms,
separated from its car park by a
footbridge across the Medbourne
Brook. Further along the stream a
medieval bridge leads to the iron-
stone Church of St Giles.
Medbourne competes each Easter
Monday with the neighbouring
village of Hallaton in an ancient
game known as bottle kicking.
The bottle – in fact an iron-bound
barrel – is on view at the Nevill
Arms (see Hallaton).

Horninghold (Leics)

The houses here, built from local
golden iron-stone, are the
creation of a wealthy farmer,
Thomas Hardcastle. He built or re-
converted them at the beginning
of the 20th century. They lie in a
secluded valley among sycamores,
chestnuts and a variety of trees
and ornamental shrubs, the focal
point of the village being the small
triangular green. Approaching the
church from the green, one can
see a restored Tudor cottage that
once served as the rectory. Far and

3 In 1.2m at entry to Hallaton turn R. (sign East
Norton). In 0.1m turn L. (sign Cranoe). In 0.2m
turn L. (sign Cranoe) and keep Str. (signs
Cranoe) for 2.1m to Cranoe. Here continue Str.
(signs Tur Langton) for 3.0m to Tur Langton.

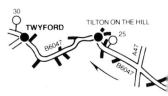

4 At Tur Langton turn R. onto B6047 (sign Melto
Mowbray). In 5.8m keep Str. across A47 (sigr
Melton) for 2.1m to Tilton on the Hill. Here kee
Str. on B6047 (signs Melton) for 4.0m to Twyf

Hallaton, the village green.

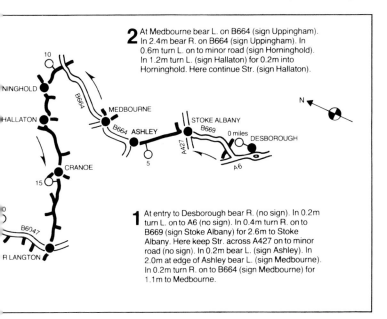

2 At Medbourne bear L. on B664 (sign Uppingham). In 2.4m bear R. on B664 (sign Uppingham). In 0.6m turn L. on to minor road (sign Horninghold). In 1.2m turn L. (sign Hallaton) for 0.2m into Horninghold. Here continue Str. (sign Hallaton).

1 At entry to Desborough bear R. (no sign). In 0.2m turn L. on to A6 (no sign). In 0.4m turn R. on to B669 (sign Stoke Albany) for 2.6m to Stoke Albany. Here keep Str. across A427 on to minor road (no sign). In 0.2m bear L. (sign Ashley). In 2.0m at edge of Ashley bear L. (sign Medbourne). In 0.2m turn R. on to B664 (sign Medbourne) for 1.1m to Medbourne.

away the most ancient building is the Church of St Peter, 700 years old but restored in Victorian times. In 1951 the coffin lid of a cross-bearer to the Knights Templar was discovered, dated 1260.

Hallaton (Leics)

From Horninghold in the valley the road rises to this hillside village with its white-railed duck pond near the Fox Inn. Nearby is the 18c grey stone Hallaton Hall, property of the Torch Trust for the Blind. By the village green is a pretty little walled garden with a plaque which tells of 'the ancient custom of Hallaton bottle kicking' (see Medbourne). This annual contest is begun with the presentation of a hare pie by the rector. Some 200 players then begin a scrummage which may last for several hours, each team attempting to move the 'bottles' to their respective villages.

Tilton on the Hill (Leics)

Much of the village lies to the right of the road, buildings which at 700 feet dominate the surrounding area. A little to the east is the hamlet of Halstead, the highest hamlet of Leicestershire. Within the golden stone parish church are the tombs of the Digbys, among them that of Sir Everard Digby of 1509, in armour with a lion at his feet. A century later his descendant, also Sir Everard, was executed for his part in the Gunpowder Plot.

Twyford (Leics)

A busy village in a lovely valley, overlooked by Burrough Hill to the north east.

The Route

A straight low-lying road for the last few miles back to Melton Mowbray.

Great Dalby (Leics)

At the heart of the village is the large triangular green and war memorial, the green surrounded by charming houses and cottages, many bedecked with flowers. Between the green and Royal Oak Inn, whitewashed with colourful window boxes, a grassy path leads to the church. Here, between tower and chancel, the 17c square nave with its mullioned windows very much resembles a typical Jacobean manor house.

Melton Mowbray, the fine parish church of St Mary the Virgin.

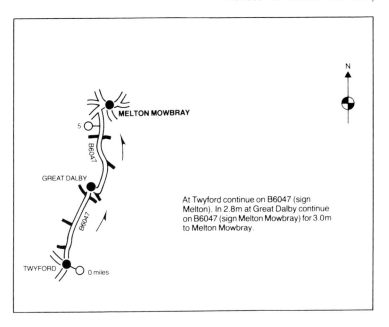

At Twyford continue on B6047 (sign Melton). In 2.8m at Great Dalby continue on B6047 (sign Melton Mowbray) for 3.0m to Melton Mowbray.

THE GREAT part of the route is confined to Lancashire's Forest of Bowland, an area that extends roughly from Lancaster in the west to the little village of Barley in the east.

The names Bowland Forest and Pendle Forest may be misleading. In fact each area is better described as a chase, an unenclosed game preserve that was once the hunting ground of medieval kings. Thus on the upland plateau sheep graze and there are few trees, the limited wooded areas being confined to the little rivers that ply their way beneath the peaty uplands, among them the Rivers Lune, Ribble, Calder and Hodder.

Many of the narrow valleys within the Forest of Bowland make ideal catchment areas for reservoirs such as the one at Abbeystead and those that lie around the villages of Sabden and Barley. There can be few lovelier roads in Lancashire than that which runs through the Trough of Bowland. Among several picturesque villages encountered early in the route are Chipping and Ribchester. Loitering in these quiet villages it seems hard to believe that they lie only a handful of miles from industrial towns such as Preston and Blackburn.

Within the eastern extremity of the Bowland Forest are the villages of Sabden, Newchurch and Barley, dominated by Pendle Hill where in 1887 beacons were lit to celebrate the Jubilee of Queen Victoria. Close to Pendle Hill is a spring known as Robin Hood's Well, also known as Fox's Well, for it was here that George Fox had a vision that led him to found the Quaker Movement in 1652.

The delightful villages of Bolton by Bowland and Slaidburn, once part of Yorkshire, now lie within Lancashire. The road from Slaidburn runs through a great expanse of open moorland where sheep graze. This road was once gated but now, happily, cattle grids divide the territories.

North of these moors are the villages of High Bentham and Burton in Lonsdale, both part of North Yorkshire and watered respectively by the Rivers Wenning and Greta. Further north still is the Lune Valley and the pleasant Cumbrian town of Kirkby Lonsdale, with its famous bridge across the river. ‐

From Kirkby Lonsdale the B, and later unclassified, road returns to Lancaster by way of Whittington and Halton. It is of interest that this latter village is described in the Domesday Book as 'the Great Manor of Halton' – Lancaster being at that time merely one of Halton's hamlets.

Lancaster

The building which dominates Lancaster is the Ashton Memorial, a round hall reached by some 100 steps and surmounted by a green copper dome. Described by Pevsner as the 'grandest monument in England', first sight of the memorial gives the impression that here

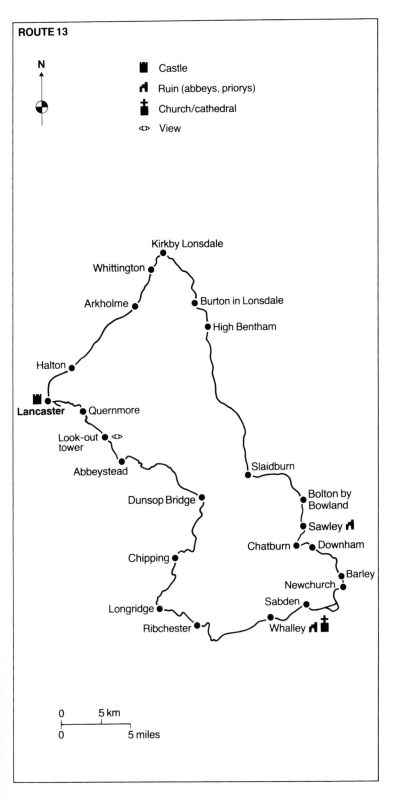

ROUTE 13

N

■ Castle

◫ Ruin (abbeys, priorys)

▮ Church/cathedral

◉ View

Kirkby Lonsdale

Whittington

Arkholme

Burton in Lonsdale

High Bentham

Halton

Lancaster

Quernmore

Look-out tower ◉

Abbeystead

Slaidburn

Dunsop Bridge

Bolton by Bowland

Sawley ◫

Chatburn

Downham

Chipping

Barley

Newchurch

Sabden

Longridge

Ribchester

Whalley ◫▮

0   5 km

0   5 miles

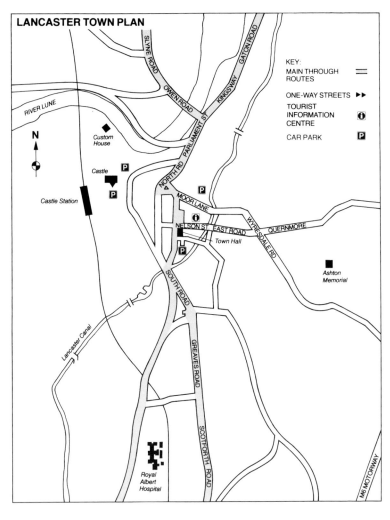

LANCASTER TOWN PLAN

KEY:
MAIN THROUGH ROUTES
ONE-WAY STREETS ►►
TOURIST INFORMATION CENTRE 🅘
CAR PARK 🅿

N

Custom House

Castle

Castle Station

Town Hall

Ashton Memorial

Royal Albert Hospital

lies a miniature St Paul's. It was built in 1909 by Baron Ashton in memory of his wife and stands in a beautiful park on the eastern fringe of the city.

The massive gatehouse of Lancaster Castle, flanked by towers 66 ft high, stands next to the priory church. The castle, part used as a prison, is open to the public for views of the Georgian court room, medieval dungeons, and the Shire Hall with its ceiling of carved stone and walls displaying some 600 heraldic shields. The Priory Church of St Mary, founded in 1094, is famous for its 14c choir stalls.

Narrow cobbled streets lead down from Castle Hill to the River Lune and St George's Quay, a thriving port in the 18c, with its stone warehouses and old Custom House that now houses a maritime museum. The River Lune is not the city's only waterway, for threading through Lancaster is the canal where boats are on hire.

Apart from the Maritime Museum, other museums of interest include the City Museum, housed in a fine old building that was once the town hall, and the Museum of Childhood where there are displays of dolls and Gillow furniture. This latter building was once the 17c Judge's Lodgings. To the east of the city, close to Williamson Park, is Hornsea Pottery where factory tours can be taken and the pottery process explained by a guide.

Some nine miles to the north of Lancaster, situated in the heart of Arnside and Silverdale, is one of Lancashire's finest country houses, Leighton Hall. This is the home of the Gillow family, Lancaster furniture designers since the 18c who became world famous with the formation of Waring and Gillow. It was Richard Gillow who built the Custom House in 1764 and the displays of furniture in the Childhood Museum are of Gillow design. In addition to the pictures and furniture at Leighton Hall, look out for the Leighton eagles which can be seen flying in the extensive grounds.

Post House Hotel, Waterside Park. T (0524) 65999. (A)

Note: Hotel accommodation in Lancaster appears to be limited and can be expensive. At Morecambe, only three miles away, there is a wide range of hotels, many well run and modestly priced.

Tourist Office, Dalton Square. T (0524) 32878.

A peaceful valley in the Forest of Bowland.

The Route

The road out of Lancaster is narrow and in places steep. Later, between Abbeystead and Dunsop Bridge, the road runs through the lovely Trough of Bowland alongside a sparkling stream with fells on either side. Quiet narrow country roads run southward from Dunsop Bridge to Chipping.

1 At Lancaster Town Hall take Nelson St, East Rd and Quernmore (see Town Plan). In 1.3m keep Str. over motorway (no sign) and in 0.4m turn L. on minor road (sign Caton). In 0.1m turn R. (sign Galgate). In 0.1m turn L. (sign Littledale). In 0.6m turn R. (sign Bayhorse). In 1.3m at Quernmore crossroads turn L. (signs Clitheroe and Trough of Bowland).

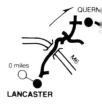

Quernmore (Lancs)

Perhaps Quernmore is better described as a region than a village. It lies to the extreme west of the Forest of Bowland, watered by the River Conder with the church, hall, houses and shop scattered over a wide area. The route passes the modern church (right). Away to the north and overlooking the Lune Valley is Quernmore Park and two small lakes. After passing the village shop the road ascends to the moors and the look-out tower (right). From the tower there are marvellous views. An inscription tells that it was constructed by the owner of nearby Hare Appletree Farm to commemorate the Jubilee of Queen Victoria.

Abbeystead (Lancs)

The road has descended from Abbeystead Fell to the reservoir and this charming hamlet, which nestles in a leafy dell. Two sturdy stone-built houses date from 1892 and face the school, which caters for some fifty children.

Dunsop Bridge (Lancs)

The little Church of St Hubert lies to the right of the road, opposite a glade of trees and remote from the village. The road to Chipping avoids the centre of the pretty village named after its river.

Centre of Abbeystead village.

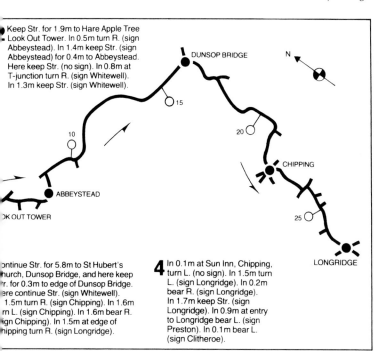

Keep Str. for 1.9m to Hare Apple Tree
Look Out Tower. In 0.5m turn R. (sign
Abbeystead). In 1.4m keep Str. (sign
Abbeystead) for 0.4m to Abbeystead.
Here keep Str. (no sign). In 0.8m at
T-junction turn R. (sign Whitewell).
In 1.3m keep Str. (sign Whitewell).

ontinue Str. for 5.8m to St Hubert's
hurch, Dunsop Bridge, and here keep
'r. for 0.3m to edge of Dunsop Bridge.
ere continue Str. (sign Whitewell).
1.5m turn R. (sign Chipping). In 1.6m
rn L. (sign Chipping). In 1.6m bear R.
ign Chipping). In 1.5m at edge of
hipping turn R. (sign Longridge).

4 In 0.1m at Sun Inn, Chipping,
turn L. (no sign). In 1.5m turn
L. (sign Longridge). In 0.2m
bear R. (sign Longridge).
In 1.7m keep Str. (sign
Longridge). In 0.9m at entry
to Longridge bear L. (sign
Preston). In 0.1m bear L.
(sign Clitheroe).

Chipping (Lancs)

This remote village in the extreme south of the Forest of Bowland is a place in which to linger. Charming stone cottages, many with mullioned windows and fronted by cobbled pavements, are scattered around without any formal pattern. The name Chipping indicates that here was once an important market place. In the 17c a variety of cottage industries began. Among these was chair-making, and today Chipping boasts a thriving century-old chair factory, located by one of the bridges across the stream. A row of terraced almshouses in Windy Street bears the inscription: 'Let him that loveth God, love his brotherhood'. The almshouses were bequeathed in 1683 by John Brabin whose house in Talbot Street is now the post office. The Church of St Bartholomew lies at the heart of the village with chancel screens made by local craftsmen. The Talbot and Sun Inns are enticing places, the latter raised high above the street and approached by steep stone steps.

Longridge (Lancs)

An expanding village with three churches and much new building. The route runs past the top of the high street, the part that represents old Longridge, with some fine stone houses that shame the modern structures scattered elsewhere.
Blackmoss Country House Hotel.
T (077 478) 3148. (B) This hotel is found by the roadside some two miles before reaching Longridge.

Dunsop Bridge, the Church of St Hubert.

The old village school and almshouses in Chipping.

The Route

*A little dull between
Ribchester and Whalley,
despite a marvellous river
view by the de Tabley Arms.
After Whalley the road
returns to the southern
extremity of the Forest of
Bowland, narrow roads but
superb scenery.*

Ribchester (Lancs)

'It is written on a stone in Rome
That Ribchester is as rich as any
town in Christendom'.

With these words William Camden
(1551–1623) recorded in his
Britannia his visit here, a village
steeped in Roman history and
tradition. The route instructions by
way of the B6245 avoid the centre
of Ribchester, but a pause here is
rewarding. The whole village is
built over the site of a Roman fort
established in 70 AD. The White
Bull Inn (1770) has a remarkable
Roman portico and stands above
Roman cellars. The most quoted
local story is of the schoolboy
truant who accidentally kicked up
a Roman helmet and visor in
1795. This is now in the British
Museum. Among interesting
exhibits in the Ribchester Museum
are handfuls of charred barley,
discovered in large granaries
capable of keeping the garrison
supplied with grain for a year. The
Church of St Wilfred has a fine
position above the River Ribble;
the pillars that support the organ
loft were constructed from stones
found among the Roman ruins.

Whalley (Lancs)

Town or village? Whichever is
correct, Whalley is the largest
place along the route. Here a wide
variety of buildings, some stone,
some mock-Tudor, lie above the

4 In 0.5m at Sawley turn L. (sign Bolton by
Bowland). In 0.2m bear R. (sign Bolton by
Bowland). In 1.8m at Copy Nook Inn at edge
of Bolton by Bowland turn L. (sign Slaidburn).
In 0.2m bear R. (sign Slaidburn). In 2.2m bear
L. (sign Slaidburn). In 1.8m turn L. on to B6478
(sign Slaidburn) for 1.3m to Slaidburn.

1 In 0.4m turn L. (sign Clitheroe). In 0.1m bear
(sign Clitheroe). In 0.7m bear R. on to B6245
Ribchester). In 2.7m at entry to Ribchester tu
on B6245 (sign Blackburn). In 1.0m cross Ri
Ribble and turn R. on B6245 (sign Blackburn
In 1.6m turn L. on to A59 (sign Whalley). Kee
on A59 and in 2.8m at roundabout turn L. on
minor road (sign Whalley).

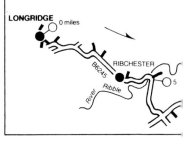

banks of the River Calder. It is to
the river that visitors flock to see
the ruined Cistercian Abbey
(1296), fragments of the walls
encompassed by stately limes and
chestnuts. Among relics of the
abbey are two gatehouses and a
part of the cloisters. The Abbot's
Lodge is now used as a
conference centre. Close at hand
is the magnificent Church of St
Mary, its origins even earlier than
those of the abbey.

Sabden (Lancs)

Neat terraced stone cottages and
a bridge over the Sabden Brook are
features of a village dominated by
Pendle Hill (1831 ft). Among
several inns is the Pendle Witch,
its name reminding that the route
has now run into an area famous

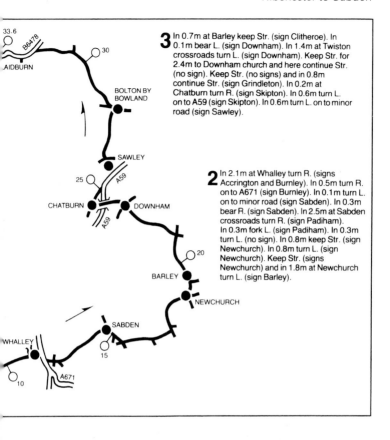

3 In 0.7m at Barley keep Str. (sign Clitheroe). In 0.1m bear L. (sign Downham). In 1.4m at Twiston crossroads turn L. (sign Downham). Keep Str. for 2.4m to Downham church and here continue Str. (no sign). Keep Str. (no signs) and in 0.8m continue Str. (sign Grindleton). In 0.2m at Chatburn turn R. (sign Skipton). In 0.6m turn L. on to A59 (sign Skipton). In 0.6m turn L. on to minor road (sign Sawley).

2 In 2.1m at Whalley turn R. (signs Accrington and Burnley). In 0.5m turn R. on to A671 (sign Burnley). In 0.1m turn L. on to minor road (sign Sabden). In 0.3m bear R. (sign Sabden). In 2.5m at Sabden crossroads turn R. (sign Padiham). In 0.3m fork L. (sign Padiham). In 0.3m turn L. (no sign). In 0.8m keep Str. (sign Newchurch). In 0.8m turn L. (sign Newchurch). Keep Str. (signs Newchurch) and in 1.8m at Newchurch turn L. (sign Barley).

The White Bull, Ribchester.

for its legend of the Pendle Witches who were reputed to cast their spells in the early 17c.

Newchurch in Pendle (Lancs)

There are fine views from this hillside village. On entry the Church of St Mary is seen (right), its churchyard sloping towards the valley. A granite monument to James Aitken tells how he took part with the Young Pretender 'in the Scottish rebellion of 1745, died and buried here in 1794'. In the centre of the village a gift shop named *Witches Galore* has featured on television. The witches of Pendle, some twenty in all, ranging from a blind old crone of eighty to a young girl of seventeen, were hanged publicly in Lancaster on 20 August 1612. Among the witches was Alice Nutter of Roughlee Old Hall, a woman of some social status. But although headstones near the church commemorate the Nutter family the place of Alice Nutter's burial remains a mystery.

Barley (Lancs)

The village lies in a valley immediately beneath Pendle Hill. It has won the Best Kept Village of Lancashire award on several occasions. On Pendle Hill is a Bronze Age burial ground. Tradition demands that anyone climbing Pendle Hill should carry a stone to add to the pile at the summit.

Downham (Lancs)

A picturesque village on the slopes of a gentle hill. In the Church of St Leonard are memorials to the Assheton family, lords of the manor and benefactors over centuries. Nearby is Downham Hall, secluded in the trees. By the

Assheton Arms is a small green with village stocks, bordered by some pretty stone-built terraced cottages, bow-shaped above the green.

Sawley (Lancs)

Once part of Yorkshire, Sawley lies beneath wooded hills, a graceful three-arch bridge spanning the River Ribble. Set among green

The War Memorial at Slaidburn.

fields near the river are the ruins of the abbey, the walls of the abbey church being the most prominent part of the remains.

Bolton by Bowland
(Lancs)

The route turns westward at an inn before entering the main part of the village. Bolton by Bowland is worth visiting. Focal point is the Church of St Peter and St Paul with a green on either side of it. The lower green, edged by a brook and the war memorial, embraces both the base of the old market cross and the village stocks. The upper green is well protected by trees and flanked by the Old Courthouse, once used to proclaim forest law.

The Route

The signpost on the road from Slaidburn indicates that it is gated. This is out of date and there are now cattle grids. There is a lovely moorland drive of some twelve miles, crossing the borders of North Yorkshire shortly before High Bentham. The road from here to Kirkby Lonsdale is narrow in places.

Slaidburn (Lancs)

A medieval bridge crosses the River Hodder into lush meadows, contrasting with the grey stone houses that form the nucleus of this charming village. The Hark to Bounty Inn occupies a central position. Its name has an amusing origin. It appears that the local vicar, a frequent visitor to the pub, owned a dog named Bounty which he would leave tied up outside. Whenever it barked he would turn to his drinking companions with the remark 'Hark to Bounty'. Slaidburn has another connection with dogs, for displayed in the church are dog whips once wielded to keep the farm dogs in order when their masters attended the service.

High Bentham (N. Yorks)

The church, 150 years old, stands on a knoll beneath tall trees. It was built originally by a mill owner to serve his employees who worked the mills on the river below. From the church the road climbs to the bustling little town, the Coach Inn indicating that this was once an important coaching stage.

Burton in Lonsdale (N. Yorks)

Georgian houses, together with some built recently, cluster above the River Greta crossed by an old

3 At town centre square turn L. and shortly L. again (sign Kendal). Shortly turn L. back on to A65 (sign Skipton). In 0.4m turn R. on to B6254 (sign Carnforth). In 1.7m at Whittington bear L. on B6254 (sign Carnforth) and continue on B6254 (signs Carnforth) for 3.2m to Arkholme.

hump bridge. Tucked away in a secluded part of the village is the spacious 19c church, fronted by a little green and maypole.

Kirkby Lonsdale (Cumbria)

The route has entered, momentarily, the extreme edge of Cumbria. Here the three-arched Devil's Bridge spans the River Lune at a lovely part of the valley. The bridge is believed to be at least 600 years old, among the most admired bridges in the north of England. Its name recalls the legend of Devil's Bridge in Wales. Here, it is said, the devil offered to build a bridge for an old cattle drover providing she would surrender the soul of the first creature to cross the bridge. The woman agreed and the devil built the bridge, hoping to gain her soul. However, the old lady cunningly enticed a dog across first, causing the devil to depart in rage. Steps from the river ascend to the churchyard of the imposing 13c

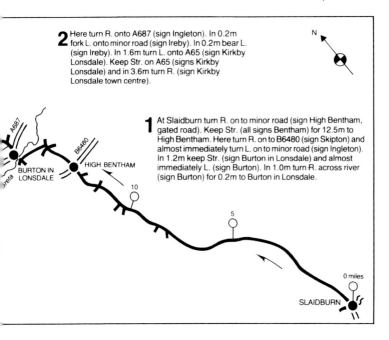

2 Here turn R. onto A687 (sign Ingleton). In 0.2m fork L. onto minor road (sign Ireby). In 0.2m bear L. (sign Ireby). In 1.6m turn L. onto A65 (sign Kirkby Lonsdale). Keep Str. on A65 (signs Kirkby Lonsdale) and in 3.6m turn R. (sign Kirkby Lonsdale town centre).

N

1 At Slaidburn turn R. on to minor road (sign High Bentham, gated road). Keep Str. (all signs Bentham) for 12.5m to High Bentham. Here turn R. on to B6480 (sign Skipton) and almost immediately turn L. on to minor road (sign Ingleton). In 1.2m keep Str. (sign Burton in Lonsdale) and almost immediately L. (sign Burton). In 1.0m turn R. across river (sign Burton) for 0.2m to Burton in Lonsdale.

A687

B6480

BURTON IN LONSDALE   HIGH BENTHAM

Greta

10

5

0 miles

SLAIDBURN

The parish church, Kirkby Lonsdale.

church. At the annual Victorian Fair everyone dresses in period costume and there is a display of Morris dancing.
Royal Hotel, Main St.
T (0468) 71217. (A)
Red Dragon Inn, Main St,
T (0468) 71205. (C)

Whittington (Lancs)

The church stands on a hillock above the hall and the quiet village. A grassy mound, even higher than the church, reminds that this was once a fortified church and the mound was once a look-out post to give warning of invaders. Within the church a window is a memorial to a Guards subaltern, born at Whittington Hall and killed in action at Flanders when only twenty.

The Route

After leaving the B6254 the minor road, straight but narrow, returns directly to Lancaster.

Halton (Lancs)

The final village before returning to Lancaster. Some ugly modern building has sprung up above Halton. By the church and inn, however, all is serenity. Here a group of 17c houses gathers beneath the church with its 15c tower. Near the church a swift-flowing stream flows from the hillside to join the River Lune. Beyond the stream a green knoll, Castle Hill, was the site of a pre-Conquest fortress.

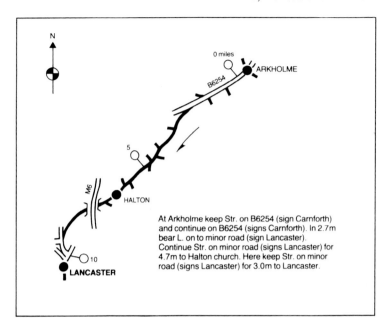

At Arkholme keep Str. on B6254 (sign Carnforth) and continue on B6254 (signs Carnforth). In 2.7m bear L. on to minor road (sign Lancaster). Continue Str. on minor road (signs Lancaster) for 4.7m to Halton church. Here keep Str. on minor road (signs Lancaster) for 3.0m to Lancaster.

The River Lune, Kirkby Lonsdale.

14 North Yorkshire, West Yorkshire, Lancashire

THE GREATEST part of the route of some 160 miles is confined to North Yorkshire. Prior to the reorganization of 1974 Yorkshire was divided into North, East and West Ridings. The reorganization meant that most of these three areas became counties in their own right. Some territory, however, went to form the new counties of Cleveland and Humberside with small outlying areas going to Durham, Cumbria, Lancashire and Greater Manchester.

Despite this upheaval North Yorkshire remains England's largest county, including the 680 square miles of the Yorkshire Dales National Park with peaks such as Whernside (2,419 ft) and Ingleborough (2,373 ft), through which much of the route runs.

'On all my travels', wrote J. B. Priestley, 'I've never seen a countryside to equal in beauty the Yorkshire Dales.' There are some sixty dales (valleys), normally named after the river or stream which flows through them, all differing in character with a wide variety of enchanting scenery.

After crossing Ribblesdale the route veers northward through the Gisburn Forest. Here, for a few miles only, the road runs through the eastern edge of Lancashire, an area that before reorganization was part of Yorkshire. At the lovely village of Clapham the road has returned to North Yorkshire.

Between Clapham and Hawes the road meanders through Widdale, with Dodd Fell Hill (2,189 ft) and Knoutberry Hill (2,203 ft) the highest surrounding features. To the east and parallel to this road is the Pennine Way, Britain's first long-distance footpath that runs some 250 miles from Edale, Derbyshire, to Kirk Yetholm, Borders region. From Hawes, capital of Upper Wensleydale, the road continues north eastward across the moors into Swaledale where at Grinton there is a fine view of the river. The charming towns of Bedale and Masham lie at the extreme eastern edge of the National Park; but from Masham the route turns westward and the road between Lofthouse and Pateley Bridge continues through Nidderdale.

Between Greenhow Hill and Otley the River Washburn flows beside the road, together with other streams and becks feeding the several reservoirs along this stretch of the route. Otley, known as the metropolis of Wharfedale, marks the entry to West Yorkshire with the large industrial town of Bradford to the south. This industrial belt is avoided by taking the moors road to Bingley before reaching Haworth and the Bronte country.

From Haworth the final few miles are by way of narrow country roads. Near Cononley there are still more Bronte associations. Lothersdale, signed just two miles off the route, features in *Jane Eyre*. Here, hidden in trees above the church, is Stonegappe, the house Charlotte Bronte called Gateshead.

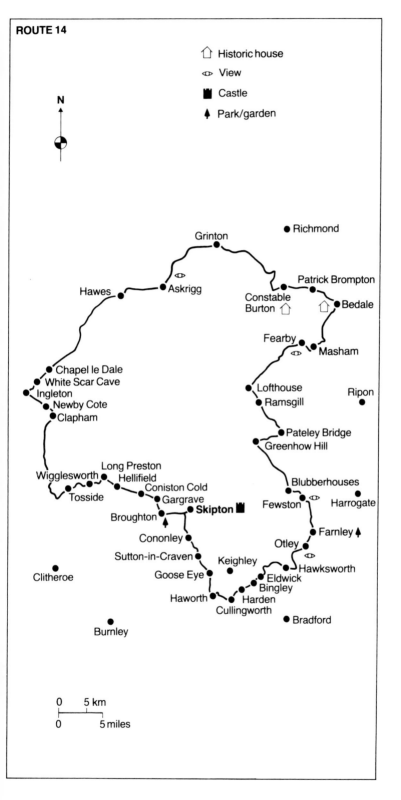

ROUTE 14

⌂ Historic house
👁 View
🏰 Castle
♠ Park/garden

N

Skipton

This busy market town stands to the south of the Yorkshire Dales National Park, 680 square miles of spectacular mountain and moorland scenery. On most days of the week the broad high street is crammed on both sides with market stalls, adding bustle and colour to a town that is steeped in history. The town's name is of Anglo-Saxon origin, deriving from the word 'scip' (sheep), for over the centuries sheep played an important part in the town's economy. At the head of the high street is Skipton Castle, its sturdy gateway engraved with the single word Désormais – 'henceforth'. This is the motto of the Cliffords, a family associated with the town for almost four centuries. The castle with its Tudor courtyard, still fully roofed and floored, is among the most complete and well-preserved medieval castles to be found in England.

Near the castle is the parish church, the impressive Clifford tombs linking church and castle. The High Corn Mill, off the Grassington Road, has been restored complete with waterwheel and obsolete machinery. Nearby a plaque records that 'Near this place John Wesley preached to the inhabitants of Skipton, 26 June 1764'.

The Craven Museum is approached through the main doors of the town hall. Among interesting exhibits is the oldest piece of cloth in Britain, recovered from a Bronze Age grave. The Leeds and Liverpool Canal runs through the heart of Skipton; scheduled boat trips are arranged to visit the surrounding countryside. Among the town's most distinguished sons was the Right Honourable Iain MacLeod MP who was born in a house in Keighley Road (see Gargrave).

Only a five-minute drive from Skipton at Embsay is the Yorkshire Dales Railway Museum Trust. Here steam trains operate on two miles of track. Among the exhibits are industrial locomotives and a model railway.

Black Horse Hotel, High St. T (0756) 2145. (B)
Red Lion Hotel, High St. T (0756) 60718. (B)

The sturdy gateway of Skipton Castle.

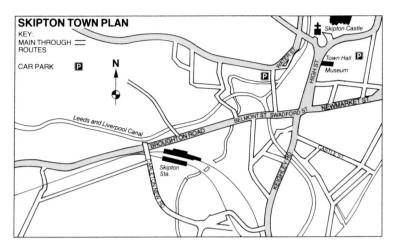

The Route

Initially the road undulates past rich pasture land to the southern extremity of the Yorkshire Dales National Park. Soon after leaving Tosside the road runs north through the Gisburn Forest. There is a car park with a fine view of the Stocks Reservoir and bird sanctuary. Here three walks in this lovely countryside are recommended, lasting respectively seventy-five, fifty and forty minutes. The construction of this huge reservoir meant that the village of Dalehead was submerged and the little church nearby, built in 1938 from the stones of the old church, acts as a memorial to the community that once lived here. The road now continues north through the heart of the National Park, re-entering North Yorkshire at Halstead Fell where there are spectacular views. Shortly before arrival at Clapham the road crosses the River Wenning.

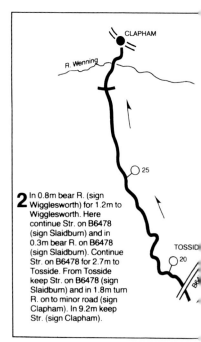

2 In 0.8m bear R. (sign Wigglesworth) for 1.2m to Wigglesworth. Here continue Str. on B6478 (sign Slaidburn) and in 0.3m bear R. on B6478 (sign Slaidburn). Continue Str. on B6478 for 2.7m to Tosside. From Tosside keep Str. on B6478 (sign Slaidburn) and in 1.8m turn R. on to minor road (sign Clapham). In 9.2m keep Str. (sign Clapham).

The Men that worked for England,
They have their Graves at Home.

Broughton (N. Yorks)

Half a mile before reaching the village is Broughton Hall (left). The extensive grounds include an Italian garden laid out by W. A. Nesfield.

Gargrave (N. Yorks)

The village stands astride the River Aire. Broad greens stretch along both sides of the river connected by bridges and stepping stones. The church is seen before crossing the river (right). In the south east extremity of the large churchyard, overlooking the fields beyond, is the grave of the respected statesman Iain MacLeod (1913–70). He was born at Skipton and died shortly after taking up office as Chancellor of the Exchequer. On his tomb stone are the moving lines of G. K. Chesterton:

Coniston Cold (N. Yorks)

A cluster of grey houses nestles in a valley amidst the moors and fells. Beyond the village (right) is a glimpse of Coniston Hall, set in woods above a twenty-five-acre lake.

Hellifield (N. Yorks)

The busy village lies at the southern extremity of the Yorkshire Dales National Park.

Wigglesworth (N. Yorks)

A handful of cottages, village shop and black and white Plough Inn straggle up the slopes of a hill in this remote little village of Ribblesdale. There is accommodation at the Plough Inn which would certainly prove a retreat for those wanting seclusion.
Plough Inn. T (072 94) 243. (C)

1 At Skipton High Street (see Town Plan) follow signs Clitheroe, bearing R. at second roundabout into Swadford St. In 1.9m turn L. on to A59 (sign Clitheroe). In 1.3m at Broughton turn R. on to minor road (sign Gargrave) for 2.3m to Gargrave. Here turn L. on to A65 (sign Settle) for 2.0m to Coniston Cold. Continue Str. on A65 (sign Settle) for 3.3m to Hellifield. At Hellifield bear R. on A65 (sign Settle) and in 1.8m at Long Preston turn L. on to B6478 (sign Wigglesworth).

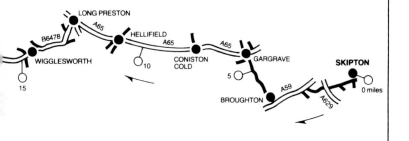

Tosside (N. Yorks)

This tiny hilltop village stands on the borders of North Yorkshire and Lancashire. Here there seems to be little more than the inn, shop and church (right). Outside the church a stone obelisk and weather vane commemorate the Jubilee of Queen Victoria.

237

The Route

The minor road from Clapham is narrow, by-passing Ingleton on reaching the B road. Ingleton, a pleasant village on the River Greta, can be visited by only a mile diversion. The road continues northward with good views of Ingleborough (right) and Whernside (left) through Widdale to Hawes.

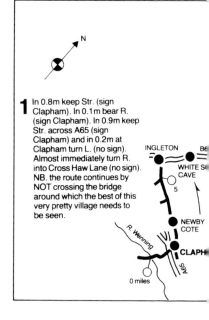

1 In 0.8m keep Str. (sign Clapham). In 0.1m bear R. (sign Clapham). In 0.9m keep Str. across A65 (sign Clapham) and in 0.2m at Clapham turn L. (no sign). Almost immediately turn R. into Cross Haw Lane (no sign). NB. the route continues by NOT crossing the bridge around which the best of this very pretty village needs to be seen.

Clapham (N. Yorks)

Charming stone houses and white cottages together with the New Inn stand by the Clapham Beck in this romantic village. Both road and footbridges cross the stream, and in the car park is the Yorkshire Dales National Park Information Centre. Before records were made it was said that Ingleborough Hill stood a mile high. In fact the hill that towers above Clapham reaches to less than half that – 2,373 ft, slightly lower than Whernside to the north. A respected botanist, Reginald Farrer, once lived here, and a popular excursion from Clapham is by way of the Reginald Farrer Nature Trail, passing for a mile through a wooded glen to Ingleborough Cave, a show cave since 1837 with guided tours.

Stone cottages in Clapham.

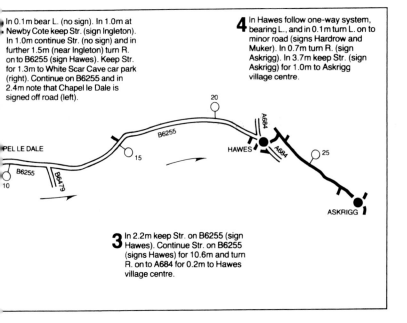

4 In Hawes follow one-way system, bearing L., and in 0.1m turn L. on to minor road (signs Hardrow and Muker). In 0.7m turn R. (sign Askrigg). In 3.7m keep Str. (sign Askrigg) for 1.0m to Askrigg village centre.

In 0.1m bear L. (no sign). In 1.0m at Newby Cote keep Str. (sign Ingleton). In 1.0m continue Str. (no sign) and in further 1.5m (near Ingleton) turn R. on to B6255 (sign Hawes). Keep Str. for 1.3m to White Scar Cave car park (right). Continue on B6255 and in 2.4m note that Chapel le Dale is signed off road (left).

3 In 2.2m keep Str. on B6255 (sign Hawes). Continue Str. on B6255 (signs Hawes) for 10.6m and turn R. on to A684 for 0.2m to Hawes village centre.

White Scar Cave (N. Yorks)

The car park lies to the right of the road. There are frequent guided tours through the floodlit caverns. Two lakes are crossed, the largest 200 ft in length. A cave chamber 700 ft long known as The Battlefield is among the largest underground caverns in the country. There are two graceful waterfalls as well as hundreds of stalagmites and stalactites.

Chapel le Dale (N. Yorks)

The remote little chapel is signed (left), a hundred yards or so off the main road. In the graveyard lie more than one hundred men, killed in accidents while building the railway between Settle and Dent Head. A plaque to commemorate these pioneers of a century ago can be seen in the chapel. Nearby is Weathercote Cove, no longer open to the public. Further along the main road (right) is the quaint Old Hill Inn, one of the rooms dating from the 16c with an inglenook fireplace.

Hawes (N. Yorks)

A delightful old town of narrow cobbled streets and squares. Hawes is said to be the second highest market town in England. It is the capital of Upper Wensleydale, famous both as a centre for the production of Wensleydale cheese and for rope making. A little to the north, close to the route and visited in *Through Britain on Country Roads* is Hardrow Force, one of Britain's most impressive waterfalls. *Fountain Hotel*, Market Place. T (09697) 206. (C)

Askrigg (N. Yorks)

This little Wensleydale town of mellow grey stone houses stands some 800 ft above sea level, sandwiched by moors and fells of a great height that overlook it. Close to the Church of St Oswald (13c) is a stepped market cross; by the side of the cross is the bull baiting stone. It was once the fashion to watch the baiting from Old Hall that stood nearby until 1935 when it was burned down.

239

The Route

*From Askrigg the road rises
steeply (1 in 4), winding across
Askrigg, Whitaside and Harkerside
Moors with superb views of
Swaledale to the north. There are
cattle grids here and sheep graze.
By taking the minor roads beyond
Grinton the town of Leyburn is by-
passed (this town was visited in
Through Britain on Country Roads).*

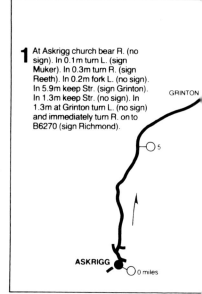

1 At Askrigg church bear R. (no sign). In 0.1m turn L. (sign Muker). In 0.3m turn R. (sign Reeth). In 0.2m fork L. (no sign). In 5.9m keep Str. (sign Grinton). In 1.3m keep Str. (no sign). In 1.3m at Grinton turn L. (no sign) and immediately turn R. on to B6270 (sign Richmond).

GRINTON

5

ASKRIGG — 0 miles

Grinton (N. Yorks)

There is a fine view of the River
Swale from the ancient recessed
bridge with its three arches. To the
north are the fells and moors of
Arkengarthdale with Calver Hill
(1,599 ft) a prominent feature. A
little further north still is Tan Hill
and England's highest inn. To the
immediate south of Grinton is
Harkerside Moor and a fortified
manor house, Grinton Lodge. The
Church of St Andrew and the
Bridge Hotel make a placid group
by the river. Everything in the
church is on a grand scale, and it
serves a parish that stretches over
a wide area. A little further along
the road is Marrick Priory (left),
founded in 1050, with its tower
the sole relic of this ancient
building. It can be approached by
a footpath along the river,
standing amid farm buildings on a
wooded stretch of the Swale.

Constable Burton (N. Yorks)

Constable Burton Hall can be seen
(left) before entering the village.
This magnificent Georgian house
was designed by the architect
John Carr; it stands in a beautiful
park of some 150 acres.

Patrick Brompton (N. Yorks)

The church, inn and cottages
mingle above a point where the
Brompton and Newton Becks join.
The church tower was built a
century ago, but parts of the
building survive from Norman
times.

Bedale (N. Yorks)

Pride of this small market town is
Bedale Hall, standing in parkland
to the north of the town. This
grand Georgian house was
requisitioned by the War
Department in the Second World
War and later, already in derelict
condition, it was occupied by
squatters. The Bedale Rural
District Council then came to the
rescue, and with grants from the
Historic Buildings Council a long-
term plan to restore the building to
its original condition was
undertaken. The programme
called for the restoration of the
staircase hall, corridor, and
ballroom. This project was
completed by 1962 and today
Bedale Hall, in addition to its
provision of council offices, caters
for the community in numerous

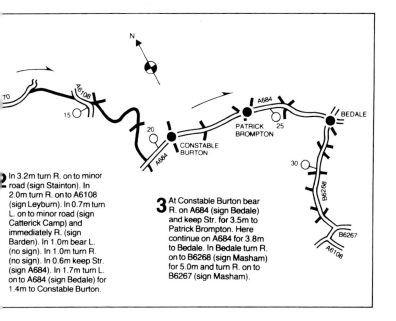

2 In 3.2m turn R. on to minor road (sign Stainton). In 2.0m turn R. on to A6108 (sign Leyburn). In 0.7m turn L. on to minor road (sign Catterick Camp) and immediately R. (sign Barden). In 1.0m bear L. (no sign). In 1.0m turn R. (no sign). In 0.6m keep Str. (sign A684). In 1.7m turn L. on to A684 (sign Bedale) for 1.4m to Constable Burton.

3 At Constable Burton bear R. on A684 (sign Bedale) and keep Str. for 3.5m to Patrick Brompton. Here continue on A684 for 3.8m to Bedale. In Bedale turn R. on to B6268 (sign Masham) for 5.0m and turn R. on to B6267 (sign Masham).

ways. The Georgian ballroom is used regularly for dances and dinners. Centrepiece of the small museum is the old fire engine with its original paintwork and lettering. The broad main street, flanked by spacious sets of cobbles, curves past splendid Georgian houses and shops with a tall stepped market cross. The Church of St Gregory faces Bedale Hall, its tall tower dominating the length of the high street.

Bedale, the main street.

The Route

After leaving Fearby there are good views of the Leighton Reservoir. Later, after leaving Ramsgill, the huge Gouthwaite Reservoir and bird sanctuary flank the left of the road. To the right of the moorland road betwen Greenhow and Blubberhouses is Thruscross Reservoir.

3 At Ramsgill bear R. (sign Pateley Bridge) for 4.8m to Pateley Bridge. Here turn R. on to B6265 (sign Grassington). In 3.1m at Greenhow Hill turn L. on to minor road (sign Blubberhouses). Keep Str. (signs Blubberhouses) and in 6.1m continue Str.-(no sign) for 1.0m to Blubberhouses.

Masham (N. Yorks)

The village stands high above the River Ure, its focal point the huge square with maypole and market cross. The broad-fronted King's Head Hotel flanks the square, while at one corner is the church beneath an imposing Norman tower and 15c spire. In the churchyard is a round pillar with figures representing Our Lord and the twelve disciples. The pillar is believed to be part of a great cross carved more than 1,000 years ago. *King's Head Hotel.*
T (0765) 89295. (A)

Fearby (N. Yorks)

Between Masham and Fearby is the lovely 300-acre Swinton Park, home of the last Lord Masham and now in use as a training centre. Fearby is a spacious hilltop village with large greens and two inns, one at each end of the village.

Lofthouse (N. Yorks)

As the name implies the village occupies a high position on the edge of the moors, clustering tightly above the River Nidd at the head of Upper Niddersdale. There is a little cross above a water fountain with various inscriptions that include:

A pint of cold water three times a day
Is the surest way to keep the doctor away.

Ramsgill (N. Yorks)

A handful of old cottages, a church built in 1842, a small green and the ivy-clad Yorke Arms Hotel where peacocks strut are the framework of Upper Nidderdale's loveliest village. Close to the Victorian church is the gabled end of a chapel that stood here centuries before the church was built. It seems hard to believe that this peaceful place formed the background to a sensational murder trial of 1745. Eugene Aram, born in a house close to the Yorke Arms, was tried and eventually executed for the murder of a local shoemaker. He became the subject of a book by Lord Edward Lytton and of lyrics by the poet Thomas Hood (1799–1845).
Yorke Arms Hotel.
T (0423) 75243. (A)

Ramsgill, the church tower.

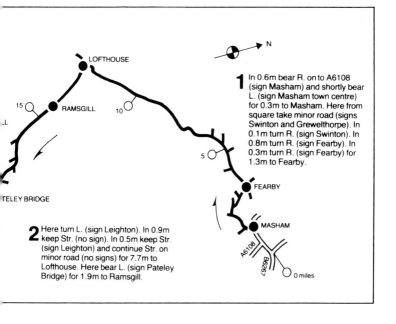

1 In 0.6m bear R. on to A6108 (sign Masham) and shortly bear L. (sign Masham town centre) for 0.3m to Masham. Here from square take minor road (signs Swinton and Grewelthorpe). In 0.1m turn R. (sign Swinton). In 0.8m turn R. (sign Fearby). In 0.3m turn R. (sign Fearby) for 1.3m to Fearby.

2 Here turn L. (sign Leighton). In 0.9m keep Str. (no sign). In 0.5m keep Str. (sign Leighton) and continue Str. on minor road (no signs) for 7.7m to Lofthouse. Here bear L. (sign Pateley Bridge) for 1.9m to Ramsgill.

LOFTHOUSE
RAMSGILL
15
10
5
FEARBY
MASHAM
TELEY BRIDGE
A6108
B6267
0 miles
N

Pateley Bridge (N. Yorks)

Narrow crooked streets rise past quaint old houses towards Pateley Moor. Pateley Bridge was constituted a market town in the 14c. Here is the Nidderdale Museum with thousands of items that relate to the Yorkshire Dales.

Greenhow Hill (N. Yorks)

The minor road that descends from Greenhow avoids Stumps Cross Caverns (visited in *Through Britain on Country Roads* and worth a diversion of a mile). Greenhow Hill features in Rudyard Kipling's *Soldiers Three*.

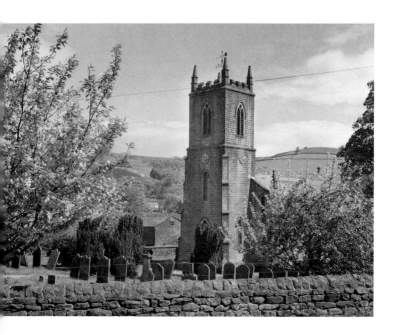

The Route

There is a good view of the Lindley Wood Reservoir after Fewston. The route from Otley to Haworth presents problems. Local advice proved fruitful in avoiding most of the industrial area. A short stretch of busy A road has to be taken; this stretch, incidentally, passes the famous Harry Ramsden fish restaurant, reputedly the largest fish and chip shop in the world. Thereafter the road crosses the Baildon Moor to Bingley.

4 In 1.0m at Bingley turn R. on to A650 (sign Keighley). In 0.1m turn L. on to B6429 (sign Harden). In 1.4m at Harden keep Str. (sign Cullingworth). In 1.8m at Cullingworth turn R. B6144 (sign Haworth). In 1.1m keep Str. acro A629 on B6144 (sign Haworth). In 1.0m turn (sign Haworth). In 0.5m turn L. (sign Haworth Follow main road, avoiding cobbled main stre 1.2m to main car park (left). From here take r road opposite park (sign Oakworth). In 0.9m R. (no sign). In 0.2m at Fleece Inn turn L. (no s In 0.1m turn L. (no sign). In 0.1m bear R. (sig Goose Eye). Continue Str. (signs Goose Eye 1.0m to Goose Eye (Turkey Inn).

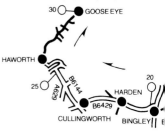

3 In 1.3m keep Str. (sign Bradford). In 0.5m ke Str. on to A65 (sign Bradford). In 0.5m bear R A6038 (sign Bradford). In 0.8m turn R. on to road (sign Hawksworth). Continue for 1.3m Hawksworth. Here keep Str. (no sign). In 0.3 keep Str. (sign Eldwick). In 0.9m turn L. (sign Eldwick). In 1.6m turn L. (sign Eldwick). In 1.6 Eldwick keep Str. (sign Bingley).

Fewston (N. Yorks)

There are spectacular views of the Fewston and Swinsty Reservoirs from the village, enfolded in wooded hills and expanses of purple moors.

Farnley (N. Yorks)

The gates of Farnley Hall, one-time home of Guy Fawkes and his descendants, can be seen at a point where the road reaches a T-junction here. It was a Thomas Fawkes who befriended the landscape artist Joseph Turner (1775–1851) and acquired many of the paintings collected here. The hall stands in a tree-clad park of 200 acres overlooking Wharfedale.

Otley (W. Yorks)

A five-span medieval bridge crosses the River Wharfe into this busy market town of cobbled streets and old inns. Thomas Chippendale, world-renowned furniture designer, was born here in 1718; a statue to commemorate him occupies a prominent position in the town. The

craftsman's first home is marked by a plaque at the Skipton Building Society in Boroughgate. The parish church has a Norman chancel and doorway. In the churchyard is a stone model of the Bramhope Tunnel, commemorating more than thirty men who were killed while constructing it. Overlooking Otley is the Chevin, a rocky hillock with panoramic views.
Chevin Lodge Hotel, Yorkgate. T (0943) 467818. (A)

Hawksworth (W. Yorks)

The village stands on a ridge on the threshold of Baildon Moor, offering good views of industrial Yorkshire to the south. Hawksworth Hall (right) with its gables and mullioned windows is now a school.

1 At Blubberhouses turn L. on to A59 (sign Harrogate). In 1.3m turn R. on to minor road (sign Fewston). In 0.5m keep Str. (no sign). In 0.2m keep Str. (sign Fewston). In 0.2m at Fewston church turn L. (no sign). In 1.2m turn R. on to B6451 (sign Otley). In 3.9m bear R. on B6451 (sign Otley).

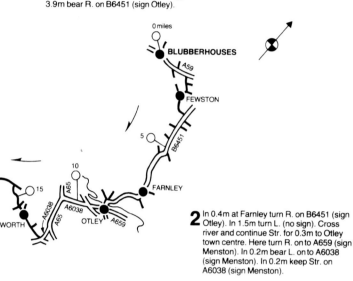

2 In 0.4m at Farnley turn R. on B6451 (sign Otley). In 1.5m turn L. (no sign). Cross river and continue Str. for 0.3m to Otley town centre. Here turn R. on to A659 (sign Menston). In 0.2m bear L. on to A6038 (sign Menston). In 0.2m keep Str. on A6038 (sign Menston).

The birthplace of Thomas Chippendale in Otley.

245

Eldwick (W. Yorks)

At the crossroads of High Eldwick is Dick Hudson's, a sturdy stone-built inn much loved by Yorkshiremen. The existing inn, built in 1900, stands on the site of an old farmhouse known as the Fleece Inn, owned from 1809 to 1878 by the Hudsons after whom the inn is now called. In the days of the Hudsons, workers from the mills flocked here, receiving hospitality from a much-loved family. Near to the inn is the home of Harvey Smith the showjumper.

Haworth (W. Yorks)

From the car park it is only a short stroll to the place everyone has come to see – the Bronte Parsonage. The Parsonage, now a museum, stands above the church. It was to here in 1821 that Charlotte, Emily and Anne Bronte moved with their parents and brother, Branwell. Among the rooms on view, furnished as when the family lived there, are Mr Bronte's study, the dining room, the kitchen, the nursery, Charlotte's room and Branwell's studio. A track leads to the moors from behind the parsonage. It was along here that the sisters would escape, dreaming and telling romantic tales that would later inspire *Wuthering Heights* and *Jane Eyre*. There is a surprising number of inns in Haworth, twelve in all. Branwell, an alcoholic in his later years, frequented the Black Bull at the top of the cobbled high street. A brass plate in the church marks the site of the Bronte vault.
Old White Lion. T (0535) 42313. (B)

The Route

There is a very steep and narrow descent after leaving Haworth. Afterwards the road remains narrow for the final few miles to Skipton, running more or less parallel with the main A629 across Keighley and Carlton Moors.

Goose Eye (W. Yorks)

The little village is cupped beneath high hills.

Sutton-in-Craven (N. Yorks)

Marks the re-entry to North Yorkshire. A little industrial town on the main road across which the minor road passes.

The Bronte Parsonage in Haworth.

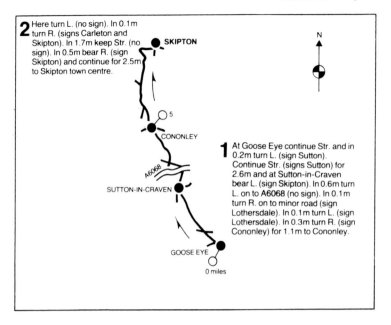

2 Here turn L. (no sign). In 0.1m turn R. (signs Carleton and Skipton). In 1.7m keep Str. (no sign). In 0.5m bear R. (sign Skipton) and continue for 2.5m to Skipton town centre.

SKIPTON

N

○5
CONONLEY

A6068

SUTTON-IN-CRAVEN

1 At Goose Eye continue Str. and in 0.2m turn L. (sign Sutton). Continue Str. (signs Sutton) for 2.6m and at Sutton-in-Craven bear L. (sign Skipton). In 0.6m turn L. on to A6068 (no sign). In 0.1m turn R. on to minor road (sign Lothersdale). In 0.1m turn L. (sign Lothersdale). In 0.3m turn R. (sign Cononley) for 1.1m to Cononley.

GOOSE EYE
○
0 miles

15   Durham, Northumberland, Tyne and Wear

THE ROUTE, among the longest in the Guide, is confined to the counties of Durham and Northumberland, encroaching only for a mile or two into Tyne and Wear.

Barnard Castle is known as the Gateway to Teesdale, an area of gentle dales, green valleys and vast expanses of moorland clad with heather and bracken. Much introductory information to Teesdale is available at both the information centre at Barnard Castle and the Bowlees Visitor Centre at Newbiggin.

Among many interesting topographical features to be seen early in the route are Gibson's Cave, Low Force, Cauldron Snout, and High Force, England's highest waterfall. When the route progresses into Northumberland there are glimpses of the historic Roman Wall, begun by Emperor Hadrian in 122 AD and extending for seventy-three and a half miles from Wallsend to Bowness-on-Solway.

After crossing the line of Hadrian's Wall the route proceeds northward, passing the Harwood Forest before descending to Coquetdale. Close to Northumberland's coastline is Warkworth Castle, immortalized in Shakespeare's *Henry IV*; and later, towering above the North Sea comes Dunstanburgh Castle, England's largest castle ruin, and mighty Bamburgh Castle.

The pretty village of Norham, the northernmost part of the route and separated from the Borders of Scotland by the Tweed, also boasts a castle in a setting of great beauty above the river. In addition to many castles and castle ruins scattered around Northumberland, reminders of threats of invasion are ever present. Everywhere there are fortified manor houses and farms. Pele towers are prominent, sometimes in the heart of the towns and villages but occasionally standing aloof on the moors between villages. Often enclosures on village greens were the assembly areas where villagers and their livestock would shelter during times of invasion.

Returning southward to Wooler and beyond there are views of the Cheviot Hills, grass-covered and rich in prehistoric remains, forming the natural boundary between England and Scotland. The return route to Durham crosses the line of Hadrian's Wall at Heddon-on-the-Wall. A little further south still, at Prudhoe, yet another castle ruin invites inspection. At Wolsingham the River Wear is crossed, the road returning to Barnard Castle by way of the great Hamsterley Forest.

Barnard Castle

This historic market town is named after the spectacular ruins of the 12c castle that towers above the River Tees. The castle, with its distinctive round tower and occupying six acres, was built by Bernard de Balliol, a Norman baron and ancestor of the founder of Balliol College, Oxford.

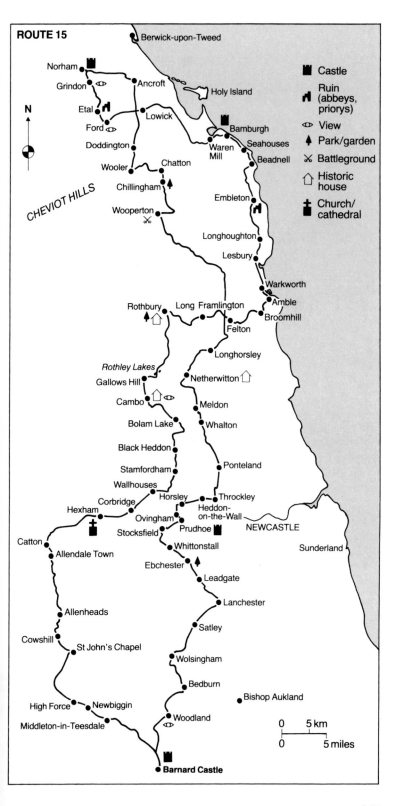

ROUTE 15

Castle

Ruin (abbeys, priorys)

View

Park/garden

Battleground

Historic house

Church/cathedral

Berwick-upon-Tweed

Norham

Grindon

Ancroft

Etal

Holy Island

Lowick

Ford

Doddington

Bamburgh

Waren Mill

Seahouses

Beadnell

Wooler

Chatton

N

Chillingham

Embleton

Wooperton

CHEVIOT HILLS

Longhoughton

Lesbury

Warkworth

Amble

Rothbury

Long Framlington

Broomhill

Felton

Longhorsley

Rothley Lakes

Netherwitton

Gallows Hill

Cambo

Meldon

Bolam Lake

Whalton

Black Heddon

Stamfordham

Ponteland

Wallhouses

Corbridge

Horsley

Throckley

Hexham

Ovingham

Heddon-on-the-Wall

Stocksfield

Prudhoe

NEWCASTLE

Catton

Whittonstall

Allendale Town

Ebchester

Sunderland

Leadgate

Allenheads

Lanchester

Cowshill

Satley

St John's Chapel

Wolsingham

Bedburn

High Force

Newbiggin

Bishop Aukland

Woodland

Middleton-in-Teesdale

0   5 km

0   5 miles

Barnard Castle

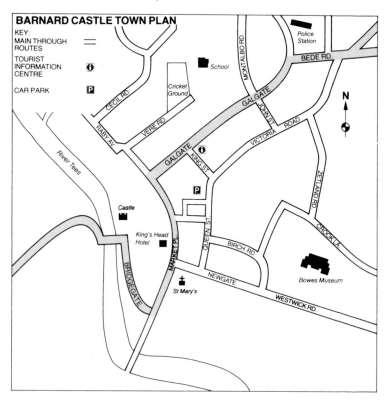

BARNARD CASTLE TOWN PLAN

KEY:
MAIN THROUGH ROUTES
TOURIST INFORMATION CENTRE
CAR PARK

Police Station

BEDE RD.

MONTALBO RD.

School

CECIL RD

Cricket Ground

VERE RD.

RABY AV.

GALGATE

GALGATE

JOHN ST.

VICTORIA

ROAD

ZETLAND RD.

River Tees

KING ST.

QUEEN ST.

Castle

King's Head Hotel

MARKET PL.

BIRCH RD.

CROOK LA.

Bowes Museum

BRIDGEGATE

NEWGATE

St Mary's

WESTWICK RD.

N

The Morritt Arms, once a coaching inn but now by-passed by the main road, occupies a delightful and peaceful position by Greta Bridge. It is well worth a visit.

Morritt Arms Hotel, Greta Bridge. T (0833) 27232. (B) Lies to the immediate south of the A66 on the Barnard Castle to Scotch Corner road.

Coach and Horses, 22 Galgate, Barnard Castle. T (0833) 38082. (C)

Tourist Office, 43 Galgate. T (0833) 690000.

The ruins of Barnard Castle overlooking the River Tees.

The octagonal market cross with supporting pillars, built in 1747, was once used for the sale of dairy produce. The administrative work of the town took place in the upper storey and surmounting the cross is a turreted fire bell and weathervane.

Close to the market cross is the King's Head Hotel, now a residential centre. It was here that Charles Dickens stayed, accompanied by his illustrator, 'Phiz', gathering information on a local school, Dotheboys Hall, and its tyrannical headmaster W. W. Shaw, whom he depicted as Squeers in *Nicholas Nickleby*.

Near the market square is St Mary's Church, established soon after the building of the castle; and Blagraves House (16c) where Oliver Cromwell was entertained with mulled wine and shortcake in 1648.

At the eastern extremity of Barnard Castle is the huge Bowes Museum, a French chateau-type building, with displays of furniture and paintings that include works by Goya and El Greco. It will be noted that one of the recommended hotels (below) lies a few miles from Barnard Castle. The Morritt Arms Hotel at Greta Bridge was founded and owned for many years by the Morritt family, owners of neighbouring Rokeby Park. It was here that their friend, Sir Walter Scott, stayed to write his romantic poem *Rokeby*, describing the locality in these lines:

Oh, Brignall banks are wild and fair,
And Greta woods are green,
And you may gather garlands there,
Would grace a summer queen.

The Route

There are numerous features of interest along the road between Barnard Castle and Langdon Beck. The moorland minor road from Langdon Beck is narrow and dominated to the east by Fendrith Hill (2,284 ft) and High Pike (1,924 ft). From St John's Chapel there is a short stretch of A road before turning northward onto the B road and crossing into Northumberland.

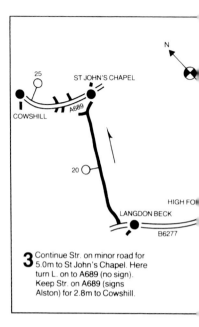

3 Continue Str. on minor road for 5.0m to St John's Chapel. Here turn L. on to A689 (no sign). Keep Str. on A689 (signs Alston) for 2.8m to Cowshill.

Middleton in Teesdale
(Durham)

Terraces of stone cottages, first built by the Quaker-run London Lead Company, stand above the wooded vale of the River Tees. Lead mining ceased here in the early 20c and Middleton House, once the headquarters of the company, is now used as a shooting lodge. Middleton, now a village rather than a town, is known as the capital of Upper Teesdale, an area acclaimed in the poetry of Sir Walter Scott and William Wordsworth. But Teesdale's own poet is Richard Watson (1833–91), born in Middleton and buried in the parish churchyard, who describes the country he knew and loved with the lines:

> Let minstrels sing till they are hoarse,
> Of Scotia's woods and dells,
> And winding streams and mountains steep,
> Where bloom sweet heather bells,
> Their strains still fail to touch my heart,
> My fav'rite ones shall be
> Those that remind me of my home,
> The Teesdale hills for me.

Teesdale Hotel. T (0833) 40264. (C)

Newbiggin (Durham)

A handful of grey stone cottages hug the road amid rugged scenery. South of Newbiggin is the River Tees, running parallel to the road with a lovely stretch of the Pennine Way, Britain's first long-distance footpath. North of the village sheep graze on the wild expanses of Middleton Common. Beyond the village is the Bowlees Visitor Centre (right), providing information of local attractions that include Gibson's Cave and Low Force Falls. Further still along the road is High Force (left), England's highest waterfall that thunders sensationally for seventy feet to the depths of a wooded gorge.
High Force Hotel.
T (0833) 22222. (B)

Langdon Beck (Durham)

This remote hamlet, surrounded on every side by splendid scenery, makes an ideal headquarters for ramblers wishing to explore the

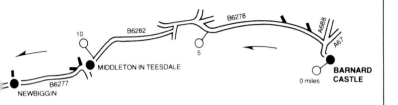

2 In 4.1m at Middleton in Teesdale keep Str. on to B6277 (sign High Force) and in 0.1m turn L. on B6277 (sign High Force). In 2.6m at Newbiggin continue Str. on B6277 (no sign). Keep Str. on B6277 for 2.0m to High Force. In 2.7m at Langdon Beck bear R. on B6277 (sign Alston). In 0.4m turn R. on to minor road (sign St John's Chapel).

1 At Barnard Castle market place take A67 (A688) (sign Darlington). In 0.1m continue into Galgate (see Town Plan) and in 0.3m turn L. on to B6278 (sign Middleton). In 4.9m keep Str. on B6278 (sign Eggleston). In 0.7m at edge of Eggleston bear L. on to B6282 (sign Middleton).

area. Some two miles to the west of Langdon Beck is Cow Green Reservoir, three miles long and covering 650 acres, approachable by the Pennine Way footpath which passes another impressive waterfall, the strangely named Cauldron Snout.
Langdon Beck Hotel.
T (0833) 22267. (C)

St John's Chapel
(Durham)

The war memorial stands on the triangular green of this Weardale village. The chapel from which the village takes its name was founded in 1465, but it was later replaced by the existing Georgian building.

Corbridge, the Roman fort.

The Route

Upon crossing the Durham/Northumberland border there are magnificent northward views of Allendale. From here the road undulates near to the River East Allen until reaching Allendale Town. The road now proceeds north eastward towards the Tyne Valley and the line of the Roman wall. Between Corbridge and Wallhouses is Aydon Castle (left), a good example of a fortified manor house, first built at the end of the 13c.

1 At Cowshill bear R. on A689 (sign Alston) and in 0.2m bear R. on to B6295 (sign Allendale). In 3.3m at Allenheads continue Str. on B6295 (sign Allendale) for 7.9m to Allendale. Here take B6303 (sign Hexham). In 2.5m at Catton keep Str. on B6295 (sign Hexham).

Allendale Town
(Northumberland)

First impression of this moorland town is of spacious greens and squares, separating the shops and houses of grey and golden stone into distinct areas. The broad main street is lined with trees and shrubs, making it hard to believe that Allendale was an important lead mining centre a century ago. St Cuthbert's Church, standing on a knoll above the river, has a sundial on the south wall giving a latitude which substantiates Allendale's claim that it occupies the precise centre of Britain. A New Year's Eve custom is the Guizers Parade. Men in colourful costumes parade around the market place carrying blazing tar barrels on their heads; these are thrown onto a bonfire at midnight to burn out the old year and welcome in the new.
The Riding. T (043 483) 237. (C)

Catton (Northumberland)

The little St Paul's Church was built at the beginning of this century as a daughter church to St Cuthbert's, Allendale.

Hexham
(Northumberland)

This charming country town lies in a green valley, south of the junction of the North and South Tyne. Pride of the town is Hexham Abbey, built in the twelfth and 13c above a crypt that dates from 674 AD. The central tower of the abbey rises more than 100 ft, climbed inside by the Midnight Stair which leads to the ringing chamber. In the chancel is a stone seat, St Wilfred's Chair, a relic of Saxon days and in medieval times used as a sanctuary seat where fugitives defied arrest. Across the market square from the abbey is

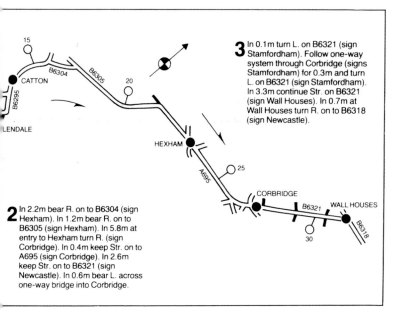

3 In 0.1m turn L. on B6321 (sign Stamfordham). Follow one-way system through Corbridge (signs Stamfordham) for 0.3m and turn L. on B6321 (sign Stamfordham). In 3.3m continue Str. on B6321 (sign Wall Houses). In 0.7m at Wall Houses turn R. on to B6318 (sign Newcastle).

2 In 2.2m bear R. on to B6304 (sign Hexham). In 1.2m bear R. on to B6305 (sign Hexham). In 5.8m at entry to Hexham turn R. (sign Corbridge). In 0.4m keep Str. on to A695 (sign Corbridge). In 2.6m keep Str. on to B6321 (sign Newcastle). In 0.6m bear L. across one-way bridge into Corbridge.

the lofty Moot Hall, built *circa* 1400 as the gatehouse of Hexham Castle, and the 14c manor house, first constructed as a prison and now housing a museum and tourist office.
Beaumont Hotel, Beaumont St. T (0434) 602331. (B)
County Hotel, Priestpopple, T (0434) 602030. (B)
Royal Hotel, Priestpopple, T (0434) 602270. (B)

Corbridge
(Northumberland)

Founded in Saxon times, the town stands on a hill overlooking the broad Tyne Valley. The Market Place is dominated by the 7c St Andrew's Church, much of it constructed from stone recovered from the neighbouring Roman fort, Corstopitum. On the south side of the churchyard is the

Vicar's Pele, one of two pele towers that remain here, in use as the tourist office with a stone staircase to an upper chamber. In the market place is the cast-iron Percy Cross with the Duke of Northumberland's emblem, a lion, on the base. The broad main street, lined with houses and bright gardens, once lay on the coaching route from Newcastle to Carlisle.
Angel Inn, Main St. T (043 471) 2119. (C)
Riverside, Main St. T (043 471) 2942. (C)

Wallhouses
(Northumberland)

Between Wallhouses and East Wallhouses can be seen a section of Hadrian's Wall (left), while to the south of the road (right) is a stretch of the defensive ditch that runs parallel to the wall, known as the vallum.

The Route

The minor road from Belsay to Wallington is narrow in places. After leaving Cambo the road touches the eastern fringe of the Northumberland National Park. Here, on both sides of the road, stretch the shimmering Rothley Lakes, now owned by the National Trust.

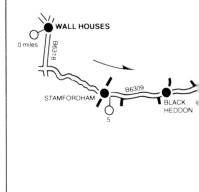

1 In 1.8m turn L. on to B6309 (sign Stamfordham). In 3.1m at entry to Stamfordham turn L. on B6? (signs Stamfordham and Belsay). In 0.2m keer Str. on B6309 (sign Belsay). In 2.7m at Black Heddon bear R. on B6309 (sign Belsay). In 1.9 turn R. on B6309 (sign Belsay).

Stamfordham
(Northumberland)

'Stamfordham welcomes you NOT LITTER' is the notice that greets the visitor. Most of this lovely spacious village lies to the left of the B road route, but is well worth visiting. There is a large sloping green, the focal point a stone-roofed market cross. At the far end of the green is the handsome Bay Horse Inn, facing the little terraced Swinburne Arms, named after the Swinburnes of Clapheaton Hall, among whose relatives was the poet Algernon Swinburne. Tucked away behind the Bay Horse Inn at the extremity of Stamfordham is the Church of St Mary, from where a path leads to the River Pont and the 'stoney ford' from which the village gets its name.

Belsay Hall and Gardens
(Northumberland)

Near the point where the B6309 joins the A696 is Belsay Hall. Home of the Middleton family for 600 years the hall stands in thirty acres of landscaped gardens, containing rhododendrons, heathers and rare trees and shrubs.

Bolam Lake
(Northumberland)

A raised walkway leads from the car park through the woods to the lake and the meadows and copses that surround it. The twenty-five-acre lake has a dam at the east end, a man-made ornamental creation formed from the marshy area of the Bolam estate.

Wallington
(Northumberland)

The car park for this National Trust-owned hall and gardens lies to the left of the road. Wallington was built in 1688, noted in particular for its exceptional plasterwork, fine porcelain, pictures and furniture, as well as an interesting collection of dolls' houses. A feature of the extensive grounds is the L-shaped walled garden, cultivated in what was once a hawthorn-filled dell.

Cambo (Northumberland)

This beautiful estate village owes much to the Blackett and Trevelyan families of neighbouring Wallington. First laid out as a model village in 1740,

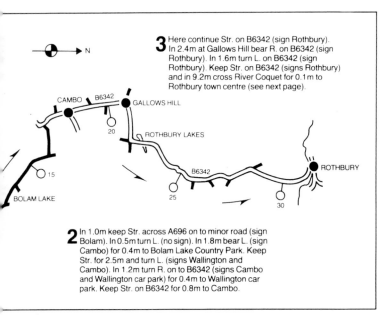

3 Here continue Str. on B6342 (sign Rothbury). In 2.4m at Gallows Hill bear R. on B6342 (sign Rothbury). In 1.6m turn L. on B6342 (sign Rothbury). Keep Str. on B6342 (signs Rothbury) and in 9.2m cross River Coquet for 0.1m to Rothbury town centre (see next page).

2 In 1.0m keep Str. across A696 on to minor road (sign Bolam). In 0.5m turn L. (no sign). In 1.8m bear L. (sign Cambo) for 0.4m to Bolam Lake Country Park. Keep Str. for 2.5m and turn L. (signs Wallington and Cambo). In 1.2m turn R. on to B6342 (signs Cambo and Wallington car park) for 0.4m to Wallington car park. Keep Str. on B6342 for 0.8m to Cambo.

Cambo stands to the right of the route in a secluded and commanding position, presenting panoramic views from the churchyard as well as from the post office and line of terraced cottages that adjoin it. The old schoolhouse was altered and enlarged as a reading room by Sir George Trevelyan in 1911; its most celebrated pupil was Lancelot 'Capability' Brown, the landscape gardener who was born at Kirkharlein in 1716.

Wallington Hall.

The Route

There are fine views of Rothbury where the road begins to descend from the hills above the town. After leaving Warkworth there is an excellent view of Alnmouth Bay.

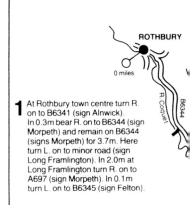

1 At Rothbury town centre turn R. on to B6341 (sign Alnwick). In 0.3m bear R. on to B6344 (sign Morpeth) and remain on B6344 (signs Morpeth) for 3.7m. Here turn L. on to minor road (sign Long Framlington). In 2.0m at Long Framlington turn R. on to A697 (sign Morpeth). In 0.1m turn L. on to B6345 (sign Felton).

2 In 2.4m bear R. on B6345 (sign Felton) for 1.8m to Felton. Here turn R. on to A1 (sign Morpeth) In 0.2m turn L. on to B6345 (sign Amble). In 1.7m bear L. on B6345 (signs Acklington and Broomhill). Keep Str. on B6345 (signs Broomhill) and in 3.5m at Broomhill turn L. on t A1068 (sign Alnwick).

Rothbury
(Northumberland)

The little town of grey stone houses, encircled by wooded heather-clad slopes, is known as the Capital of Coquetdale. The broad main street (through which the direct route does not pass) is flanked by a green adorned with sycamores. Upon leaving the town the road passes directly by the National Trust-owned Cragside House and Country Park. This Victorian house stands in a 900-acre park created by its owner, the first Lord Armstrong. Some thirty rooms are on view in the house, the first in the world to be lit by hydro-electricity. Lord Armstrong developed his own hydro-electric system in the grounds with man-made lakes and miles of underground piping. The park above the river embraces woodland paths as well as magnificent azalea and rhododendron shrubberies. *Coquet Vale*, Station Road. T (0669) 20305. (C)

Long Framlington
(Northumberland)

Two miles to the south of Long Framlington, by a loop in the river, is the 12c Brinkburn Priory, restored a century ago. It is probable that the priory was built by Walter de Framlington who was also responsible for Long Framlington church, built *circa* 1190, that stands among trees to the left of the road.

Felton (Northumberland)

The village of grey stone houses stands close to the busy A1 across which the route passes. Here two bridges span a lovely stretch of the River Coquet.

Amble (Northumberland)

This coastal village stands to the immediate south of Warkworth Harbour, at the mouth of the River Coquet. It is worth diverting from the main road for a good view of Coquet Island, a mile out to sea, where the lighthouse was at one time in the charge of Grace Darling's brother (see Bamburgh).

Warkworth
(Northumberland)

The village with its tree-lined street of 18c stone houses stands at a point where the River Coquet flows into the North Sea. Dominating the scene are the magnificent ruins of Warkworth Castle with its impressive gatehouse and tower.

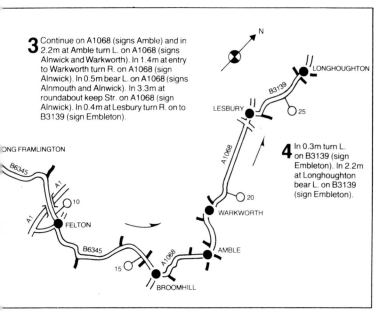

3 Continue on A1068 (signs Amble) and in 2.2m at Amble turn L. on A1068 (signs Alnwick and Warkworth). In 1.4m at entry to Warkworth turn R. on A1068 (sign Alnwick). In 0.5m bear L. on A1068 (signs Alnmouth and Alnwick). In 3.3m at roundabout keep Str. on A1068 (sign Alnwick). In 0.4m at Lesbury turn R. on to B3139 (sign Embleton).

4 In 0.3m turn L. on B3139 (sign Embleton). In 2.2m at Longhoughton bear L. on B3139 (sign Embleton).

Warkworth Castle, the keep.

259

The Route

Initially there is no direct coast road. Beyond Beadnell the road runs close to the sea, offering views of the Farne Islands. After turning inland from Bamburgh the road to Warren Mill flanks Budle Bay. The route does not pass directly through the busy town of Belford, veering northward with views of Holy Island.

2 In 0.6m continue Str. on B1340 (sign Bamburgh). In 1.8m at Seahouses bear R. and immediately L. on B1340 (signs Bamburgh) for 3.5m to Bamburgh. Here keep Str. on B1342 (signs Warren Mill and Belford). In 2.5m at Warren Mill turn L. on B1342 (sign Belford).

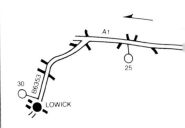

3 In 2.2m turn R. on to A1 (sign Berwick). In 5.4m turn L. on to B635 (sign Lowick). In 3.7m at Lowick continue Str. on B6353 (no sign).

Embleton
(Northumberland)

There is no direct coastal road between Longhoughton and Embleton. The link road to Craster, however, is signed to the right. Here whitewashed terraced cottages face the sea, encircling the tiny harbour. The area between the cottages and harbour is enriched by pretty sunken flower gardens. Close to the harbour, on the shore's edge, is the Jolly Fisherman Inn and the kippering sheds where the famous Craster kippers are produced. From the harbour walls is a good view of Dunstanburgh Castle, built in the early 14c and the largest of all the Northumbrian castle ruins. It can be reached by a footpath of about one mile. Within the parish church of Embleton are memorials to the Greys of Falloden, among them that to Edward Grey, Foreign Secretary from 1905 to 1916, who after failing to secure a settlement with Germany in 1914 is remembered by his words: 'The lamps are going out all over Europe; we shall not see them lit again in our lifetime.'

Beadnell
(Northumberland)

The route does not pass directly through the village; both village and harbour are signed (right). At Beadnell Harbour, in the care of the National Trust, are a group of 18c lime kilns within which fishermen store their gear. At the heart of Beadnell Village is the charming inn (below), its beer cellar standing at the base of a 15c pele tower.
Craster Arms. T (0665) 720075.
(C)

Seahouses
(Northumberland)

This fishing harbour adjoins North Sunderland, both of them popular summer resorts. On the coastline are the National Trust-owned St Aidan's and Shoreston Dunes, sixty acres of sand dunes with views of the Farne Islands. These islands, also National Trust, are reached by motor boat from

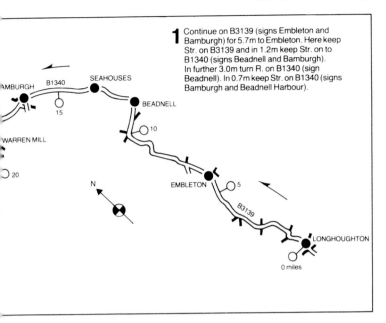

1 Continue on B3139 (signs Embleton and Bamburgh) for 5.7m to Embleton. Here keep Str. on B3139 and in 1.2m keep Str. on to B1340 (signs Beadnell and Bamburgh). In further 3.0m turn R. on B1340 (sign Beadnell). In 0.7m keep Str. on B1340 (signs Bamburgh and Beadnell Harbour).

Seahouses. At the northern extremity of the Farne Islands is the Longstone lighthouse, recalling Grace Darling, the lighthouse keeper's daughter (see Bamburgh). Today the islands provide a summer home for one of the largest and most varied colonies of seabirds found along the coasts of Britain.
Beach House, Sea Front. T (0665) 720337. (B)
St Aidans. T (0665) 720355. (C)

Bamburgh
(Northumberland)

Bamburgh Castle, an enormous building of red sandstone, stretches for almost a quarter of a mile along the cliffs. The castle began as a wooden structure in 547 AD. After enlargement to its present size in Norman times, it was bought in 1894 by Lord Armstrong who restored it extensively. All that now remain of the Norman buildings are the massive keep and the well, sunk from the basement through 150 feet of solid rock. The street beneath the castle, lined with Victorian houses, leads to the tree-shaded triangular village green. Memories of Grace Darling are everywhere. It was she who with her father, lighthouse keeper on Farne Islands, battled through the seas in 1838 to rescue survivors from a stricken steamer. Grace was born here in 1815. A plaque on an antique shop tells that this was the house where she died when only twenty-seven. Her canopied monument stands to the north of the windswept churchyard. Close to the church is the Grace Darling Museum, among the exhibits the lifeboat used by the Darlings.

Lord Crewe Arms. T (066 84) 243. (B)
Victoria Hotel. T (066 84) 431. (B)
Sunningdale. T (066 84) 334. (C)

The Route

Quiet country roads throughout. After Norham the route runs almost due south with fine views of the Cheviots as Wooler is approached.

Norham
(Northumberland)

> Day set on Norham's castle steep,
> And Tweed's fair river, broad and deep,
> And Cheviot's mountain lone;
> The battled towers, the donjon keep,
> The loop-holed walls where captives weep,
> In yellow lustre shone.

The rose-coloured ruins of Norham Castle stand proudly above the River Tweed, immortalized in the words of Sir Walter Scott's epic poem *Marmion*. This border stronghold was first built as a wooden structure in the early 12c. Some fifty years later, in 1160, Bishop Pudsey of Durham rebuilt the castle with its massive walls, gateway and keep, and today the impressive ruins stand among spacious lawns encircled by beech trees. The castle dominates the village of stone houses that cluster around a number of greens; among them a triangular green graced by a market cross surmounted by a weathervane in the form of a fish, a symbol of the importance of fishing here in the River Tweed. The Church of St Cuthbert was built in the same period as the castle. On the south wall of the church is a model of a coble (a flat-bottomed fishing boat) inscribed: 'God Bless the Tweed Fisheries'.
Mason's Arms. T (0377) 86644. (C)

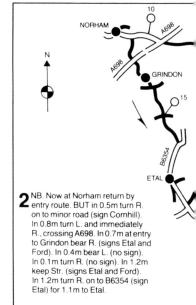

2 NB. Now at Norham return by entry route. BUT in 0.5m turn R. on to minor road (sign Cornhill). In 0.8m turn L. and immediately R., crossing A698. In 0.7m at entry to Grindon bear R. (signs Etal and Ford). In 0.4m bear L. (no sign). In 0.1m turn R. (no sign). In 1.2m keep Str. (signs Etal and Ford). In 1.2m turn R. on to B6354 (sign Etal) for 1.1m to Etal.

Grindon
(Northumberland)

The little village comprises a line of pleasant slate-roofed grey stone bungalows. Good views from here of the Cheviots.

Etal (Northumberland)

This estate village lies on either side of a single road that runs above and parallel with an entrancing section of the River Till. At one end of the street is the manor house; at the other are the ruins of Etal Castle. The castle, one of several local strongholds against the Scots, fell to James IV of Scotland in 1496, seventeen years before his defeat at Flodden. The impressive ruins stand on a mound from which there is a spectacular view of a salmon leap. The village houses that link the castle and manor are graced by lawns, well-tended flower gardens and trim hedges. Thatched buildings are

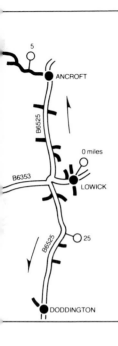

1 In 0.7m turn R. on to B6525 (sign Berwick). In 3.6m at Ancroft turn L. on to minor road (sign Norham). In 1.2m bear R. (sign Norham). In 1.4m keep Str. (sign Norham). In 2.7m keep Str. across A698 (sign Norham) for 1.7m to Norham.

3 Here continue Str. on B6354 (no sign). In 1.4m keep Str. on to B6353 (sign Ford) for 0.5m to Ford. In Ford continue Str. on B6353 (no sign). In 4.0m turn R. on to B6525 (sign Wooler). Keep Str. on B6525 (signs Wooler) for 4.8m to Doddington.

Thatched cottages and castle ruins in Etal.

263

uncommon in Northumberland, so it is of interest that several here are thatched, among them the whitewashed Bull Inn.

Ford (Northumberland)

The model village was built by Louisa, Marchioness of Waterford, in memory of her husband who was killed in a riding accident in 1859. The broad main street is lined by stone houses, lawns and colourful gardens. The Lady Waterford Hall, once the school and now open to the public, has walls covered by watercolours painted by Lady Waterford. The paintings depict biblical scenes in which the villagers served as models, the artist paying her child sitters sixpence and a 'gilly piece' (bread and jelly). A glimpse of Ford Castle can be seen from the main road above the village. This former defensive stronghold was rebuilt in the 18 and 19c and is now in use as an adult education centre. There are magnificent views from the lofty churchyard of St Michael's Church. Here the panorama includes the distant Cheviot Hills and Flodden Field, scene of the memorable battle in 1513 when James IV and his army were defeated by the English. In a field close to the church are the remains of a pele tower, once the priest's fortified house.

Doddington
(Northumberland)

Stone cottages nestle in an arbour of trees. There is an ancient spring, Dod Well, surmounted by a stone cross 20 ft high from the base of which water trickles. Beyond the village (left) is Dod Law, a bracken-covered hill with the remains of a prehistoric fort on the summit.

1 At Doddington continue on B6525 (no sign). In 2.6m at entry to Wooler turn L. on to A697 (sign Morpeth). In 0.2m turn L. on to B6348 (sign Chatton). In 4.7m at entry to Chatton turn R. on minor road (sign Chillingham). In 1.4m at Chillingham continue for further 0.3m to Chillingham Castle.

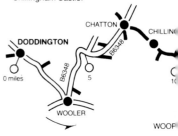

2 Here keep Str. (sign Alnwick). Continue Str. on minor road (signs Alnwick) and in 3.8m turn R. (sign Wooperton). In 1.9m bear L. (no sign). In 0.2m turn L. on to A697 (sign Morpeth). Continue on A697 (signs Morpeth) and in 4.3m turn L. on to minor road (sign Bolton).

The Route

Apart from two short stretches on A roads, the route runs through pleasant wooded countryside.

Wooler (Northumberland)

The little market town stands on the slopes of a hill above Wooler Water. It lies to the extreme north east of the Cheviot Hills and the Northumberland National Park, an unspoilt area of moorland and lush grassland that spreads southwards from the Cheviots in the direction of the historic Roman Wall. On a grassy mound in the centre of the town are the remains of a medieval castle.
Tankerville Arms. T (0668) 81581. (B)
Ryecroft. T (0668) 81459. (C)

Chatton
(Northumberland)

The road veers southward at the edge of the village. Chatton comprises grey stone houses and

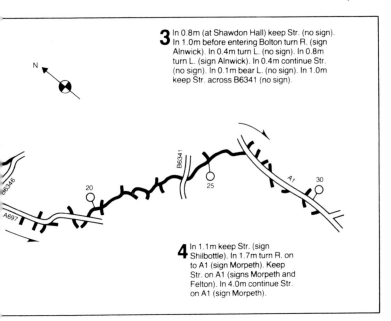

3 In 0.8m (at Shawdon Hall) keep Str. (no sign). In 1.0m before entering Bolton turn R. (sign Alnwick). In 0.4m turn L. (no sign). In 0.8m turn L. (sign Alnwick). In 0.4m continue Str. (no sign). In 0.1m bear L. (no sign). In 1.0m keep Str. across B6341 (no sign).

4 In 1.1m keep Str. (sign Shilbottle). In 1.7m turn R. on to A1 (sign Morpeth). Keep Str. on A1 (signs Morpeth and Felton). In 4.0m continue Str. on A1 (sign Morpeth).

well-tended gardens, a picturesque scene that sprawls along the west bank of the River Till.

Chillingham
(Northumberland)

The church and a handful of cottages nestle outside the walls of Chillingham Castle, ancestral home of the Earl of Tankerville. The Wild White Cattle of Chillingham, descendants of prehistoric wild oxen, roam the castle's 300-acre wooded park. The herd is maintained by a voluntary organization, the Chillingham Wild Cattle Association, which employs a warden, from whom tickets can be bought for a conducted tour of the park. The eighth Earl of Tankerville has written a pamphlet describing the cattle and their history. They have crescent-shaped horns and are the only white cattle that breed true to type, never having produced a coloured calf. The herd graze through the idyllic surroundings, sheltering in copses

when the weather is bad and overlooked to the north east by a steep conical hill known as Ros Castle (owned by the National Trust), the site of an Iron Age fort. Before leaving Chillingham it is worth looking in on the little Church of St Peter; here is the splendid tomb of Sir Ralph Grey (died 1443), engraved on all sides with a variety of saintly figures.

Wooperton
(Northumberland)

The moorland expanse to the immediate south of this main road village was once the scene of a great battle of the Wars of the Roses. Here in 1464 the Yorkists defeated the Lancastrians under Sir Ralph Percy. Shortly after leaving the village is a walled enclosure (right). The two huge rocks within the enclosure are said to define the length of the leap of Sir Ralph's charger at the height of the Battle of Hedgeley Moor. Nearby is a 10 ft cross marking the spot where Sir Ralph was slain.

The Route

Unspoilt country roads to Whalton and beyond. From here the southward route has been planned to avoid Newcastle's industrial belt as much as possible. The county of Tyne and Wear is entered briefly at Throckley, some five miles to the west of Newcastle, before veering westward and re-entering Northumberland at Heddon.

1 In 3.6m turn R. on to minor road (sign Longhorsley). In 2.8m at Longhorsley keep Str. across A697 (sign Netherwitton). In 0.1m keep Str. (no sign). In 1.1m bear L. (sign Netherwitton) In 0.1m bear R. (sign Netherwitton). Keep Str. (signs Netherwitton) and in 3.5m at T-junction turn R. (sign Rothbury) for 0.3m to Netherwitton.

2 Here turn L. (sign Longwitton). In 1.2m turn L. (sign Meldon). In 0.7m keep Str. (sign Meldon). In 0.9m keep Str. (sign Meldon). In 1.3m turn L. and immediately bear R. (signs Meldon and Whalton). In 0.9m bear R. (sign Meldon) for 0.2m to Meldon.

Longhorsley
(Northumberland)

The prettiest part of this little main road village is seen after crossing the A697. Here, on the left, are two greens, facing which an old pele tower has been converted into a private residence. The parish church is not passed – it lies to the left of the Longhorsley to Morpeth road at the edge of the village.

Netherwitton
(Northumberland)

The approach to this charming village is by way of much wooded countryside. Before reaching the village (right) is stately Netherwitton Hall where Cromwell's troops camped for a night in 1651. The hall lies in Newpark Wood, site of two of the largest oaks in the country – the King's Oak, thirteen feet round, and the Queen's Oak, eleven feet round. On entry to Netherwitton some picturesque terraced cottages adjoin a huge derelict mill (right), scheduled for conversion to dwellings. The River Font glides through the village, and in one of the gardens are the remains of the village cross.

Meldon (Northumberland)

The little church of St John the Baptist stands on a wooded knoll (left). By the font in the church is the effigy of Sir William Fenwick (died 1652), whose grandson was executed in 1716 for supporting the Jacobite cause. Apart from the church there are only a few houses, scattered on the hillside with views of the Cheviots.

Whalton
(Northumberland)

A spacious village where the bulk of the houses are of brown stone and lie along a broad tree-lined street. Many buildings date from the 17c and 18c, a group on the north side of the street being raised on a grassy terrace. At one end of the street is the manor house (not open to the public), a combination of four small houses designed by Sir Edwin Lutyens. Whalton has the unique distinction of preserving the Bale Festival every 4 July. Bale is from

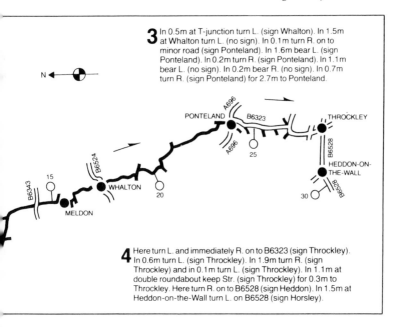

3 In 0.5m at T-junction turn L. (sign Whalton). In 1.5m at Whalton turn L. (no sign). In 0.1m turn R. on to minor road (sign Ponteland). In 1.6m bear L. (sign Ponteland). In 0.2m turn R. (sign Ponteland). In 1.1m bear L. (no sign). In 0.2m bear R. (no sign). In 0.7m turn R. (sign Ponteland) for 2.7m to Ponteland.

4 Here turn L. and immediately R. on to B6323 (sign Throckley). In 0.6m turn L. (sign Throckley). In 1.9m turn R. (sign Throckley) and in 0.1m turn L. (sign Throckley). In 1.1m at double roundabout keep Str. (sign Throckley) for 0.3m to Throckley. Here turn R. on to B6528 (sign Heddon). In 1.5m at Heddon-on-the-Wall turn L. on B6528 (sign Horsley).

Stone houses in Whalton, with the Manor House behind.

267

an Anglo-Saxon word meaning 'great fire', and the bonfire lit on the village green on Bale Night stems from the custom of driving cattle through the fire to rid them of vermin. Today the bonfire ceremony is an occasion when folk-dancing takes place accompanied by the music of Northumbrian pipers.
Beresford Arms. T. (067 075) 225. No accommodation.

Ponteland
(Northumberland)

The route avoids most of this busy main road village, crossing the River Pont by way of a handsome bridge.

Throckley (Tyne and Wear)

The busy village lies on the Newcastle to Carlisle road, part of it built over the foundations of the Roman Wall. This was the boyhood home of George Stephenson (1781–1848), father of the railways, who at the age of fourteen worked in a local colliery for a shilling a day.

Heddon-on-the-Wall
(Northumberland)

The route by-passes the heart of this hilltop village. Here can be seen an outstanding section of the remains of Hadrian's Wall, some 300 yards long, a few feet high and 10 ft broad.

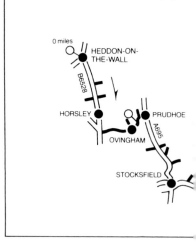

1 Continue Str. on B6528 for 2.7m to Horsley. He keep Str. (no sign). In 0.5m keep Str. (sign Ovingham). In 0.1m turn L. on to minor road (si Ovingham). In 1.4m at Ovingham turn R. (sign Prudhoe) and continue to follow signs Prudhoe through village. Cross river (one-way bridge) a continue for 0.5m to Prudhoe Castle (left).

The Route

From Stocksfield to Ebchester the route follows the old Roman road. Rather an untidy urbanized stretch between Ebchester and Lanchester, particularly around Leadgate. Thereafter the road leaves the urban belt, heading for the Wolsingham Moors.

Horsley (Northumberland)

Neat cottages are strung out along a windswept ridge. From the garden at the back of the Crown and Anchor Inn there are good views of the Tyne Valley and Horsley Wood.

Ovingham
(Northumberland)

The village stands on the north bank of the Tyne, inclining down to the narrow one-way iron bridge that links Ovingham with Prudhoe. Ovingham's church with its Saxon tower stands above the Old Vicarage, a 17c stone building

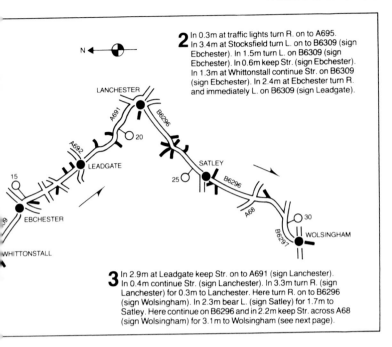

2 In 0.3m at traffic lights turn R. on to A695. In 3.4m at Stocksfield turn L. on to B6309 (sign Ebchester). In 1.5m turn L. on B6309 (sign Ebchester). In 0.6m keep Str. (sign Ebchester). In 1.3m at Whittonstall continue Str. on B6309 (sign Ebchester). In 2.4m at Ebchester turn R. and immediately L. on B6309 (sign Leadgate).

3 In 2.9m at Leadgate keep Str. on to A691 (sign Lanchester). In 0.4m continue Str. (sign Lanchester). In 3.3m turn R. (sign Lanchester) for 0.3m to Lanchester. Here turn R. on to B6296 (sign Wolsingham). In 2.3m bear L. (sign Satley) for 1.7m to Satley. Here continue on B6296 and in 2.2m keep Str. across A68 (sign Wolsingham) for 3.1m to Wolsingham (see next page).

that lies on the site of a cell of Hexham Priory. The most famous pupil of the church school that was started in the Old Vicarage was Thomas Bewick (1753–1828), renowned for his wood engravings of animal life and in particular his *British Birds*. In the chancel of the church is a marble inscription: 'Thomas Bewick, whose genius restored the art of engraving on wood. The most perfect specimens of his skill are shown in his history of quadrupeds and British birds'.

Prudhoe (Northumberland)

First sight of this sprawling town of the River Tyne is its ancient castle, sited on the hillside above the river and defended by a moat and deep ravine. The castle was built in Norman times, covering an area of some three acres.

Ebchester (Durham)

The River Derwent defines the boundary between Northumberland and Durham.

Here a glorious ten acres of woodland on the river bank are now the property of the National Trust. Much of the village stands on the site of what was once a Roman fort, an area that covered four acres and was known as Vindomara. The Norman church stands at the southern corner of Vindomara, partly built from the stones of the fort. In the churchyard a marble cross marks the grave of Robert Surtees (1803–64), creator of Jorrocks, the sporting grocer who features in *Jorrocks and Jollities* (published 1838).

Lanchester (Durham)

Focal point of this one-time Roman encampment is the huge triangular green. By the green is the magnificent church, its 15c tower containing stones from the Roman fort. A further Roman connection is seen in the south porch, a Roman altar discovered at Hurbuck Farm to the north of the village.

The Route

Quiet country roads throughout. From Bedburn to Woodland the road passes along the eastern fringe of Hamsterley Forest.

1 At Wolsingham turn R. (no sign). In 0.1m turn L. to minor road (sign Hamsterley Forest). In 1.9[m] bear R. (sign Hamsterley Forest). Keep Str. fo[r] 2.8m to Bedburn and here continue Str. (no si[gn]). In 0.1m turn R. (sign Woodland). In 0.7m turn [L.] (sign Woodland). In 0.4m keep Str. (no sign). In 2.9m keep Str. (no sign) for 0.8m to Woodla[nd]

Wolsingham (Durham)

The road descends sharply to this delightful Weardale village. On the hill before the final descent, the Redgate Cross is approached by a flight of stone steps with an inscription that reads: 'Near this spot Venerable John Duckett was arrested. He was afterwards tried at Sunderland and taken to Tyburn where he was executed for being a priest 7 September 1644.'

Bedburn (Durham)

The Bedburn Beck flows beneath the bridge in a woodland glen, the setting for this peaceful hamlet that lies at the north eastern tip of the Hamsterley Forest. Entry to the forest is signed here (right). Hamsterley Forest occupies 5,500 acres, and the Forestry Commission welcomes the public into some 1,000 acres in the heart of the forest. There are picnic areas on the banks of a stream, a four and a half mile forest drive, forest walks and a visitor centre.

Woodland (Durham)

The village straggles along a ridge at the edge of Hamsterley Forest. From the heights are good views of Teesdale and Deepdale.

Derwent Reservoir near Ebchester, on the Durham/Northumberland border.

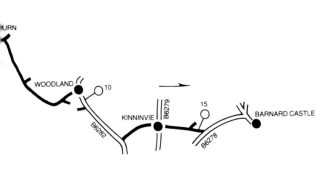

2 Here turn R. on to B6282 (no sign). In 0.8m bear L. (sign Middleton). In 1.7m turn L. on to minor road (signs Kinninvie and Barnard Castle). In 1.5m at Kinninvie keep Str. on minor road (sign Barnard Castle). In 1.5m turn L. on to B6278 (sign Barnard Castle) for 2.0m to Barnard Castle.

FOR ADMINISTRATIVE purposes Sussex is now divided into two counties, East and West Sussex, having their headquarters at Lewes and
Chichester respectively. The county is rich in woodland, root and
cereal crops are grown, and cattle and sheep reared. Sandwiched as
it is between London and many popular seaside resorts, inevitably a
number of major roads link the capital with the coast, running almost
parallel to each other through the county. This 120-mile route has
been planned to avoid these busy roads, meandering through picturesque Sussex villages by way of the many country roads which still
exist.

At Flimwell the route crosses into Kent for a glimpse of the western
extremes of the county of orchards, hop fields and market gardens
that has been described as the Garden of England. It would be difficult
to single out the most beautiful of the many villages encountered in
both counties. In Sussex those that impress include Alfriston, Wilmington, Mayfield and Burwash. And although the route only passes
through a fragment of Kent it seems unlikely that the county would
claim many fairer villages than Goudhurst, Brenchley and Matfield.

At least three notable ruins lie along the route, Wilmington and
Michelham Priories and Bayham Abbey, all three sited in areas of
exceptional beauty.

The route runs by, or close to, two National Trust gardens, Sprivers
and Nymans, as well as the Forestry Commission's Bedgebury
Pinetum. Among the many pleasant village pubs passed are two in
particular to note – the Wheelwright's Inn at Matfield and the George
Inn at Frant.

Brighton (East Sussex)

George, Prince of Wales, later Prince Regent and George IV, came to
Brighton some 200 years ago. From that time the seaside resort's
popularity was assured.

Brighton's most famous building, of course, is the Royal Pavilion
with its domes, spires and minarets in the eastern style; its banqueting
room, set out and equipped as if for a royal banquet; and its huge
apartments, furnished lavishly, the whole designed by John Nash to
cater for George's extravagant tastes. It was here that George lived,
both as Regent and King, entertaining Mrs Fitzherbert whom he
married secretly and whose room is among those on view. Brighton
Pavilion, acquired by the town in 1850, was the fore-runner of the
many attractive Regency squares and terraces that sprang up here
and at neighbouring Hove in the early 19c.

Another of Brighton's heritages is The Lanes, narrow footpaths
between bow-fronted shops, pubs and restaurants that criss-cross a
wide area between the Pavilion and the sea front, a delightful maze
in which it is a pleasure to lose oneself.

ROUTE 16

♠ Park/garden
⌂ Historic house
👁 View
⛪ Church/cathedral
🏰 Ruin (abbeys, priorys)

N

0   5 km
0   5 miles

Matfield   Brenchley
Royal   Horsmonden
Tunbridge Wells
East Grinstead   Groombridge   Bayham   Hook
Weir   Abbey   Green   Goudhurst
Wood Res.   Hartfield
Turners Hill   Withyham   Frant   Bells Yew   Bedgebury
West Hoathley   *ASHDOWN*   Green   Pinetum
Handcross   *FOREST*   *Bewl*   Flimwell
Staplefield   *Bridge Res.*   Ticehurst
Haywards Heath   Mayfield   Burwash
Ansty   Batemans
Burgess Hill   Heathfield ♠
Ditchling   Horam
Hassocks
Ditchling Beacon
Michelham   Bexhill
Priory
⌂   Wilmington 🏰
Brighton   Rottingdean   Alfriston ⌂
Newhaven   Seaford 👁

273

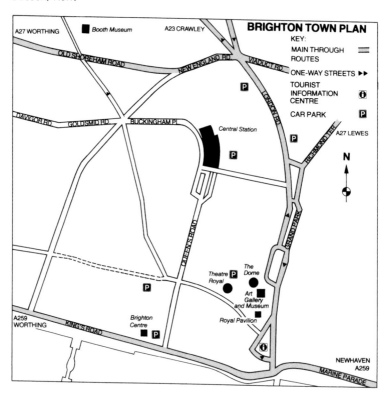

Among many other buildings and places of interest is Preston Manor, rich in history, furniture and paintings; Brighton Art Gallery and Museum with displays of art nouveau; the Booth Museum of Natural History, containing the finest collection of British birds in the country; the Dolphinarium, seating 1,000 with shows every day of the year; and the Theatre Royal, a famous Regency playhouse where many plays are staged before their London premier.

Among Brighton's modern buildings is the Brighton Centre, on the sea front and equipped for dancing, concerts, ice spectaculars and many varieties of sport.

Brighton has hundreds of hotels and boarding houses. It is stressed, once again, that this guide does not pretend to take the place of a hotel guide, only occasionally referring to hotels and pubs of particular interest. The three hotels shown below vary in price range.

Old Ship Hotel, Kings Road. T (0273) 29001. (A)
Beach Hotel, 3 Regency Square. T (0273) 23776. (B)
St Catherine's Lodge, Kingsway. T (0273) 26302. (B)
Tourist Office, 54 Old Steine. T (0273) 23755.

The Seven Sisters can be seen from the Downs above Seaford.

The Route

Brighton covers a wide area in all directions. It is necessary to take the busy coast road for the first thirteen miles. Thereafter enchanting country road. Good views of the Cuckmere Valley from the hills above Alfriston.

Rottingdean (E. Sussex)

The famous girls' school of Roedean towers above the road (left) before reaching Rottingdean. Celebrated former inhabitants of this small seaside village, once a haven for smugglers, include Rudyard Kipling who wrote *Kim* here, and the painter and designer Sir Edward Burne-Jones.

Newhaven (E. Sussex)

Best known as the channel port that provides a regular ferry service to Dieppe.

Seaford (E. Sussex)

This busy seaside town straggles along some three miles of front. There are two golf courses. One is laid out on the coast, the other occupies high ground on the Sussex Downs with glorious seaward views.

Alfriston (E. Sussex)

The narrow High Street is flanked by many old buildings, some timber-framed with overhanging storeys. Among several ancient inns is the Market Cross Inn, close to the medieval village cross and once the haunt of the Alfriston smugglers; the 15c Star Inn adorned with quaint carvings including a figurehead of a ship in the shape of a lion; and the timbered George Inn. At the end of the high street is the spacious village green, one corner

2 In 3.3m at Alfriston branch R. (no sign), passing car park on right. In 0.3m turn R. on minor road (sign Litlington). In 0.1m turn R. (sign Litlington). In 0.7m turn L. (sign Wilmington). Remain on minor road for 1.5m to Long Man and Priory car park (left). In 0.4m keep Str. across A27 on minor road (sign Abbot's Wood).

1 In Brighton take A259 (sign Newhaven) for 3.8m to Rottingdean. Here keep Str. on A259 (signs Newhaven) and in 5.9m at Newhaven remain on A259 (signs All Directions and Seaford). In 3.8m at Seaford stay on A259, passing railway station and war memorial (left). In further 0.5m turn L. on to minor road (sign Alfriston).

displaying a mine washed up in the River Cuckmere in 1943. Dominating the green is the 14c St Andrew's Church, a building of such size that it has become known as the Cathedral of the South Downs. Alongside the church and close to the river is the thatched oak-framed Clergy House. Designed for a community of parish priests, it was built in about 1350 with separate apartments and a large communal dining and recreation hall. In 1896 it was bought by the National Trust for £10 and restored; it is one of the few clergy houses to have survived. After leaving Alfriston on the minor road a signpost directs the footpath to Lullington Church (half a mile to the left), one of the smallest parish churches in England.

Star Inn. T (0323)   870495. (A)
Deans Place. T (0323) 870248. (A)

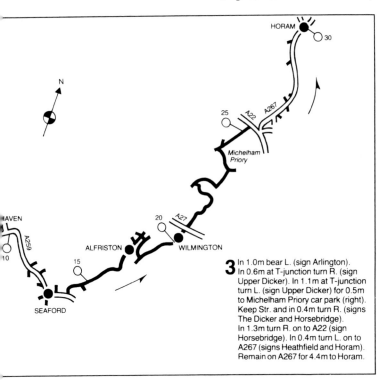

3 In 1.0m bear L. (sign Arlington).
In 0.6m at T-junction turn R. (sign
Upper Dicker). In 1.1m at T-junction
turn L. (sign Upper Dicker) for 0.5m
to Michelham Priory car park (right).
Keep Str. and in 0.4m turn R. (signs
The Dicker and Horsebridge).
In 1.3m turn R. on to A22 (sign
Horsebridge). In 0.4m turn L. on to
A267 (signs Heathfield and Horam).
Remain on A267 for 4.4m to Horam.

Wilmington (E. Sussex)

The car park for the Wilmington
Long Man and the Priory is on the
left of the road before entry to this
picturesque small village. The car
park offers an excellent view of the
Long Man, cut in chalk on the
green turf of Windover Hill. The
tall figure, more than 200 ft high,
stands with staves on either side.
In an 18c manuscript the staves
are described as being a rake and
a scythe, suggesting an Iron Age
agricultural fertility figure. Some
believe that the Long Man dates
from Roman times, others attribute
the figure to the monks of
Wilmington. Although the Long
Man's age is disputed, it does
appear that he represents the
largest image of a man in Europe.
Between the car park and the
Church of St Mary and St Peter are
the ruins of the medieval priory,
begun in the 12c. Church and
priory were once linked by a
covered cloistered walk. Beneath
the walls of the priory is a stone
seat presented in memory of the
writer John Jeffrey Farnol
(1878–1952) by his widow. An
inscription from one of his best
known novels, *The Broad
Highway* reads: 'The Truth of Life
is Good Works which abide
everlastingly.'

Michelham Priory (E. Sussex)

The car park is found to the right
of the road. The one-time
Augustinian priory is approached
by way of a moat and Norman
gateway, situated by a lake and a
glorious stretch of the River
Cuckmere. There is also a working
water-mill, restored in 1972, that
grinds wheat into flour by water
power.

277

The Route

Apart from a dull stretch in the immediate vicinity of Heathfield, quiet country roads, many wooded. The route to Burwash was chosen in order to join the one-way system past Bateman's before reaching the village.

Heathfield (E. Sussex)

There is nothing remarkable about this small town. To the north east of the closely packed buildings is Heathfield Park, and just visible in the trees above the high walls of the park is a folly, Gibraltar Park, built in honour of a former governor of Gibraltar.

Mayfield (E. Sussex)

The main street lies along a ridge above the Weald of Sussex, medieval buildings on all sides. There is a fascinating village sign, depicting a maid among children at play, perhaps accounting for the village name, meaning 'Maid's Field' (old English Maghfeld). Among prominent buildings are Walnut Tree House and the Tudor inn, Middle House Hotel. Across the road from the inn is the 15c gatehouse to a school, the site of a former palace of the Archbishops of Canterbury.
Middle House Hotel.
T (0435) 872146. (B)

Burwash (E. Sussex)

The car park to Bateman's lies to the right of the minor one-way road before entering the village. This Jacobean house with mullioned windows and brick chimney stacks, now the property of the National Trust, was bought in 1902 by Rudyard Kipling who lived here until his death thirty-four years later. Here can be seen the study where the author wrote,

1 At Horam bear R. on to B2203 (sign Heathfield). In 3.0m at Heathfield turn R. on to A265 (sign Burwash). In 0.2m turn L. on to minor road (sign Mayfield). In 3.6m turn R. on to A267 for 0.7m to Mayfield. Here at end of high street keep Str. on to minor road (sign Witherenden). In 0.2m bear R. (sign Witherenden).

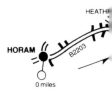

2 In 1.0m turn L. (sign Witherenden). In 1.8m kee (sign Witherenden). In 0.9m turn R. (sign Burw Common). In 0.3m turn R. (no sign). In 0.2m tu (no sign). In 2.0m turn R. on to A265 (sign Heathfield). In 0.1m turn L. on to minor road (si Batemans) for 0.4m to Batemans car park (righ

describing the local countryside in *Puck of Pook's Hill*. The little Dudwell stream flows through the gardens, laid out with yew hedges, lawns and rose gardens by Mrs Kipling. The village of Burwash lies a mile away, the long high street lined with brick and timber-framed shops and cottages. In the south aisle of the parish church is a bronze tablet in memory of John Kipling, son of the writer, who was killed in action at Loos in 1915 aged eighteen years and six weeks.

Ticehurst (E. Sussex)

A spacious village with some notable weather-boarded houses and cottages. A feature of the 13c parish church is the medieval glass Doom window, showing souls of the damned being dragged down to hell by the devil.

Bedgebury Pinetum (Kent)

The car park lies to the right of the road. The Pinetum is part of the 3,000-acre Bedgebury Forest, run

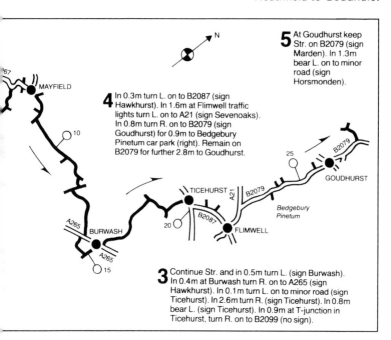

5 At Goudhurst keep Str. on B2079 (sign Marden). In 1.3m bear L. on to minor road (sign Horsmonden).

4 In 0.3m turn L. on to B2087 (sign Hawkhurst). In 1.6m at Flimwell traffic lights turn L. on to A21 (sign Sevenoaks). In 0.8m turn R. on to B2079 (sign Goudhurst) for 0.9m to Bedgebury Pinetum car park (right). Remain on B2079 for further 2.8m to Goudhurst.

3 Continue Str. and in 0.5m turn L. (sign Burwash). In 0.4m at Burwash turn R. on to A265 (sign Hawkhurst). In 0.1m turn L. on to minor road (sign Ticehurst). In 2.6m turn R. (sign Ticehurst). In 0.8m bear L. (sign Ticehurst). In 0.9m at T-junction in Ticehurst, turn R. on to B2099 (no sign).

by the Forestry Commission. Here broad avenues and occasional narrow paths lead between varieties of trees and shrubs, among them pines, birch, cypress, oak and rhododendrons.

Goudhurst (Kent)

The direct route does not pass through the centre of the village. If time allows it is worth parking the car near the duck pond to stroll up the narrow main street – just a little perilous as both street and pavements are extremely narrow. At the top of the street of tiled, weather-boarded and half-timbered houses is the square-towered Church of St Mary, once the scene of a fierce battle between the militia and the dreaded gang of Hawkhurst smugglers. By the church, approached by a flight of steps, is the timbered 14c Star and Eagle Hotel, believed at one time to have been connected to the church by an underground passage.
Star and Eagle Hotel.
T (0580) 211512. (A)

The village of Goudhurst.

The Route

The road from Horsmonden to Brenchley is narrow. The same applies to that between the A21 and Hook Green. From Hartfield to West Hoathly the road runs from east to west through the Ashdown Forest.

Horsmonden (Kent)

The village surrounds a handsome square green. Horsmonden's best known son was John Browne, gunsmith for Charles I, the local hammer pond providing power for what was once a thriving industry. The inn on the green is named, appropriately, the Gun Inn. Signed half a mile away (not on the direct route) is Sprivers, a National Trust-owned 18c house set in 108 acres of parkland, orchards and woods.

Brenchley (Kent)

'Brenchley bells, across the meadows, will always be music, whereas Big Ben's booming is an automatic episode in the calendar.' Thus wrote Siegfried Sassoon, poet, First World War hero and subsequent pacifist, who spent his boyhood years here. Brenchley is the 'Butley' of his semi-autobiographical novel *Memoirs of a Fox Hunting Man* (1928). In the novel he vividly describes hunting and playing cricket on local village grounds. Focal point of Brenchley is the small green and oak tree. Among impressive buildings is the Old Palace, now a restored half-timbered line of separate dwellings that was once the home of the lords of the manor. The path to the sandstone church is fringed by yew trees, shaped like sentinels and said to be 400 years old.

4 Here continue Str. on B2110 (sign Hartfield). In 1.7m at Hartfield branch R. on B2110 (sign Forest Row). In 1.9m turn L. on to minor road (sign Wych Cross). In 0.2m keep Str. (sign Wych Cross). Keep Str. for 1.7m to Ashdown Forest Information Centre (right). In 0.9m keep Str. across A22 (sign West Hoathley). In 1.3m turn L. (sign West Hoathley). In 2.3m at edge of West Hoathley continue Str. (sign Turners Hill).

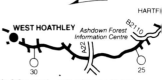

HARTF

WEST HOATHLEY Ashdown Forest Information Centre

30   25

3 In 0.9m turn L. on to minor road (sign Groombridge). In 1.1m turn R. and immediately L. across A26 on minor road (sign Groombridge). In 2.8m at edge of Groombridge turn L. on to B2110 (sign Withyham). In 0.4m bear R. on B2110 (sign Withyham) and keep Str. on B2110 (signs Withyham) for 2.2m to Withyham.

Matfield (Kent)

The village lies round an enormous green. At one end of the green is a duck pond and the picturesque weather-boarded Wheelwright's Arms. First built as a farmhouse in 1602, the building later served as a grocer's store and ale house. It was not until 1850, when bought by a wheelwright, that it took on the role of village inn. An interesting notice gives the names of all the owners since 1602, among them the landlady who hanged herself in 1920, her ghost allegedly now walking the premises *Wheelwright's Arms.*
T. (089 272) 2129. (C)

Hook Green (Kent)

Half a mile past the village (signed to the right) are the ruins of Bayham Abbey, beautifully situated in the wooded valley of the River Teise. The abbey was begun in the 13c by monks from Premontre in north east France. Among surviving remains are the church, cloisters and gatehouse.

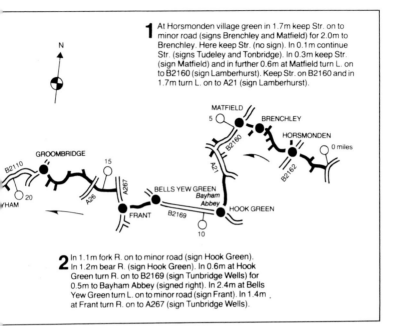

1 At Horsmonden village green in 1.7m keep Str. on to minor road (signs Brenchley and Matfield) for 2.0m to Brenchley. Here keep Str. (no sign). In 0.1m continue Str. (signs Tudeley and Tonbridge). In 0.3m keep Str. (sign Matfield) and in further 0.6m at Matfield turn L. on to B2160 (sign Lamberhurst). Keep Str. on B2160 and in 1.7m turn L. on to A21 (sign Lamberhurst).

2 In 1.1m fork R. on to minor road (sign Hook Green). In 1.2m bear R. (sign Hook Green). In 0.6m at Hook Green turn R. on to B2169 (sign Tunbridge Wells) for 0.5m to Bayham Abbey (signed right). In 2.4m at Bells Yew Green turn L. on to minor road (sign Frant). In 1.4m at Frant turn R. on to A267 (sign Tunbridge Wells).

Frant (E. Sussex)

The village lies round two greens, one large enough to accommodate a cricket ground. The most charming aspect is seen along the road from the smaller green to the church, passing the village school, with a quotation from *Proverbs*, and a pleasant inn.

The Dorset Arms in Withyham.

Brenchley, one of the prettiest villages in Kent.

Withyham (E. Sussex)

In a hollow is the Dorset Arms, built in 1790. Some 200 yards past the inn a narrow road leads to the church on a hill (left). There is a breath-taking view from here across a lake and miles of undulating meadows and woods. Within the church is the Sackville Chapel with memorials to the Earls of Dorset who once lived here. Among the most interesting is the monument by Cibber, depicting the figure of Thomas Sackville who died when only thirteen. His hand rests on a skull, indicating that he died before his parents.

Hartfield (E. Sussex)

Stands to the edge of Ashdown Forest, famous in that it was once the home of A. A. Milne and Christopher Robin. There is a Pooh Bridge Walk, starting from Gill's Lap car park (along the B2026 to the south of Hartfield). The walk, five miles in length, leads past the 'enchanted place' and Pooh Bridge where Pooh and Christopher Robin would often go to play Pooh Sticks.

Ashdown Forest Information Centre (E. Sussex)

The information centre is found by the car park (left) in a modernized barn. The centre lies in the heart of the forest, an area of heathland and woodland with clumps of Scots pine, oak, birch and beech trees. Some 250 fallow deer roam the forest, once the hunting ground of kings.

West Hoathly (E. Sussex)

The route avoids the centre of the village. Here a one-time medieval vicarage, the Priest's House, has a museum of interest.

3 Keep Str. on B2116 (no signs) and in 1.7m at Ditchling crossroads turn R. (no sign). In 0.1m turn L. on to minor road (sign Ditchling Beacon). In 0.9m keep Str. (sign Ditchling Beacon) for 0.9m to Ditchling Beacon. Here keep Str. (no sign). In 2.4m turn L. and immediately R. on minor road (no sign). Keep Str. (signs Town Centre) and in 3.4m turn L. for 1.0m to Brighton Town Centre.

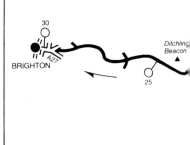

The Route

The minor road between the B2114 and Ansty is very narrow. The road on both sides of the Beacon is steep and narrow but well surfaced.

Turners Hill (W. Sussex)

Sir Aston Webb (1849–1930), British architect best known for his design of the new front of Buckingham Palace, built the tower of the church here as a memorial to the fallen of the village. It stands proudly, a landmark between the Surrey border to the north and the Ardingly Reservoir to the south.

Handcross (W. Sussex)

At a point where the route joins the B2114 at Handcross are Nymans Gardens (left). The gardens were bequeathed to the National Trust in 1954 by L. C. R.

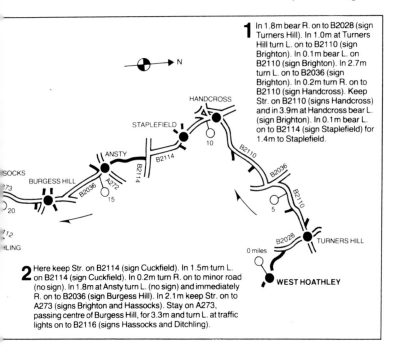

1 In 1.8m bear R. on to B2028 (sign Turners Hill). In 1.0m at Turners Hill turn L. on to B2110 (sign Brighton). In 0.1m bear L. on B2110 (sign Brighton). In 2.7m turn L. on to B2036 (sign Brighton). In 0.2m turn R. on to B2110 (sign Handcross). Keep Str. on B2110 (signs Handcross) and in 3.9m at Handcross bear L. (sign Brighton). In 0.1m bear L. on to B2114 (sign Staplefield) for 1.4m to Staplefield.

2 Here keep Str. on B2114 (sign Cuckfield). In 1.5m turn L. on B2114 (sign Cuckfield). In 0.2m turn R. on to minor road (no sign). In 1.8m at Ansty turn L. (no sign) and immediately R. on to B2036 (sign Burgess Hill). In 2.1m keep Str. on to A273 (signs Brighton and Hassocks). Stay on A273, passing centre of Burgess Hill, for 3.3m and turn L. at traffic lights on to B2116 (signs Hassocks and Ditchling).

Messel, son of Ludwig Messel who began planting here in 1885. Over three quarters of a century father and son assembled rare trees, shrubs and plants from all over the world. Features include the Pinetum with a garden temple; a rose garden; an Italian archway leading to a walled garden; and designated walks, one devoted to spring flowers, the other to summer perennials, converging at an Italian fountain.

Downs amid hundreds of acres of gorse-clad common. Small lanes twist past lovely timbered cottages. A half-timbered house by the church gate was the home of Anne of Cleves, Henry VIII's discarded queen. To the south west of the village, on Ditchling Common, the two windmills are known as Jack and Jill. A little to the east is Plumpton with a popular National Hunt race course.

Staplefield (W. Sussex)

Here a handful of houses and the pub are scattered close to a huge green, the war memorial at one corner. The church is tucked away to the left of the road.

Ditchling (E. Sussex)

Burgess Hill, an ever-growing conglomeration of buildings, appears to have little to commend it. The reverse applies to Ditchling. It lies beneath the lofty Sussex

Ditchling Beacon (E. Sussex)

This superb viewpoint (813 ft), site of one of many beacons lit to give warning of the arrival of the Spanish Armada in 1588, is part of four acres of hillside owned by the National Trust. Traces of the ramparts and ditch of a prehistoric fort remain.

Overleaf: a breathtaking view from Ditchling Beacon.

17   Dumfries and Galloway

THIS AREA of some 2,500 square miles, the extreme south west of Scotland, embraces the former counties of Dumfries, Kirkcudbright, Wigtown and South Ayrshire. The climate is the most temperate in Scotland. More than half the region comprises mountainous moorland and forest, including the famous Glentrool Forest, now part of the Galloway Forest Park.

In this area of natural beauty between the mountains and the sea, lochs abound. Some, like Clatteringshaws, Lock Ryan, and Lock Ken are clearly visible from the highway; many others crouch beneath the Merrick and Rhinns of Kells mountain ranges in spectacular forest

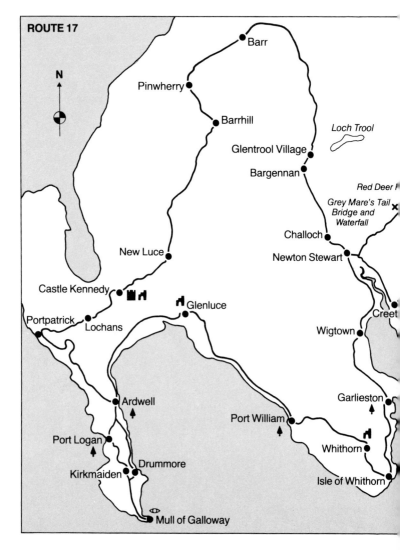

scenery, only approachable by remote footpaths.

Thus the greater part of Galloway has a scanty population, the more populated areas being confined to the coastline. Stranraer and Cairnryan, to the west, provide the ferry link with Ireland, a two and a half hour journey. To the south Galloway is girdled by the sea from the Mull of Galloway, stretching eastward to Luce Bay, Wigtown Bay and the Solway Firth.

Tourists from all over the world flock to Scotland; but the physical geography of Dumfries and Galloway is the reason, perhaps, that this lovely area escapes the attention of many of them.

When considering my tour of Scotland for *Through Britain on Country Roads* I sought the advice of many Scottish friends. Opinions were divided. I decided, ultimately, that for this book I would explore the better trodden areas to the north and west, mindful that many people felt that Galloway, relatively unknown, should have featured in the guide. I am grateful, in particular, to my friend Dr Bill Thom,

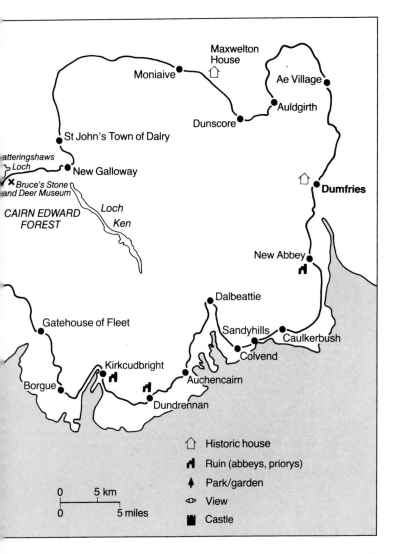

Mull of Galloway, the most southerly point in Scotland.

born and bred in Galloway, for the advice and encouragement that persuaded me to include the beautiful region of Dumfries and Galloway in *The New Through Britain on Country Roads*.

Here historic associations abound. The wild terrain in the heart of Galloway proved ideal for the type of guerrilla warfare that Robert the Bruce waged against the English. At Loch Trool and nearby Bruce won several encounters against superior forces, battles which were the prelude to his famous victory at Bannockburn in 1314.

Two and a half centuries later Mary Queen of Scots is known to have made at least three excursions through Galloway, visiting a number of places along the described route. In 1563 Mary and her courtiers progressed from Glenluce Abbey and Whithorn Priory to Dumfries. Two years later she visited Sweetheart Abbey. On her final fateful journey to exile and ultimate execution she spent the night of 15 May 1568 at Dundrennan Abbey, her last resting place upon Scottish soil.

A hundred years later, at the Restoration, Charles II revived episcopacy in Scotland. Ministers faithful to presbyterianism were evicted, preaching in conventicles in remote hills and caves, ignoring the Act of 1670 declaring this treasonable. Today, scattered throughout Galloway, are memorials and tombs of hundreds of persecuted Covenanter martyrs.

Final mention is of Robert Burns (1759–96), Scotland's beloved dialect poet, who in 1788 began farming at Ellisland near Dumfries, before moving to the town of Dumfries. Burns stayed and wrote at several of the inns mentioned in the guide, among them the Globe Inn, Dumfries, which might almost be described as a Robert Burns museum.

Dumfries

The busy market town, standing beside a broad sweep of the River Nith, makes an ideal starting point for touring Galloway. There is much to see. Fortunately the many places of interest lie in a compact area, meaning that a stroll through Dumfries is a rewarding experience.

The tourist office lies on the east bank of the Nith. After crossing the Devorguila foot-bridge one arrives at Old Bridge House, the town's oldest house built in 1660, which now serves as a museum featuring kitchens of 1850 and 1900, an early dentist's surgery, and Victorian childhood. Close at hand is the Robert Burns Centre, opened in 1986 in an 18c water-mill, telling the story of the poet's last years in the town; and the Dumfries Museum, located in a windmill tower with a camera obscura where on the table-top screen can be seen a panorama of Dumfries and many miles around.

After re-crossing the river by St Michael's Bridge one arrives at Burns House, the small sandstone cottage where Robert Burns spent the last years of his life. The tomb where he was laid to rest in 1796 can be seen at nearby St Michael's Church.

Approaching the centre of the town other places of interest include the Midsteeple, built in 1707 as a court house and prison; the Robert

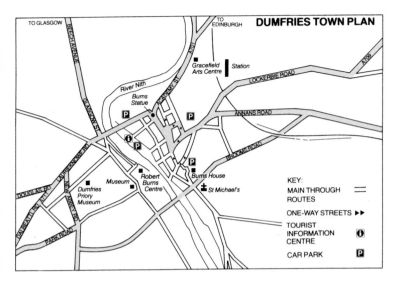

Burns statue; and the Globe Inn, tucked away in an alley off the high street, almost a museum in itself, for many of the rooms in this three storey building have been preserved much as they were when Burns stayed here.

Nearby, at a modern supermarket, is a reminder of an event that took place centuries before Robert Burns's time. Here a plaque tells that this was the spot where Robert Bruce slew the 'Red' Comyn, representative of the English crown, at first expressing a doubt that he had finished him off properly. His friend Sir Roger Kirkpatrick, coming to his aid, plunged his sword repeatedly into the body with the words: 'I mak siccar'. (I'll make sure).

Finally, by the side of the indicated route before leaving the town, is Dumfries Academy where former pupils include J. M. Barrie of *Peter Pan* fame.

Station Hotel, 49 Lovers Walk. T (0387) 54316. (B)
Skyline, 123 Irish St. T (0387) 62416. (C)
Swan at Kingholm, Kingholm Quay. T (0387) 53756. (C)
Tourist Office, Whitesands. T (0387) 53862.

The Route

Initially through the Ae Forest. By the edge of the forest is Loch Ettrick (right), cupped beneath hillocks of forest on every side. The only section where traffic is encountered is the three-mile stretch of the A76, this road running parallel to the River Nith. Thereafter the road follows Cairn Water with the Dalmacallan Forest and Bogsie Hill (1,417 ft) to the south.

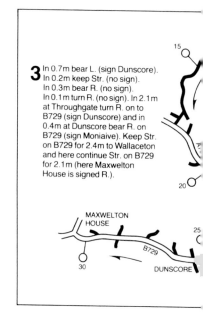

3 In 0.7m bear L. (sign Dunscore). In 0.2m keep Str. (no sign). In 0.3m bear R. (no sign). In 0.1m turn R. (no sign). In 2.1m at Throughgate turn R. on to B729 (sign Dunscore) and in 0.4m at Dunscore bear R. on B729 (sign Moniaive). Keep Str. on B729 for 2.4m to Wallaceton and here continue Str. on B729 for 2.1m (here Maxwelton House is signed R.).

Ae (Dumfriesshire)

A huddle of foresters' cottages make up this village with a name which must surely be the shortest anywhere. The Forest of Ae covers twenty-five square miles, producing more than 20,000 tonnes of timber annually. A little past the village the forest car park is signed (right). From here coloured markers indicate walks of four miles, two and a half miles, and one and a half miles through a forest of Sitka spruce, Scots pine, Norway spruce, and Japanese larch. Sitka spruce predominates. It was first introduced to Great Britain in 1831, taking its name from an Alaskan seaport. Wildlife in the forest includes roe and fallow deer, foxes and hares.

Dunscore (Dumfriesshire)

The remote village, birthplace of Jane Haining who won fame for her work in Poland during World War Two, lies in the heart of an agricultural area. Five miles to the east of Dunscore, on the banks of the River Nith, is Ellisland Farm where Robert Burns farmed from 1788 to 1791. On 14 March 1788 Burns wrote to a Miss Chalmers

concerning his new occupation: 'I begin at Whit-Sunday to build a house, drive lime etc, and Heaven be my help! for it will take a strong effort to bring my mind into the routine of business.' Despite his labours Burns found the time to compose *Tam O'Shanter* and *Auld Lang Syne* while at Ellisland. Today the farm and small museum are open to the public on specified occasions.

Maxwelton House (Dumfriesshire)

The house is approached by a drive to the right of the road before reaching Moniaive. Maxwelton was formerly the home of the Laurie family, its most famous member being Annie Laurie, whose lover William Douglas of Fingland wrote the first version of the ballad:

Maxwelton braes are bonny
They're a-clad ower wi' dew,
Where I and Annie Laurie
Made up the promise true.

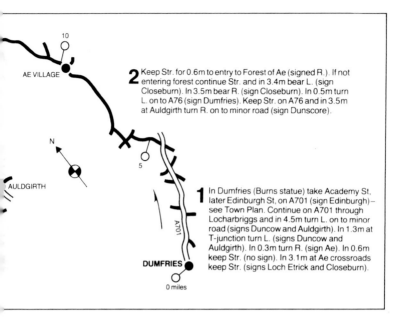

2 Keep Str. for 0.6m to entry to Forest of Ae (signed R.). If not entering forest continue Str. and in 3.4m bear L. (sign Closeburn). In 3.5m bear R. (sign Closeburn). In 0.5m turn L. on to A76 (sign Dumfries). Keep Str. on A76 and in 3.5m at Auldgirth turn R. on to minor road (sign Dunscore).

1 In Dumfries (Burns statue) take Academy St, later Edinburgh St, on A701 (sign Edinburgh) – see Town Plan. Continue on A701 through Locharbriggs and in 4.5m turn L. on to minor road (signs Duncow and Auldgirth). In 1.3m at T-junction turn L. (signs Duncow and Auldgirth). In 0.3m turn R. (sign Ae). In 0.6m keep Str. (no sign). In 3.1m at Ae crossroads keep Str. (signs Loch Etrick and Closeburn).

The house has now been restored to look much as it was when Annie was born here. It is open on occasions during the summer months, together with a delightful little chapel that lies by the lake in the grounds of Maxwelton.

The old bridge and weir over the River Nith, Dumfries.

The Route

Some two miles after leaving Moniaive is a house named Craigdarroch (left), the one-time married home of Annie Laurie of Maxwelton House. From here the forest gives way to moorland and Fingland Hill (left). Later good views of Kendoon, Carsfad and Earlstoun Lochs (right). From New Galloway the Queen's Way, once travelled by Mary Queen of Scots, runs westward to Clatteringshaws Loch.

Moniaive (Dumfriesshire)

Colour-washed cottages line the narrow street towards the small square and market cross. The Craigdarroch and Dalwhat Waters meet here to form the Cairn Water, and by the river is the George Inn, dating from 1638 and claiming to be among Scotland's oldest inns.

Dalry (Kirkcudbrightshire)

The route is by way of a street that slopes sharply down to another old inn, the Clachan Inn, at the heart of the village. At the top of this street stands, unobtrusively, a small stone block where according to legend John the Baptist once rested. The village, in fact, is often known as St John's Town of Dalry. It was once also known as Old Galloway, a reminder that Dalry is older than neighbouring New Galloway. *Lochinvar Hotel.* T (064 43) 210. (C)

New Galloway

This one-time royal burgh is reached by crossing the Water of Ken where, by the river bank, a standing stone is believed to date from the Bronze Age. Sandwiched between handsome lochs to the north and south, with vast hilly forests to the west, New Galloway makes an ideal centre for

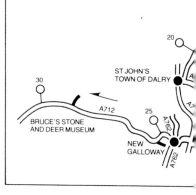

2 In 2.5m turn R. on to A712 (sign New Galloway). In 0.7m at entry to New Galloway bear R. on A712 (sign Newton Stewart). Continue on A712 and in 5.7m (signed R.) is car park for Bruce's Stone and Deer Museum.

exploration in every direction. Kenmuir Castle, a mile to the south, was once the seat of the Gordon of Lochinvar. *Leamington Hotel*, Main St. T (064 42) 327. (C)

Bruce's Stone (Kirkcudbrightshire)

The car park for the Stone is signed (right), immediately before the Queen's Way reaches the edge of Clatteringshaws Loch. A footpath leads from the park to the Stone, the place where Robert the Bruce is said to have rested after defeating an English army in 1307, one of several battles that culminated in his famous victory at Bannockburn seven years later. From the car park a lane leads in the opposite direction to the Stone, towards the Deer Museum where a Forestry Commission display relates to wildlife, ecology and forest management. Close to the museum is an interesting replica of a Romano-British homestead, the original discovered when the loch was drained.

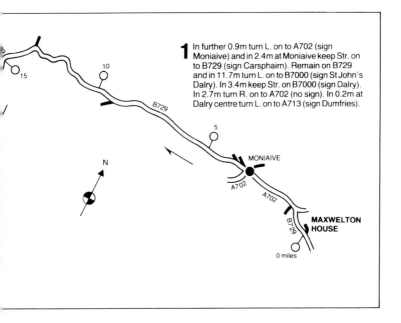

1 In further 0.9m turn L. on to A702 (sign Moniaive) and in 2.4m at Moniaive keep Str. on to B729 (sign Carsphairn). Remain on B729 and in 11.7m turn L. on to B7000 (sign St John's Dalry). In 3.4m keep Str. on B7000 (sign Dalry). In 2.7m turn R. on to A702 (no sign). In 0.2m at Dalry centre turn L. on to A713 (sign Dumfries).

Loch Trool and the Bruce Stone.

The Route

The road to Newton Stewart is known as the Queen's Way. Although designated as an A road it is quiet with little traffic. This scenic route is named after Mary Queen of Scots who is known to have travelled here during her visits to south west Scotland in 1563 and 1568. The minor road northward from Bargrennan is narrow but well surfaced and traffic-free. Many spectacular views.

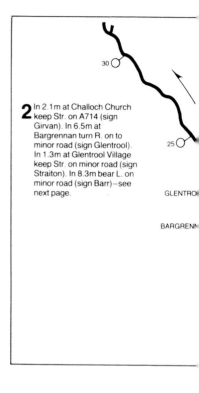

2 In 2.1m at Challoch Church keep Str. on A714 (sign Girvan). In 6.5m at Bargrennan turn R. on to minor road (sign Glentrool). In 1.3m at Glentrool Village keep Str. on minor road (sign Straiton). In 8.3m bear L. on minor road (sign Barr)—see next page.

30

25

GLENTROO

BARGRENN

Red Deer Range
(Kirkcudbrightshire)

The Galloway Forest Park is the only sanctuary for red deer outside the Highlands of Scotland. The car park for the Red Deer Range lies by the road (right). Two nearby observation hides allow close inspection of these elusive animals in their natural surroundings. A little further west is the Wild Goat Park where a herd of feral goats can also be seen.

Grey Mare's Tail Bridge
(Kirkcudbrightshire)

Close to the bridge the Grey Mare's Tail waterfall cascades down some 60 ft – not to be confused with the larger fall of the same name near Moffat. Towering above the bridge is Murray's Monument, erected in memory of Alexander Murray (1775–1813), the shepherd's son who due to short-sightedness was unable to follow in his father's occupation. This led to boyhood study of such brilliance that Murray eventually became Professor of Oriental Languages at Edinburgh University. The remains of Murray's simple home, Dunkitterick Cottage, are signed off the Queen's Way (left) and approached by a well-preserved footpath.

Newton Stewart
(Wigtownshire)

The busy market town is approached by a fine recessed bridge across the River Cree. Here, at the foot of the town, is a monument to Randolph, ninth Earl of Galloway, the focal point of a

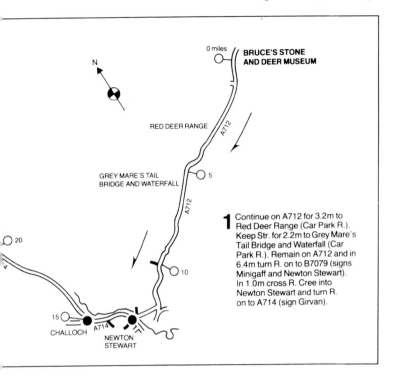

1 Continue on A712 for 3.2m to
Red Deer Range (Car Park R.).
Keep Str. for 2.2m to Grey Mare's
Tail Bridge and Waterfall (Car
Park R.). Remain on A712 and in
6.4m turn R. on to B7079 (signs
Minigaff and Newton Stewart).
In 1.0m cross R. Cree into
Newton Stewart and turn R.
on to A714 (sign Girvan).

well-tended rose garden.
Surrounded by wooded hills,
Newton Stewart takes its name
from William Stewart who
obtained a charter for the town as
a burgh from Charles II. There is
an excellent folk museum.
Bruce Hotel, Queen St.
T (0671) 2294. (B)
Creebridge House, Minnigaff.
T (0671) 2121. (C)

Challoch (Wigtownshire)

The churchyard (left) lies in a
peaceful setting, overlooked to
the north by the Glentrool Forest
and the lofty Rhinns of Kells. Here
are memorials to the eleventh and
twelfth Earls of Galloway, and to
the son of the twelfth Earl, killed
in action while serving with the

Black Watch during World War
One.

Glentrool Village
(Kirkcudbrightshire)

The village lies at the south west
corner of the Glentrool Forest, now
incorporated into the Galloway
Forest Park. From here it is
possible to divert three miles
eastward in order to visit lovely
Loch Trool, with superb views
from the Bruce Memorial to the
east of the loch. Some two and a
half miles past the village the
Palgowan Open Farm is signed
(right). Items of interest to be seen
at this 7,000-acre hill farm include
hill cattle, blackface sheep
handling, working sheepdogs,
and walking-stick making.

The Route

*The road, initially, is narrow
with passing places,
running northward
towards Ayrshire through
the lovely Minnoch Valley.
There is a good eastward
view of the Merrick Range
with the highest hill in south
Scotland (2,770 ft). Further
north the road runs past
Carrick Forest before
following the course of the
River Stinchar to Barr and
onwards. At Pinwherry, a
village of no particular note,
a serious choice had to be
made. From this village a
popular route to Stranraer
would be by way of the
A765 and A77, along the
shore of Loch Ryan. Local
people, however, describe
the A77 as being
overpopulated with heavy
vehicles on their way to the
busy seaport. Thus the
chosen route, southward,
was by way of Barrhill and
the traffic-free minor road
towards New Luce. At first
this road runs through
forest, later giving way to
open moorland with
numerous cattle grids before
reaching the Cross Water of
Luce.*

2 At Barr T-junction turn R. (no sign). In 0.1m turn L. on to B734 (sign Pinwherry). In 3.8m fork L. (no sign). In 1.8m turn L. on to A714 (sign Barrhill). In further 1.8m continue Str. (sign Barrhill). In 0.4m at Pinwherry turn R. on A714 (sign Barrhill).

3 In 4.0m at entry to Barrhill turn R. on to minor road (sign New Luce). Continue for 13.6m on minor road to New Luce—see next page.

30

● **NEW LUCE**

Barr (Ayrshire)

The road has trespassed,
momentarily, into Ayrshire and this
picturesque village. Two pleasant
inns, the King's Arms and the Jolly
Shepherd, lie side by side together
with neat whitewashed stone
cottages across from the bubbling
River Stinchar. The gate to the
churchyard is in memory of a
vicar's son who died when only
fifteen. Immaculate bowls and
putting greens stand near the
church, built in 1878 to replace
the former building which had
become uninhabitable. By the
gate a notice proclaims: 'This
church is always open' – a
welcome truth because regrettably
many of the churches in south
west Scotland remain securely
bolted. More than a century ago
Barr was the site of Kirkdandie
Fair, an ancient annual gathering
when smugglers from the coast as
well as local shepherds made
merry. According to the church
history this one-time happy
occasion had by the mid-19th
century become 'little more than a
common booze-up' and by the
1860s the fair had ceased to exist.

Castle Kennedy, Wigtownshire.

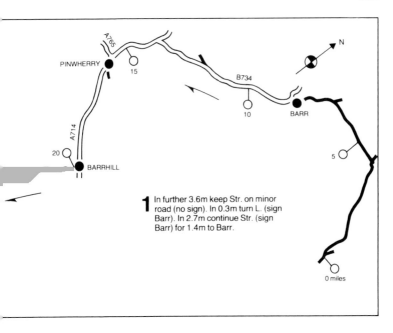

PINWHERRY

A765

15

B734

N

10

BARR

A714

20

BARRHILL

5

1 In further 3.6m keep Str. on minor road (no sign). In 0.3m turn L. (sign Barr). In 2.7m continue Str. (sign Barr) for 1.4m to Barr.

0 miles

The Route

From Castle Kennedy the road avoids busy Stranraer, running south westward directly towards Portpatrick. Later it follows the coast, narrow with marked passing places, before crossing the mainland by minor roads to the coast of Luce Bay.

3 Continue Str. on A77 for 5.2m to T-junction at Portpatrick harbour (from here car park is signed L.). From this point re-trace route and in 0.4m turn R. on to minor road (sign Caravan site).

4 In 1.9m keep Str. (no sign). In 0.6m bear slightly left (no sign). In 1.0m turn R. on to B7042 (sign Sandhead). In 0.7m turn R. on to minor road (sign Ardwell). In 3.1m at crossroads continue Str. (sign Drummore). In 0.7m keep Str. (no sign).

5 In 1.2m keep Str. (no sign). In 0.8m at crossroads keep Str. (sign Ardwell). In 0.8m continue Str. (no sign) for 1.0m to Ardwell.

New Luce (Wigtownshire)

The small village is known as the Capital of the Moors district of Galloway, lying at a point where the Main Water of Luce and the Cross Water of Luce join. Among many of the Covenanter preachers was Alexander Peden (1626–86), described as a peppery prophet, who suffered with many others when the post-Restoration troubles arose. Peden preached his final fiery sermon here in 1662 before his ejection and retreat to hiding places in neighbouring dens and caves.

Castle Kennedy
(Wigtownshire)

The village is named after the castle, the seat of the Kennedy family until it was destroyed by fire in 1716. The ruins stand on a peninsula between the White and Black Lochs, close to the modern Lochinch Castle, home of the Earl of Stair and built to replace the old castle. Castle Kennedy Gardens in their magnificent setting are open to the public during the summer months. The gardens are famous for their displays of rhododendrons (thirty-five different species by the Round Pond), azaleas and magnolias.

Portpatrick
(Wigtownshire)

The picturesque fishing harbour lies only some twenty-one miles from Northern Ireland, the shortest crossing place but no longer in use as a channel port due to the gales that rage round it. Fittingly this historic harbour has a lifeboat exhibition. Legend has it that Saint Patrick 'strode here from Ireland', giving the village its name.
Fernhill. T (077 681) 220. (B)
Portpatrick. T (077 681) 333. (B)
Mount Stewart. T (077 681) 291. (C)

Ardwell (Wigtownshire)

The village straggles along a rugged coastline. The Ardwell Gardens, open to the public, specialize in spring flowers, flowering shrubs, and rock plants. From the large pond there are good views of Luce Bay.

Portpatrick, the fishing harbour.

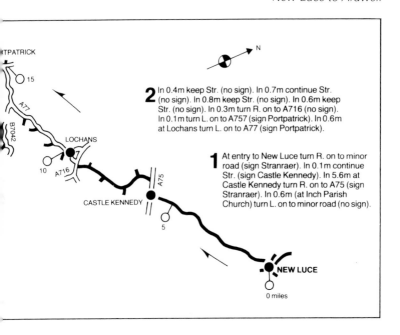

2 In 0.4m keep Str. (no sign). In 0.7m continue Str. (no sign). In 0.8m keep Str. (no sign). In 0.6m keep Str. (no sign). In 0.3m turn R. on to A716 (no sign). In 0.1m turn L. on to A757 (sign Portpatrick). In 0.6m at Lochans turn L. on to A77 (sign Portpatrick).

1 At entry to New Luce turn R. on to minor road (sign Stranraer). In 0.1m continue Str. (sign Castle Kennedy). In 5.6m at Castle Kennedy turn R. on to A75 (sign Stranraer). In 0.6m (at Inch Parish Church) turn L. on to minor road (no sign).

The Route

The southerly route from Ardwell to Port Logan and the Mull of Galloway is by quiet inland minor roads with few distinguishing features. The return northward journey from Drummore to Ardwell clings to the coast with good views of Luce Bay. Some three and a half miles past Ardwell (signed left) a minor road of little more than a mile leads to the Kirkmadrine Stones, after those at Whithorn the earliest Christian memorials in Scotland.

3 From Mull of Galloway re-trace route by minor road and B7041. In 4.2m turn R. on B7041 (sign Drummore). In 0.7m bear L. on B7041 (sign Drummore). In 0.1m at Drummore turn R. on to A716 (sign Stranraer). In further 0.1m turn L. on A716 (sign Stranraer).

4 In 5.0m bear R. on A716 (sign Stranraer). In 3.7m after returning to Ardwell continue Str. (no sign).

10
C

MULL OF GALLOWAY

Port Logan
(Wigtownshire)

Before reaching Port Logan the Logan Botanic Gardens are signed (right). This famous walled garden, administered by the Royal Botanic Garden, Edinburgh, contains many exotic plants, among them palms and tree ferns. There are woodland and water gardens. Refreshments are available at an excellent salad bar. A mile further along the route is the small fishing village of Port Logan, a trim line of cottages sheltering beneath the raised road that runs along Port Logan Bay. There is a pleasant picnic area by the harbour. To the north of the bay is an interesting tidal fish-pond where tame fish, responding to a bell, are fed by hand. In the late summer of 1987 the pond was closed. Perhaps it will be open to the public once more in 1988.

Mull of Galloway
(Wigtownshire)

The drive here, by way of a narrow minor road, means retracing the route. The visit to this narrow isthmus, however, is rewarding. The lighthouse marks the most southerly point in Scotland, with magnificent views of the Isle of Man and Ireland less than twenty-five miles away. The Mull is noted both for its bird life and for a number of prehistoric fortifications.

Drummore
(Wigtownshire)

The village street leads down gradually to a sheltered sandy bay, overlooked by the Ship Inn and a short line of whitewashed terraced cottages. The little harbour to the edge of the bay is the headquarters of the Kirkmaiden Boating Club.

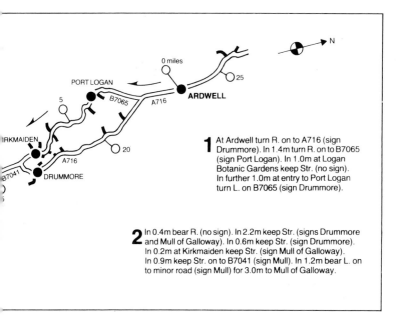

1 At Ardwell turn R. on to A716 (sign Drummore). In 1.4m turn R. on to B7065 (sign Port Logan). In 1.0m at Logan Botanic Gardens keep Str. (no sign). In further 1.0m at entry to Port Logan turn L. on B7065 (sign Drummore).

2 In 0.4m bear R. (no sign). In 2.2m keep Str. (signs Drummore and Mull of Galloway). In 0.6m keep Str. (sign Drummore). In 0.2m at Kirkmaiden keep Str. (sign Mull of Galloway). In 0.9m keep Str. on to B7041 (sign Mull). In 1.2m bear L. on to minor road (sign Mull) for 3.0m to Mull of Galloway.

Port Logan Bay.

The Route

The road from Glenluce to Port William follows the coast for much of the way. Very little traffic despite the A road designation. Near the sea's edge the tiny Chapel Finian (left) was a pilgrims' landing place chapel named after a Celtic saint. From Port William the road turns inland, passing the White Loch of Myrton and Monreith House that lie sheltered in the trees to the south.

Glenluce (Wigtownshire)

The abbey is signed (left) before entering the village. The magnificent ruins, in a secluded setting of great beauty, stand on the bank of the Water of Luce. Glenluce Abbey was founded before 1192 by Roland of Galloway, Constable of Scotland, as a Cistercian monastery of at least thirteen monks and an abbot.

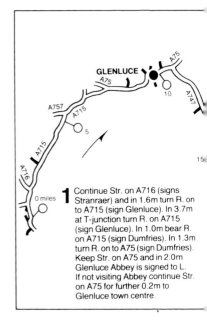

1 Continue Str. on A716 (signs Stranraer) and in 1.6m turn R. on to A715 (sign Glenluce). In 3.7m at T-junction turn R. on A715 (sign Glenluce). In 1.0m bear R. on A715 (sign Dumfries). In 1.3m turn R. on to A75 (sign Dumfries). Keep Str. on A75 and in 2.0m Glenluce Abbey is signed to L. If not visiting Abbey continue Str. on A75 for further 0.2m to Glenluce town centre.

Best preserved of the ruins is the chapter house, lit by two fine Gothic windows and entered by an ornamented doorway. From this doorway there is a distant view of the Castle of Park, a tall

The ruins of Glenluce Abbey.

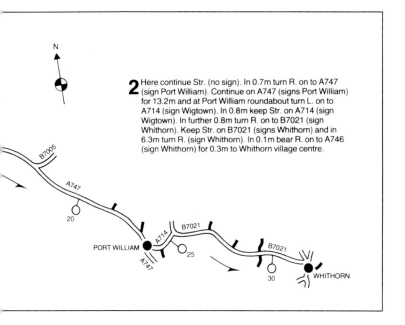

2 Here continue Str. (no sign). In 0.7m turn R. on to A747 (sign Port William). Continue on A747 (signs Port William) for 13.2m and at Port William roundabout turn L. on to A714 (sign Wigtown). In 0.8m keep Str. on A714 (sign Wigtown). In further 0.8m turn R. on to B7021 (sign Whithorn). Keep Str. on B7021 (signs Whithorn) and in 6.3m turn R. (sign Whithorn). In 0.1m bear R. on to A746 (sign Whithorn) for 0.3m to Whithorn village centre.

fortified mansion outlined on the hillside. The Castle of Park, or Park Hay, was built in 1590 by the son of Thomas Hay who was constituted abbot here in 1560. Thomas Hay will have been the host to Mary Queen of Scots and her nobles who spent the night of 9 August 1563 here when on their way to Whithorn. Among many interesting features of the small abbey museum are the medieval water pipes, some of them still in situ near the area which once served as the monks' refectory and kitchen. After returning to the main road the route runs directly through Glenluce, a quiet village to the immediate east of the Water of Luce which flows past St Helena Island into Luce Bay. *King's Arms*, 31 Main Street. T (058 13) 219. (C)

Port William
(Wigtownshire)

Overlooking the square by this small seaport of Luce Bay are the Maxwell Gardens and War Memorial – fine views from the top of the gardens. The gardens are named after Sir William Maxwell who founded the harbour in 1770. *Monreith Arms*. T (098 87) 232. (C)

Whithorn (Wigtownshire)

The village is the site of Scotland's first recorded Christian church, built by St Ninian *circa* 410 AD. During the 12th century a new priory church was built, and the shrine of St Ninian attracted pilgrims from far and wide over the centuries, among them Mary Queen of Scots who made her last visit here in 1563. From the broad main street of the village a fine 16c gateway leads to the priory ruins and the site of the early church, an area of excavation known as the Whithorn Dig. In 1986 the Whithorn Trust was established to explore, over a five-year period, the secrets of Whithorn's past. Visitors are welcome to see the dig from an observation platform. An audio-visual display explains Scotland's Christian history.

The Route

The quiet B road follows the coastline of Wigtown Bay for much of the way. There is little habitation through this remote undulating countryside. At Kirkinner the church on the hill (right) is a prominent feature.

Isle of Whithorn
(Wigtownshire)

The little coastal village lies on a promontory, once an island, defining the extreme south east of Wigtownshire. After passing a pleasant inn, The Steam Packet (good bar snacks), a footpath leads through the community playground to the small Chapel of St Ninian, built in the early 13c. In common with the Chapel of St Finian this chapel, perched on a headland above the rugged shore, was a focus for pilgrims from Ireland on their way to Whithorn.

Garlieston
(Wigtownshire)

The route by the B road by-passes this sheltered small port, though there is a diversion of only half a mile to the harbour. Before reaching the village the road passes Galloway House Gardens. These historic gardens (1740), open to the public every day of the year, contain fine trees, shrubs, rhododendrons, camelia house, and walled garden.

Wigtown (Wigtownshire)

Once the county town of Wigtownshire. Wigtown is a spacious place with a central square above Wigtown Sands. The route turns through the heart of the town until reaching the

1 At Whithorn continue Str. In 0.2m bear L. (sign Isle of Whithorn). In 0.6m keep Str. (sign Isle Whithorn). In 1.1m turn L. on to A750 (sign Isle Whithorn). In 1.6m at Isle of Whithorn car park L. on to B7063 (sign Garlieston). In 2.2m turn on B7063 (sign Garlieston).

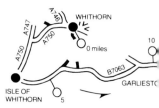

2 In 3.6m turn R. on to B7004 (sign Garlieston). In 1.0m turn R. on B7004 (sign Garlieston). In 0.4m at entry to Garlieston turn L. on B7004 (sign Wigtown). In 4.0m turn R. on to A746 (sign Wigtown) for 0.6m to Kirkinner Church. In 0.7 keep Str. on to A714 (sign Wigtown).

parish church at the town's edge. In the churchyard, railed off, are tombs of five of the Wigtown martyrs – three male Covenanters who were hanged and two females who were drowned. Among several well-preserved inscriptions is that to Margaret Willson, aged 18:

> Let earth and stone still witness beare
> There lies a vergine Martyr here
> Murtered for owning Christ suprame.

A little further along the road past the church is the Martyr's Stake car park (right). From here a footpath leads by way of steps and footbridges to a stone stake erected in 1937 to mark the traditional site of the martyrdom. Here sixty-three-year-old farmer's widow Margaret Maclachlan and eighteen-year-old Margaret Willson were drowned.

Newton Stewart
(Wigtownshire)

The route does not enter the centre of the town.

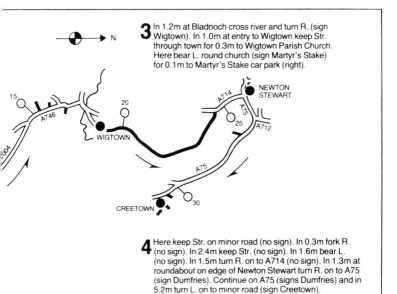

3 In 1.2m at Bladnoch cross river and turn R. (sign Wigtown). In 1.0m at entry to Wigtown keep Str. through town for 0.3m to Wigtown Parish Church. Here bear L. round church (sign Martyr's Stake) for 0.1m to Martyr's Stake car park (right).

4 Here keep Str. on minor road (no sign). In 0.3m fork R. (no sign). In 2.4m keep Str. (no sign). In 1.6m bear L. (no sign). In 1.5m turn R. on to A714 (no sign). In 1.3m at roundabout on edge of Newton Stewart turn R. on to A75 (sign Dumfries). Continue on A75 (signs Dumfries) and in 5.2m turn L. on to minor road (sign Creetown).

Wigtown, the Martyrs Stake.

The Route

*The minor road ascends from
Creetown before following the
course of the old railway line
across the moors (the old railway
station is now a private house).
From the moors the road descends
to the Valley of Fleet through
enchanting wooded countryside.
Along this twelve-mile stretch no
vehicle was encountered.
Approaching Kirkcudbright Bay
there is a car park (right). Here
from the sheltered and secluded
bay is a good view across to St
Mary's Isle, visited by Mary Queen
of Scots during her tour of 1563.*

1 In 1.2m at Creetown clock tower turn L. and
immediately bear L. on to minor road (sign
Gatehouse of Fleet via Rusko). In 0.1m bear l
(sign Gatehouse). In 5.3m turn R. on to B796 (s
Gatehouse). In 3.5m continue Str. (sign
Gatehouse). In 2.1m keep Str. (no sign).

Creetown
(Kirkcudbrightshire)

Once known as Ferrytown of Cree,
this charming village stands
between the Cree estuary and
wooded hills through which the
Moneypool and Battoch Burns
join the river and flow into
Wigtown Bay. From the village the
minor road turns inland, passing
the interesting Gem-Rock
Museum (left). The museum
exhibits minerals and gemstones
collected over a fifty-year period,
as well as a lapidary workshop
where the cutting and polishing
of the exhibits takes place. There
is an art gallery with paintings by
local artists.

Gatehouse of Fleet
(Kirkcudbrightshire)

Set amid grand forest scenery the
small town lies at the mouth of the
Water of Fleet. Focal points of the
town are the Murray Arms and
adjacent granite clock tower built
in 1871. The Murray Arms existed
as a coffee house pre-1642, the
keeper of the 'gait' and road to the
ford across the river living in what
was then the only house here –

hence Gatehouse of Fleet. James
Murray built the Murray Arms as
a coaching inn in 1760, and facing
the modernized hotel are terraced
cottages, once the posting stables.
Among the public rooms of the
hotel is the Burns Room where,
reputedly, Robert Burns wrote
Scots Wha Hae. After crossing the
Fleet bridge there is a Forest
Information Centre (signed right).
Here is a small wooden hut at the
edge of the forest, providing
information about the locality and
indicating forest trails.
Murray Arms Hotel, High St.
T (055 74) 207. (A)

Kirkcudbright
(Kirkcudbrightshire)

Many consider this estuary town
to be the most picturesque in the
whole of Galloway. Dominating
the colourful harbour are the ruins
of McLellan's Castle, built 1581–2
on the site of the Monastery of
Greyfriars. Between castle and
harbour are two whitewashed
cottages, formerly fishermen's
cottages known as But and Ben,

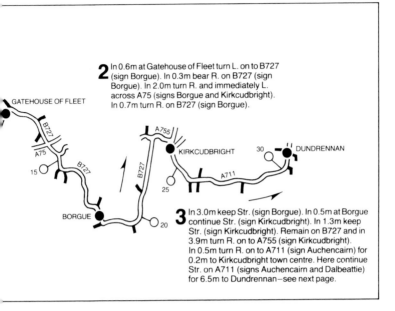

2 In 0.6m at Gatehouse of Fleet turn L. on to B727 (sign Borgue). In 0.3m bear R. on B727 (sign Borgue). In 2.0m turn R. and immediately L. across A75 (signs Borgue and Kirkcudbright). In 0.7m turn R. on B727 (sign Borgue).

3 In 3.0m keep Str. (sign Borgue). In 0.5m at Borgue continue Str. (sign Kirkcudbright). In 1.3m keep Str. (sign Kirkcudbright). Remain on B727 and in 3.9m turn R. on to A755 (sign Kirkcudbright). In 0.5m turn R. on to A711 (sign Auchencairn) for 0.2m to Kirkcudbright town centre. Here continue Str. on A711 (signs Auchencairn and Dalbeattie) for 6.5m to Dundrennan—see next page.

now serving as an art gallery. The Stewartry Museum contains an interesting display of local antiquities. At the Selkirk Arms there are further reminders of Scotland's bard for it was here in 1794 that he stayed and wrote the Selkirk Grace:

Some hae meat, and canna eat,
And some wad eat that want it,
But we hae meat and we can eat
And sae the Lord be thanket.

Selkirk Arms Hotel, Old High St.
T (0557) 30402. (C)
Royal Hotel, St Cuthbert St.
T (0557) 30228. (C)

The hills around Gatehouse of Fleet.

The Route

The road to Auchencairn is quiet with little traffic. Along this stretch the Ministry of Defence coastal firing range is hidden from view by woods. After leaving Auchencairn there are good northerly views of the wooded hills, with Bengairn Cairn and Screel Hill the dominating features. The road reaches the coast once more at Sandyhills.

1 At Dundrennan continue Str. and in 1.0m bea on A711 (sign Dalbeattie). In 3.7m at Auchenc keep Str. on A711 (sign Dalbeattie). In 6.9m t R. on A711 (sign Dalbeattie). In 0.6m at outsk of Dalbeattie turn R. on to A710 (sign Solway Coast). In 3.3m at Barnbarroch continue Str. A710 (sign Rockcliffe).

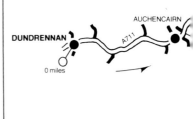

Dundrennan
(Kirkcudbrightshire)

The abbey ruins lie in solitude, a little removed from the village. This Cistercian abbey was founded in 1142, with a chapter house added a century later. Among the many monuments is one to a murdered abbot. Mary Queen of Scots spent her last night in Scotland at the abbey before departing to exile in England.

Auchen Cairn
(Kirkcudbrightshire)

The village of whitewashed cottages sweeps down a hillside, high above Auchencairn Bay. This sheltered bay may well have been a haven for smugglers, the Smugglers Inn here acting as host to them.

Dalbeattie
(Kirkcudbrightshire)

The route avoids the centre of Dalbeattie, a town of 19c grey granite houses built from local stone. In the last century the River Urr was navigable, ships conveying the quarried granite for use in Manchester, Liverpool and London. Local products include Dalbeattie cheese, haggis and Galloway beef.

Colvend
(Kirkcudbrightshire)

From this main road hamlet a minor road leads (right) to the Colvend Coast where Rockcliffe is a popular holiday resort.

Sandyhills
(Kirkcudbrightshire)

There is a car park and splendid sandy beach, culminating at the rocky entrance of Rough Firth, the estuary of the River Urr. The nearby caves and coves were once favourite haunts for smugglers.

The Abbey at Dundrennan where Mary Queen of Scots spent her last night in Scotland.

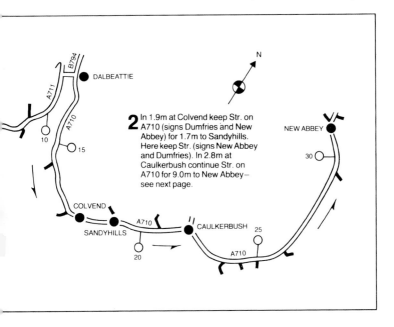

2 In 1.9m at Colvend keep Str. on A710 (signs Dumfries and New Abbey) for 1.7m to Sandyhills. Here keep Str. (signs New Abbey and Dumfries). In 2.8m at Caulkerbush continue Str. on A710 for 9.0m to New Abbey— see next page.

313

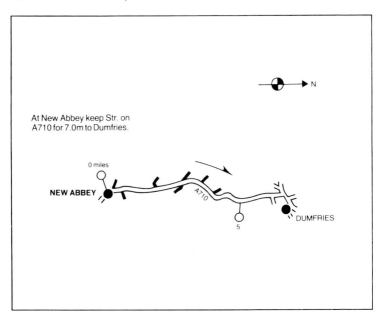

At New Abbey keep Str. on
A710 for 7.0m to Dumfries.

0 miles

NEW ABBEY

A710

DUMFRIES

5

The Route

*Little traffic encountered
along the final few miles to
Dumfries.*

New Abbey
(Kirkcudbrightshire)

Sweetheart Abbey lies at the
fringe of the village, a massive ruin
of red sandstone founded as a
Cistercian abbey in the 13c by
Devorguila, wife of John de Balliol
of Barnard Castle. John de Balliol
had been buried at Barnard Castle
several years before the abbey's
foundation. Devorguila embalmed
the heart of her husband,
depositing it in a silver casket and
carrying it wherever she went. At
her request she was buried in front
of the high altar of the abbey, the
heart of Balliol laid upon her
breast. Thus arose the name of
Dulce Cor or Sweetheart Abbey.
The narrow street of New Abbey
winds past picturesque cottages,
among them on the left of the
small square the old village smithy
with the motto: 'By Hammer and
Hand All Arts do Stand'. The
Shambellie House Museum of
Costume displays women's
fashion of the 1880s.
Abbey Arms. T (038 785) 215. (C)

Index